CONNOISSEUR VIDEO
The Best in World Cinema

our releases include films by Kurosawa (**The Seven Samurai**),
Fassbinder (**Martha**), Renoir (**Le Crime de Monsieur Lang**),
Antonioni (**L'Avventura**) and Visconti (**Ossessione**)

ACADEMY VIDEO
The Best of Non-Fiction

with documentaries on Pasolini, Sturges and Scorsese -
Brownlow and Gill on Chaplin, Keaton and Griffith,
The Century of Cinema series, including Martin Scorsese's
Personal Journey Through American Movies.

other titles include Claude Lanzmann's **Shoah** and **From The
Pole To The Equator** directed by Gianikian and Lucchi
"perhaps the single most welcome video release of the year"
Dennis Lim **Independent on Sunday**

 Films

For further information or to obtain a catalogue of over 200 titles please call 0171 957 8957

GRANTA 61, SPRING 1998

EDITOR Ian Jack
DEPUTY EDITOR Robert Winder
MANAGING EDITOR Karen Whitfield
EDITORIAL ASSISTANT Sophie Harrison

CONTRIBUTING EDITORS Neil Belton, Pete de Bolla, Frances Coady,
Ursula Doyle, Will Hobson, Liz Jobey, Blake Morrison, Andrew O'Hagan

Granta, 2–3 Hanover Yard, Noel Road, London N1 8BE
TEL (0171) 704 9776, FAX (0171) 704 0474
SUBSCRIPTIONS (0171) 704 0470

FINANCE Geoffrey Gordon
ASSOCIATE PUBLISHER Sally Lewis
SALES David Hooper
PUBLICITY Gail Lynch, Rebecca Linsley
SUBSCRIPTIONS John Kirkby, Mark Williams
PUBLISHING ASSISTANT Jack Arthurs
TO ADVERTISE CONTACT Jenny Shramenko 0171 704 9776

Granta US, 1755 Broadway, 5th Floor, New York, NY 10019-3780, USA

PUBLISHER Rea S. Hederman

SUBSCRIPTION DETAILS: a one-year subscription (four issues) costs £24.95 (UK),
£32.95 (rest of Europe) and £39.95 (rest of the world).

Granta is printed in the United States of America. The paper used in this publication
meets the minimum requirements of American National Standard for Information
Sciences—Permanence of Paper for Printed Library Materials, ANSI Z39.48-1984. ∞

Cover design by The Senate
Cover photograph: SuperStock

ISBN 0 903141 16 7

Once in
a house on fire

INTRODUCTION

The sea can still make us scared and wistful—the *Titanic*, Charles Trenet singing *La Mer*—but it also seems to have lost its power. The tide of its images, metaphors and stories has been steadily retreating. There are some great and popular exceptions—the novels of Patrick O'Brian, Hollywood's new *Titanic*—but even these see the sea as history, evocations of the way we were. Why should this be? One obvious answer is that as travellers we no longer need the sea. Only the poor in the East, hopping islands in the Pacific, still use it as a means of urgent human transport. Another is that ships have deserted great cities and their shorelines: not Hamburg yet, nor Rotterdam or Bombay, but the Hudson in New York and the Thames in London (where Marlow told the *Heart of Darkness*), the Clyde in Glasgow—all almost empty rivers now. With the ships have gone the men who sailed them, their waterfront bars long closed, the old piers turned into museums or marinas. Even the terminology of the sea seems antique (which, of course, it is): bow and stern, abaft and abeam, hawser, port and starboard, fathoms, ship ahoy! Modern writing feels uncomfortable with this—hey, what century are we in?—unless it is being self-consciously historic: *Mr Smith sir, I should be obliged if you would furl those topgallants and be sharp about it.* Joseph Conrad wrote for his contemporary reader: *And I looked upon the true sea—the sea that plays with men till their hearts are broken, and wears stout ships to death.* A lovely sentence, and perhaps at the time an accurate sentiment; but how many people would feel its truth now?

Men are in some ways the barrier. The sea, as the province of male work, has also been the province of male sentiment, male adventure, male stoicism. All three have been undermined by social change and fashion. And yet the sea still matters to us as much as, if not more than, ever. The world's economy couldn't thrive without its cargoes, or the world's diet without its fish. There may well soon be more of it. If predictions of its rise are correct, many island states in the Pacific and Indian Ocean will disappear. It is still dangerous. The largest loss of life at sea in peacetime is not owed to the loss of the *Titanic* (1,523 dead) in 1912, but to the wrecking of the Philippines ferry *Dona Paz* (4,386 dead) in 1987. The sea is still mysterious. Who can predict El Niño? Its deeps remain to be explored.

This year, as it happens, has been dedicated by the United Nations as the International Year of the Oceans. The tide of our imagination may be turning.

THE SEA

Royal Festival Hall
Queen Elizabeth Hall
Purcell Room

Literature Events
March - June 1998

A truly International line-up of writers for the spring including:

Toni Morrison, **Malcolm Bradbury**, **Irina Ratushinskaya**, **Michael Ignatieff**, **Richard Dawkins**, **Erica Jong**, **Germaine Greer**, **Terry Eagleton**, **Romesh Gunesekera**, **Will Self**

plus writing from the **Caribbean**, **Greece** and **South Africa**

Hayward Gallery
on the South Bank • London

Exhibitions

FRANCIS BACON: THE HUMAN BODY
and
HENRI CARTIER-BRESSON: EUROPEANS
5 February – 5 April

ANISH KAPOOR
30 April – 14 June

BOX OFFICE **0171 960 4242**
BROCHURE LINE **0171 921 0734**
(Literature Bulletin and Exhibitions Leaflet)
OR SURF **www.sbc.org.uk**

GRANTA

JAMES HAMILTON-PATERSON
SEA BURIAL

Do you remember this?
A broken engine; the hours' becalming; an empty ocean still as a lake of mercury. It was soundless to the horizon and our small noises placed us at the centre of the universe, unique in our activity. From time to time a spanner clinked, a bare foot bumped a thwart. From the vinyl-scented shade of a rigged tarpaulin we watched our tiny ripples become visible only as they left the *Medevina*'s shadow, trembling outward, as if the shadow's edge were the actual hull, our whole craft insubstantial, no more than an airy nothing which had briefly come between sun and sea. The mutter of voices (*Try this. It's rusty. The gasket's ruined.*), the rasp and flare of a match, the incense of a cigarette. The small splash of a handful of waste. And then, emerging from the shadow into gorgeous colour like the tip of a kingfisher's wing, an iridescent oil-stain flashing its molecules, splitting the spectrum and creeping out across the water. Do you remember how dazzling it was? That spreading puddle of hues in a still world of primary blue? Greens and purples, golds and pinks, rubies and violets, forming and re-forming, pooling and glittering minutely so the fascinated mind drew ever closer to its surface and fell into a microscope's gaze such that the twinkle and sputter of evaporation almost became visible, the spirituous fractions boiling off in order of their volatility.

The sun climbed and remained stuck at the top of the sky. Sometimes we stood up or wandered aft to peer at the dismantled carburettor. The parts were black with oil and rust—deformed, even: corroded artefacts turned up by a plough rather than precision-engineered components. Our shifting weight as we moved about the narrow boat made one bamboo outrigger gently dent the water, the other rise and shed a line of droplets. The brilliant oil-stain fractured. Feathers and petals broke off, some drifting perversely back into our shadow and winking out. A flotilla of melding islets moved into the glare beyond the outrigger, sending back scorching chromatic flashes. The hours passed. Fish and rice to eat, the bowls washed over the side and fat replenishing the film until—do you remember?—a peacock sheen surrounded our soundless universe, marbled and swirled and striated. In a halo of specious glory our little boat sat and baked, breathing out its rainbowed anima.

No, you will not have forgotten; not in the light of what was to happen later, not in the particular isolating light in which individual events were picked out with such intensity.

Now and then a fish rose, but languidly, as if its head had difficulty breaking the surface tension, so thick was the water's skin. Several pairs of eyes would remain on the resealed hole where snout or fin had protruded for an instant. At length a flying fish broke completely out, tail whirring the water's surface like the propeller of a planing speedboat and leaving a straight scar of irregular dashes for sixty yards before vanishing into an invisible notch. This was a fishing boat, after all, and at last someone aroused himself out of his lethargy enough to bait a hook and drop it into the rectangle of water enclosed by an outrigger. It was as much for something to do as a gesture of habit.

It was mid-afternoon before the engine started. Our companions murmured their relief. We had lost six hours. The blocks of ice in the insulated chests would be that much smaller. Nobody had opened the lids to look, for fear of accelerating the process. Now we could spend fewer than four hours at the lobster beds, even if the motor kept going and took us there before midnight. You will not have forgotten how precarious these trips were, ninety miles each way. If all went well we could fill half the chests with lobsters, having transferred the remaining ice to the other half to pack around fish. Any serious delay on the way back might mean the fish were lost. And this quite apart from the usual risks of dodging coastguard cutters alert for illegal fishermen. Edgy times; but grounded in comradeship and marked, as always, by heightened senses.

How vivid, still, are the seagoing smells? Oily bilges, fish entrails, a freshly lit cigarette drawn through salt paper? And at night, if you were not diving, the compressor's exhaust fumes, its lethal monoxides, barking and blattering our darkened boat's position for anyone to hear. But a shift of wind might gently lay its hand on a cheek and turn your head like a weathervane, pointing your nostrils into the smell of unseen land: forest and rot and copra, jasmine, mimosa and ylang-ylang. And you may have thought of the strangeness of it, sitting there in night's scented cocoon, propped up by nails and timber in the middle of the water while men you knew like brothers worked away in the fish mines far beneath the boat, their dim torchlight opening up fugitive seams and corridors. Their wooden goggles and floating hair.

And behind everything, the economics: the tanks of fuel we carried set against the miles we needed to cover; the ice matched with that and the anticipated size of the catch; the future price of fish in the market half a week away; profits eaten up by repairs. The fisherman's immemorial equations, whose hidden term is time. Tides and currents, nightfall and winds, the rising of the moon: all determine whether he is too early, too late, or punctual for the flow of fish he is banking on at his journey's end.

So we were already late; but the captain said Push on. Push on, go (pointing with jutting lips to the speckless ocean's rim). To turn and head for home was too safe, too undisguised a loss of fuel and effort. Follow the sun, now curving a south-westering course. In this way we reached the moment when our prow was aimed directly at where, in one corner of the day-long featureless sky, evening clouds were beginning to form a range of wool mountains above an invisible coast. It was still too early for pinkish colours. The peaks were white and blue-and-white, undershadowed with pearl: glittering snowfields which convection was thrusting into pinnacles and spires even as we watched, transforming the alps into the skyline of an impossible town. There, among amorphous towers and eroding castles, an insane architect was busy opening up sly passages, glimpses of alleys, vistas of tall windows and bent porticoes whose very act of moulding held out the constant promise of disclosure. Glancing away for a moment and then looking back, the eye would catch these apertures at the tantalizing instant of being sealed by vapour, blocked by soundless landslides, erased for ever. Even as the gaze scrambled back down crumbling stairways leading nowhere, the great gates were slamming all around in silence. And always, as they closed or melted, they left behind the faintest air of having successfully denied, of having withheld a view of some innermost chamber or secret courtyard now buried deep within palisades.

Meanwhile, the mercury ocean across which we had been heading was gone. In its place a glassy violaceous swell reflected this soft metropolis so that the one image leaned above the other,

11

the lower scarcely distorted. And it was on this, dead ahead, you will remember we first saw the tiny black insect of another boat. The only visible object on the ocean's face, it lay in our path with the punctuality of an omen. Without needing to alter course by a degree we gradually overhauled the lone fisherman as he sat in the celestial city's mirrored thoroughfares.

The captain eased the nylon string which held the throttle so the engine note fell to a mutter and the *Medevina* lost way. With the rudder slightly over we began a gentle curve which took us within hailing distance of the fisherman, but not so close that our wake would swamp him. As to what we already thought, can you remember that? Even though we had passed many identical craft on previous expeditions, can you remember if you had taken in the absence of a mast and rice-sack sail, or the fact that the boat's smallness and the man's position in it made it obvious there could be no engine? Even as we came abreast thirty yards off, had you appreciated that nobody under paddle-power alone would allow himself to drift so far out to sea that no land was visible at any point of the compass? A stocky man, the boat's occupant was wedged comfortably low on the bottom boards, watching our approach from beneath the brim of a hat shaped like a straw lampshade. A fishing line was stretched the freeboard's short distance between one hand and the water.

'Oy, *paré*!' called our captain, allowing us to laze across his bows, then around to the other side. The fisherman's face did not turn, however, and something about his posture had forestalled any jocular shouts of '*Hoy gising!* Wake up there!' The captain only said for all of us, softly, '*Yari na. Patay na.*' And so we completed our circle, staring at the dead man, the water at our stern dimpling and crawling above the scarcely revolving screw. There was still no breath of wind; but possibly even at a saunter our own larger vessel with its spread awning leaned against enough air lazily to displace it, for by the time we had gone entirely around the fisherman a waft of corruption had reached us. There, in the early evening light amid the shattered debris of clouds, he sat and exhaled the gases of his own corporeal breakdown.

2

It is well known in these parts that fish choose not to speak, in order to risk nothing worse at men's hands. Being wrenched from the depths into thin and bitter light to drown slowly in air is bad, but not bad enough to merit speech. Suffering put into words merely takes up an additional burden of pathos. Even being laid alive on coals may induce them to writhe but to utter only occasional squeaks of steam. Hereabouts, people say fish are wise not to give tongue and express a reasonable protest at such treatment. If they did, they would lose the last refuge of dignity which stoicism confers: the right to die unobserved by the faces poised over them, fanning and chatting and waiting for their supper. To enter a mild reproach would excite their captors' amazement and curiosity, so that henceforth the fishermen would bring their catches to the point of speech in delighted competition to see whose was the wittiest, whose the most touching. Sensibly, the fish remain silent, lest men either patronize them or redouble their torture. Nor do they mourn either themselves or their fellows. By such means, it is said, they keep their spirits intact.

As the *Medevina* slowly circled the fisherman we appreciated how in the end he had learned from a lifelong identification with his prey. His own muteness surrounded and exalted him. He was sitting deep in a tiny boat which was anyway lower than ours, his buttocks wedged below water level, in a sense already partly submerged. Objects found in mid-ocean sometimes look larger than they are, as though defiant at being so consummately dwarfed. This fisherman's silence girt him about like the ring of ornamental chains surrounding a great monument in a public park. And as the chains mark off a space where the horizontal becomes the vertical, delineating a change in the mode of looking as well as a boundary preventing intrusion, this man's towering privacy and immobility kept us at a distance until we could work out a way to approach him. He had a paralysing effect. The very fact that there was nothing to be done left us with everything to decide.

(In these parts, then, the spirits of stoical fish rise up from their driftwood pyres and eddy about the eaters, listening to the mirth and chatter, trying to understand their executioners. Some float off down the beach to the sea, where they creep out across the water and wait for the time when they can be reabsorbed. This needs complete darkness, the black of an overcast and moonless night. If, as so often happens, the sea is bright with the reflected light of galaxies, the fish-spirits hang sadly above the surface, unable to return to their world. With the first real darkness, though, they slip below, where at once they turn into the tiny phosphorescent granules foreigners mistake for dinoflagellates. Gradually they sink, and are reborn into fry of their original species.)

From afar the fisherman had been sitting reflectively in a dreamy cloudscape. Now that we were close, the angle of vision had changed and the pinkening cloud city had receded, leaving him starkly present and casting his own shadow. He had acquired power. His first act had been to summon us to him from over the horizon, his second to have thrown us into confusion. Now he presented us with a dilemma. The things which people said (and which you will certainly be able to recall since you yourself said some of them) included:

'We don't know who he is.'

'We haven't the time.'

'If we touch him we'll have to get rid of him. And the boat. They'll pin it on us.'

'How do you know he was murdered?'

'We can't just leave him.'

'I say leave him.'

'He must have a Christian burial.'

'Are you a priest, then?'

'How do you know he isn't a Muslim?'

'Ho, are you an imam?'

'We really haven't the time. The sun's setting.'

'At least let's find out who he is. We can let his family know.'

'Volunteering, are you? Perhaps he died of AIDS. You want to touch him?'

'We can't just leave him.'

'We haven't the time.'

'It'll bring us bad luck if we don't.'

'It'll bring us worse if we do.'

'I say turn back.'

'We haven't the time.'

And meanwhile we kept describing slow circles in the water around this monument, following our own fudged wake in a circularity of thought.

Even in these regions the dead are encountered with a frisson. People under the influence of startlement usually say nothing unexpected; in terms of what is expressed death merely jars loose the predictable. Nobody observed of our fisherman that he was the colour of clouds. Hypostasis had caused his blood to sink so that the upper half of his body was wax-pale. Still less did they say that his spirit had powerfully engaged with us and, no matter what we did now, was setting the terms of our entire trip and maybe even those of future ones. Our fear and uncertainty made us dither and go on drawing and redrawing the tedious outline of the problem he had set us.

We stopped the engine to save fuel. The ring of silence which surrounded the dead man expanded. The captain resignedly tied a T-shirt over his mouth and nose and lowered himself from the prow into the dead fisherman's craft, which skidded lightly away with him to a distance of several yards.

We watched him gingerly approach the sitting figure from behind. Maybe his stealth was from having to keep his balance in a tiny craft designed only for a single occupant, his high centre of gravity making the bamboo outriggers alternately rise and smack. From where we sat his hesitant progress looked as though he feared the fisherman might suddenly turn at the touch of a hand on his shoulder. In the silence we could hear our captain's low mutter behind the mask: Catholic prayers or else respectful requests for permission from the sea-spirits clustering around the little boat. Perhaps he was simply talking to the fisherman into whose face he was peering, apologizing and asking forgiveness for crouching down to put his hands briefly into the pockets of his shorts. When the fisherman had set out on his last voyage the shorts would have been loose. Now his distended stomach made it hard to perform this intimate search. In a moment the captain was rinsing his hands over the side and standing up again.

'Nothing,' he called. 'Not even a cigarette.'

'No blood?'

'Not a mark on him that I can see. There's nothing in this boat except for him and this fishing line—' he lifted a short length of thick bamboo around which the nylon filament was wound. 'Oh, and a bailer.' Delicately he stretched past the man and retrieved a red plastic pot, the ubiquitous one-litre engine oil container with its top cut off. Then he hesitated before again reaching between the sprawled legs and straightening up with a piece of paper in his hand. He put this in the pot and made his way back to the stern, where he lay and began paddling with both arms. So light was the skiff and so calm the sea that he and his dead passenger were soon alongside. Our captain reached up and swung himself on board the *Medevina*. At his involuntary kick the fisherman once more scooted away, adrift and rocking.

The scrap of paper was blank. It had been torn from a school exercise book, lined in alternate pink and blue feint. Creases suggested it had been screwed around a small container—pills perhaps.

'Heart medicine,' somebody said.

But you will remember a voice at once said, 'No,' and faces turned at the speaker's apparent certainty. 'No, because there's no bait, is there?' which made the captain glance sharply towards the drifting back beneath the straw hat. 'Who goes fishing without bait? What does a bare hook catch?'

'Perhaps he kept it in the bailer and had finished it. In any case he's fishing, isn't he, Mots? He's holding the line.'

Mots was stubborn. 'Then where's his catch? He's not fishing. That's not what he's doing.'

'He's not *doing* anything.'

'Yes, he is. He's being dead, just as he intended. The paper contained poison. He came out here to die, only that. So naturally he brought nothing else with him. After a while he must have thrown the paddle away and just drifted. Boat empty, pockets empty. Why catch fish you'll never eat?'

All the while the sun was sinking amid the city's vermilion and cinnamon rubble. Soundlessly the towers and palaces had been shaking themselves down, flattening into featureless broad terraces of farewell colour through which the sun settled like a marble in oil. Behind us the night was hurrying up over the Pacific. In silence we watched the dead man darken until he became an outline, an emblem, a timeless and purposeful shape, the patient unmoving fisherman. Without warning, without word or grunt, our captain started the engine and in the shocking blare we took up our course.

There was no one aboard whose gaze was not fixed aft. For a great while, it seemed, our wake went on opening up between us without the fisherman's figure diminishing. Then suddenly he had shrunk from a monument to a miniature chessman, whittled away as much by the withdrawing of light as by increasing distance. There came a brief period when he would vanish and reappear as the invisible swell raised him high enough to catch a last smoulder. Then he descended into troughs and wells already pooled with night. Even when he dissolved entirely and was lost, our eyes still watched the place like Sir Bedevere straining for a last glimpse of his dead king's boat.

'I still think we should have buried him,' a voice said at last above the engine's din.

'I don't think he committed suicide at all,' someone else said indignantly. 'He was killed and robbed, like always. There're lots of ways of killing a man without blood. Pirate scum. They stole his catch and everything else, but the boat wasn't worth a tow so they just left him.'

'But *we* oughtn't to have left him . . . '

'We didn't have the time. We're already late as it is.'

'This trip was jinxed from the start.'

'We had no time.'

'No time.'

3

They say death has changed for modern man, that it has been deconstructed and, like him, become postmodern. Sometimes when the day is bright and blue and hot enough to be quite empty, and the rocks shimmer in the sun, the conviction comes that at their heart human societies are just elaborate fabrications for suppressing a knowledge of death—conspiracies sufficiently complex and beguiling that the dark secret of our own mortality no longer obtrudes. This huge artifice protects the race against its Achilles heel—the certainty that all its affairs are nothing.

On the morning wind we seem to hear the creak of a million treadmills, the squeak of rowing machines, the trilling and drilling of an endless aerobics class. It is the dawn chorus of anxiety. A kind of insurance is being enacted, that private/public investment in keeping fit and being seen to be keeping fit. Apart from exacting its own toll in humourless tedium, it turns ill health into a personal failure, so that death is seen as just deserts for not having taken the trouble to be sufficiently alive. The body as machine, the unread user's manual, the culpable lack of maintenance: they all form a nexus of irresponsibility and downfall. Someone fails to turn up at the gym as usual in their Lycra leotard. After a few days their name escapes us. It is understood there was always something more they might have done: another few yards' jogging a day, many fewer beers and cigarettes, a further notch of health reached in order to carry on being fit indefinitely. (What was it we failed to grasp even as we hung punitively from wall bars? Does the mind rot atop its splendid torso?)

In what pathetic fragments we move, believing ourselves whole! The precious 'I' disappears for long stretches each day and entirely vanishes during sleep. In one of our registers something never forgets that in default of the ocean deeps, a refrigerator door is always yawning for us as the prelude to spade or flames. Here, at least, the old mythologies no longer work as they did. It is not possible to envisage a private survival. There can be no magic left in prophecies of paradise. That all life was held to have begun in a garden and—if we are good—will likewise end in one convinces hardly anyone. Soon, two-thirds of the world's people will be town-dwellers, to whom rural metaphors are no longer instinctive. Since most people who imagine life after death think of their ordinary life transfigured, a townie would find the myth of the celestial city more plausible than that of a garden paradise.

There is pathos in the way religions of the book have become immovably beached on the littorals of far away and long ago. To desert-dwellers, what more natural than to see heaven as a sublime oasis which owes its existence to nothing more mystical than *water*? Here we are, the deserving, eternally at peace in a lush garden, sprawled in the shade and recovering after life's gruelling journey. The essence of paradise will always be conflated with that of lost Eden, since the future is unimaginable and the present unmythic. The very word 'paradise' comes from Persian via Greek and means a park. What could the modern world offer by way of a matching tranquil and timeless vision? Are we to recline for ever in some leafy municipal square, where the sun filtering through the trees dapples us in a bearable radiance, where traffic noise has ceased, where litter-free paths are strolled by the righteous eating ambrosial hamburgers? It doesn't work. Nor does a Southern Californian dream of bronzing our cancer-proof skin beside Hockney-blue pools, endlessly dating and mating and clinching deals. Besides lacking depth, such visions have no ecstasy. In any case, our bodily needs are now largely catered for. It is impossible to imagine any central image as simple and important as *water* which might resonate for us as a condition of life itself. And this is the triumph of material mastery: that it supersedes and blots out the symbolic to the extent that the only resounding things left are absences. Nature has fallen beneath *Homo*'s power, and in doing so has left him without an image of heaven.

In distant archipelagos there are often days of heat and dazzle powerful enough to wipe out thought, to leach away everything that is not planetary furniture: trees, rocks, clouds and water, to the horizon. To people who skitter about these gulfs of ocean in pea-pod craft—a few sheets of marine plywood tacked together with copper nails—death is an imminent presence. So it is for those hacking at their stony fields high above the glittering shoreline. Subsistence throws things into bright relief. At the end of the day's work either there are fish and maize cobs to be laid over charcoal or there are not. Infants are born, linger for a week, vanish into the ground. There are no hidden deals. Everything— shelter, food, water—is plain. The facts are dealt with by private treaty. The woman pounding her washing on a stone in the stream, the plodder behind his buffalo knee-deep in a rice paddy, the lone fisherman far out in the sun's glare: each might harbour wistful dreams, but none pretends to be proof against the cancellation which can descend in an instant, whimsically, without notice or reprieve. The beaches on which their children romp and tumble are composed of the dead. The whole landscape is a cemetery. Diatom, mollusc, foraminifer, cuttlebone, dog jaw, pig tooth, and all by the trillion ton. Daily they walk on the deepening past, mend nets on it, fall asleep on it, make cement blocks with it, shit into it. The sea turns over and over, a geological machine smoothly meshing its gears and grinding up time itself. At night it sparkles with energy. Sit beside it under the stars, and fan the driftwood embers and watch very seriously the broiling fish as slowly they curve upwards from the heat. Not as dead as they look, some of them, for now and then one leaps off the coals the instant it is laid across them. *'Buhay pa!'* and a child's delighted scurry to retrieve it and place it on the fire again. 'Lie down! Go to sleep!' Companionable laughter. The incense of smouldering fish oil drifts across the constellations and brings the village dogs from far down the beach.

Despite the skinniness of this living, for all its rigour, there can exist in these rural and marine backwaters a certain ebullience. Not to sentimentalize it, it is that peculiar freedom which descends like a gift on those so constantly menaced that they slip off the burden of mere worry. A strange security results when death is so close a companion. It can be felt while crunching along a beach, a skeleton walking on skeletons with the time machine turning in step, wavefalls and footfalls. A gleeful levity at being so brief, at feeling so exempt. Freedom from what, then? Certainly not from the irreducible pact of living. Rather, from the heaviness of having to share in metropolitan anxieties, the contaminating conspiracy, the yearning. Freedom, too, from the corroding suspicion that the extra time bought by wall bars has already gone on wall bars.

4

On into night we went, nakedly starlit, without even the stealth of a light overcast. The equatorial sky blazed with local stories. Little Turtle lay helplessly and wept a stream of stars which fell

beyond the sea's edge. She had been overturned by the turbulent
rush of Tig-it, the giant manta whose eye—to other folk in distant
lands—was Achernar in the constellation of Eridanus. Little
Turtle wept because, being on her back, she could now see only
the darkness of Earth and nothing of the guiding sky with its
brilliant lamps and beacons, and knew she would never reach
home. Far away from her was the Brazier with its frozen rag of
ionized gases drifting for hundreds of parsecs, through whose
smoke Cry-Baby was being passed three times to dry his tears.
Into the Brazier had been sprinkled incense, seaweed, fish bones
and chips of scented wood. The enchanted perfume filled the
heavens, reaching the nostrils even of the Octopus. The Octopus
was sunk deep over the horizon, biding his time. He waved his
tentacles menacingly, their suckers marked by stars. Now and
then sparks from the Brazier shot across the sky. Whenever these
meteors fell into the sea they changed instantly into pearls, which
sank, still glowing, to await a lucky fisherman.

Over everything such orderly dramas shed a stark, revealing
glare, a million suns lighting up a single Earth night in which a
fishing boat was hoping to poach some lobsters from another
nation's territorial waters. The noise of its engine reached all parts
of the universe, like the Brazier's incense. You will remember that
sensation, something of stateliness as well as apprehension. The
fear of coastguard cutters, naturally: of an impounded boat,
confiscated tackle, jail, diplomacy, bureaucrats and fines—
whatever else, the fines. But behind all that, like the Octopus
hunkered down in his lair beneath the horizon, lay the shadow of
the man we had left in his boat. He was there somewhere behind
us, still sitting in his broad-brimmed hat, the fishing line with its
unbaited hook trailing from his dead hand. Unwaked and
unburied, far out beneath the stars he sat, lifting and falling in the
long Pacific swell. So must he have sat many thousand times
before. Nights of moon, nights of rain, nights of angry chop
sending water spilling over the low freeboard, obliging him to
loop the line over a copper nail and set to bailing with the plastic
motor oil container. Nights when he could see into the depths
with his eyes shut, sense the eddies of ten thousand tails and drop
his hook right among them. Cold, too, on other nights, sitting

there in the empty wind, now and then fumbling a cigarette alight with the tiny companionable flame which flickered deep in a sawn-off mayonnaise jar.

Some nights he and his colleagues would remain within hailing distance, their yellow lights so low in the water they winked out in the troughs of passing wavelets, then on and again off, with the steady persistence of fireflies. The water beneath them might have been empty of life. As if drawn together by a mutual acceptance that no one was going to get fat on this night's fishing, the boats stayed within conversational distance. Gossip was exchanged, cigarettes, matches, a spare jersey. A flat bottle of rum was passed around. There they would sit in that enclosed world which sprang into being, even in the nowhere of mid-ocean, when men talked like survivors of a series of grim accidents ashore. The sicknesses, the deaths, the separations; the plot of unyielding land whose scant crops were tithed by a landlord; the truant son, the feud with the policeman's family. Over and over again stories were told that everyone knew. Their retelling, and the long reflective silences falling between each, were a description of that other world whose reach seemed absolute, yet outside which it was still possible to sit. The lamps of land could not always be seen. The fishermen's night lights danced their flames within their sooty, improvised chimneys, marking out the coordinates of an existential annexe as temporary as it was shifting. Within it, something invisible and unspoken came into being. For a while the flames were the bars of its cage and it could not escape until the cage fell apart or the blanch of dawn disclosed a loose knot of tired, stiff men floating on the sea. This unspoken, this invisible— which sometimes smelt of tobacco and sometimes as though incense and fish bones were burning—was the pact. It was the silent deal done with the sea and the stars, with what welled up from below and sifted down from above, with immeasurable gulfs. The deal could never be expressed. Into its secret balance nothing weighty was thrown, simply the piecemeal fragments of what each inner mind held in safe keeping: a particular smile with a hand half raised in neither greeting nor farewell; a receding wave draining sand and fragments of shell from around bare feet and undermining the toes crawlingly; the shimmer of a cooking fire at dusk and a child's laugh; the gecko's grating call—the cry the dinosaurs knew and which would not stop until after the human race, when the planet ran down: ' . . . loves me, loves me not; loves me . . . ' (as European children once blew dandelion clocks). And heaped into the balance as these fragments might be, the deal remained always the same, imperturbably. The Octopus's suckers twinkle; his arms await. They embrace the sky. The playlets overhead are scanned for portents, warnings and news of all kinds. The playlets enacted below are watched by no one and nothing.

All these things were turned over by the living about the dead, until the lone fisherman bobbing far behind at our wake's end grew in stature like a fable. There was not a soul aboard without guilt for the uncompromising corpse we had left. His boat was clustered around with spirits: they had been practically visible, perched like transparent vultures along the outriggers, fidgeting at bow and stern. Some would have jumped ship—would even now be swaying atop the black poles supporting *Medevina's* tarpaulin roof or hunched on the fuel tank of the temperamental Briggs & Stratton sixteen-horsepower motor which had already caused us delay. And, causing that delay, had engineered the encounter with the unknown suicide who had now adopted us. What trip starting thus could turn out well? So you will no doubt remember the thrill of portent with which you abruptly discovered that the bank of cloud low above the sea to starboard was land, that we were now in foreign waters, that a new playlet was about to begin.

When the motor falls abruptly silent it is the time for stretching, for scanning the scene with ears as well as eyes. No cutter's masthead light crawls across the nearby bulk of cliff, no angry hum of motorized pursuit. Just the slap of water under prow and outrigger noses. Our intermittent, eventful journey has brought us here, late; our stubborn captain's calculations can almost be heard. Half past one: tide change in thirty-five minutes. We'll need the anchor. Throughout these archipelagos, in a thousand straits and sounds, channels and passages, the current switches direction. Twice a day it streams, races and eddies, often forming boiling demarcations where two contrary currents intersect. To sit there with divers deployed in relays, working the lobster beds, the boat must remain on station. It cannot be allowed to drift. Our captain must have Bajau blood, they say. He does not even possess a compass, yet he has brought us back over his secret patch of seabed after almost twenty hours of travel. Nobody aboard has the slightest doubt that when the first two men go down, their torch beams will fall on familiar terrain.

The anchor is thrown from the prow. It is made of inch-thick reinforcing rods stolen from a construction site, knobby with crude welding and rust. Two men paddle in the slack water to bring the line taut so that when the current begins at tide-turn we will already be nosing into it and can drift no further. With a tyre lever a boy is slipping off the frayed fan belt which drives the propeller shaft. He eases it instead over the pulley of a compressor bolted to the deckboards. This, too, is a rusty lump of engineering. It is connected to a converted cooking gas cylinder whose tap has twin nozzles. Men are breaking out two coils of thin polythene tubing whose insides are mottled with mould, pushing the ends over the tank's outlets, tightening clips. The first two divers are already in the water. Their wet knuckles gleam as they hold on to the boat. In addition to T-shirts and shorts, they are wearing home-made goggles carved from wood, the eyepieces set with a lozenge of glass embedded in pink marine epoxy. They carry torches waterproofed by a motorcycle inner tube and lengths of stout wire with one end bent into a sharpened hook. A lidded basket on a rope is handed to each. At the captain's signal the still-hot engine is swung, fires, backfires, splutters, blares into life. On its continued running the divers' lives depend. They will be working at between sixty and a hundred feet. Lobsters are most abundant at about 1,000 feet. Puny half-naked men with ramshackle compressors and cheap Chinese flashlights can do no more than skim off the topmost handful, concentrating on the two main species which can be found on these comparatively shallow reefs: slipper lobsters and spiny lobsters.

The Briggs & Stratton has been throttled back to a slow blatting. The ends of the tubes are tossed to the men in the water and thrash about, fizzing, until caught. Each man folds over the last inch and grips it between his teeth, regulating the air pressure by clenching or relaxing his jaws. In the water's uppermost ten or fifteen feet they will have to bite quite hard; below that, their grip must gradually slacken to allow more of the foul-tasting air to gush into their mouths and counteract the sea's growing squeeze. Looking over the edge of the boat, the rest of us follow the small, wavering green puddles of their torchlight until they are extinguished in the blackness beneath.

We who are left behind. The phrase carries both anxiety and mourning, ready to shift emphasis in an instant, and into the bargain flies a modest pennant of heroism. The sea captain's wife, her lantern casting up her strained features, paces the widow's walk on her roof and stares into the gale for her man's returning gleam. The ground crew watch in silence as the departing squadron lifts from a darkened airfield somewhere in wartime Europe with its cargo of bombs and boys—teenagers, some of this squadron, children sitting or lying prone in vibrating alloy nests. And we, too, go on staring at the patch of sea beneath which our friends have vanished, each mind anxiously drawing on the black surface its own sketches of misadventure. The direction of the tubes and ropes gives no real clue to where the divers might be. The two older men paying out the coils have already put overboard fifty yards apiece, passing it steadily through their hands and easing out kinks as it goes. They are waiting for the tide change, to see which way the boat will swing. The divers went over on the starboard side, the tubes vanish over the stern. Suddenly the men are paying out to port, and with a shock of reorientation you discover that the dark mass of land now lies off to the left.

Can you remember how many times you have watched this? And have yourself gone down with that hissing pipe clenched in your molars until your jaw aches? The torch beam lights around itself the pale black cell in which you descend, heading down and down. Twinkling dinoflagellates bounce off your bare hands and arms in crumbs of cold light. The spirits of martyred fish, they stream from the invisible plastic tube as though on your trajectory through space you had crossed the path of a meteor shower. Head-down you descend, eyes behind the oval glass peering for focal points, imposing patterns on nothingness, until one of the patterns catches. It gives you a queer pick-up at the heart to see it harden into a detail of rock with small nocturnal fish going their

ways, a cantle of this universe which hides itself from the world
above. This place is not simultaneous with the realm of air. It can
never be reached by anchors and plumb lines. It happens at
different wavelengths and is full of a vividness that remains
invisible to the air-breathing human, his ears plugged with water
and his eyes as dim as his weakening torch. He is an interloper in
a land full of playlets he cannot quite see and stories he just fails
to hear. Unsensed, a teeming sexuality surrounds this visitor, who
can smell nothing, nor taste anything but mould and exhaust
fumes. All he can ever bring back from this ancient domain are
beautiful banalities like pearls and lobsters, and even these are
more beautiful than he knows.

You are not going down tonight, though, but instead will sit
in the darkened boat with the others who are left behind. After
twenty minutes the first diver emerges. His basket is hauled aboard
and emptied in a cascade of claws and carapaces.

'OK?' our captain calls to the man in the water, who has
removed his air hose and is taking breaths of clean night air.

'We're behind the Madonna. The first of those gullies. It's
good.'

'One more and then Mots goes down.'

The diver's pale hand waves, replaces the air hose, grabs the
empty basket and drags it under the water. A single plywood
flipper thrashes the surface briefly and he is gone in a swirl of
luminescence. The boys begin picking lobsters out of the bilges,
tying their claws with a double loop of plastic straw, packing
them into the first of the iceboxes. Among them is the flaccid
mass of an octopus. By starlight the boys look for the marks left
by the diver's teeth where he killed it. They are difficult creatures
to tease out of a hole and nobody would waste time doing so on a
lobster hunt. The diver's light must have caught it in the open, a
dark pink and pallid umbrella flowing desperately over the
exposed coral, tentacles searching for a crevice into which to furl
itself. It is possible to take them then, to grasp the bulging pulpy
head in one hand and bite the narrow neck which joins it to the
tentacles. The flesh is tough and rubbery and our diver would
have had to remove his air hose before chewing at the creature. If
you can detach the octopus entirely from the rock before killing

it, it will clamp its arms about yours, pulling its hooked beak towards your hand. Biting at this fleshy club is even less pleasant since it immediately transfers some of its sticky grapples to your head, welding itself over your face as you try to get a mouthful of the vulnerable part. Yet an experienced fisherman can kill a small octopus with his teeth quicker than he can with a knife, for even the sharpest blade can skid off the gristle and gash his own hand.

The second diver soon surfaces and his basket is emptied. 'Not far from the Madonna,' he says as he disappears again. 'The Madonna', we all know, is the name someone on a previous trip has given to a curious coral formation, a slender pillar some fifteen feet tall which in outline, seen from one aspect, resembles a statue even to the extent of having a texture like the petrified folds of a robe. On her seaward side the reef falls away into a series of steep gullies, in the first of which our divers are working, and she forms a useful marker.

When each man has filled two baskets the divers come in and are replaced by a second pair. Our captain is strict about this. Each pair dives for roughly forty minutes, rests for the same, then goes down for a final forty minutes. Whatever theory he is working on, it bears little relation to the rigid decompression rates on which an alien medical science insists. Transient headaches are a matter of course, yet nobody in his crews ever gets the bends, though there are crippled young men further up the coast. It is mysterious.

The engine chugs on, the compressor's worn cylinder clatters, the valve on the tank bleeds with a chattering hiss. The boys go on packing the scrabbling lobsters in ice. A loud sizzle is heard aft. In the galley (a sheet of tin on which stands a cement cooking stove large enough for a single pot) someone has tossed the first pieces of chopped octopus into a wok of hot oil. The domestic smell of frying drifts across the boat and over the sea. Faces are dimly illumined by the red glow of the stove's mouth, across which a hand with a palm-leaf fan flaps rhythmically. The captain and others go on scanning the darkness for the first signs of a coastguard cutter. Yet the deployed divers and the cookery would make a quick getaway impossible, and after the initial tension a calm insouciance overtakes us until we almost forget the dead man over the horizon.

5

As he was to relate in his autobiography *Viaticum* ('Life has written me, not I my life'), Justus Forfex (Giusto Forbici) was shipwrecked eight times in his wanderings between 1842 and 1867. One way and another, he was able to observe burial customs from the Subang Gulf through New Castile to what he whimsically dubbed 'Cholynesia, or the Bile Islands'. He also had the opportunity, over long months' tattered living off crabs and coconut juice on deserted atolls, to reflect on how the significance of water pervades both soul and body.

Years later, as Giusto Forbici, he passed his scholarly retirement in a gaunt, book-lined palace in Arezzo. When asked why he had chosen that particular city (he was born in Salerno) he replied that there was no part of Arezzo from which one could possibly see the sea. In his most notorious essay, 'De atramento et oceanis morteque', he writes of the relation between ink, oceans and death. For those with a little Latin his title makes the connections less apparently strained since the word for ink, *atramentum*, would call to mind the adjective *atratus*, meaning 'darkened' or 'wearing mourning'. This essay had its roots in the circumstances of Forbici's last and most desperate shipwreck, when he was the sole survivor washed up on a coral strand in the heart of 'Cholynesia'. Washed up with him was more than his fair share of irony: nine large straw-covered glass carboys which he remembered having glimpsed in the ship's hold. These, he knew, contained fresh water. His elation was short-lived. They turned out to be full of ink, part of a consignment destined for Dutch bureaucrats in Batavia. The ink was made of dried sepia extracted from thousands of cuttlefish, purified, mixed with lampblack and thinned with spirits and water. It smelt of bad fish. Forbici thus found himself alone on an islet with many gallons of a substance scarcely more drinkable than the ocean surrounding him.

With immense effort he trundled the great flasks up above the high-tide mark and buried them. He hoped to prevent the direct heat of the sun from evaporating the alcohol through the cork bungs and thereby stop the liquid's fishy component from putrefying still further. For nearly three months he eked out survival by drinking small tots of rotten ink. They made him retch as well as leaving a slight hangover. He produced occasional sooty turds full of carbon, until towards the end as he grew weak and feverish he was seized with stomach cramps accompanied by a Stygian leakage. Not only was he drinking ink but he seemed to be excreting it as well.

How formative is illness for the imagination! Entering what should have been his final delirium (he later wrote), he saw himself as quite conventionally encompassed on all sides by death. Yet suddenly he perceived it as a distillate of that very death—as produced by octopuses and cuttlefish—that was keeping him alive by a kind of homeopathy. Was this proof of the eccentric Dr Hahnemann's 'Law of Similia'? How did these cephalopods extract their black essence from clear sea water? Since it was impossible to make an element such as carbon, did this not imply that the world's oceans already consisted of highly dilute ink which the creatures then concentrated? Two-thirds of the planet was a fatal inkwell.

These thoughts seemed to him very clear and satisfactory as he sat under a sparse canopy of thorny macrophyllum, whose mildly hallucinogenic leaves he now and then chewed. Much later, after being rescued and having recovered his wits, he remembered Varelius's little monograph on the presence of gold in the sea. Forbici then made the leap which was to give his own essay its fame. He reasoned that if the sea acted as a body of solvent, leaching out of rocks their auriferous veins, then its clear depths must contain all the essence of land [il nocciolo della terra], down to its last molecular constituent. If the human body itself was composed only and wholly of chemicals and minerals that occurred in the Earth's crust, then it followed that the sea must also contain all the component parts of a person. In theory, therefore, a wizard, alchemist or divine agent would be able to assemble a human being from a quantity of sea water. Nothing would be lacking but the Soul; and who knew but that also might be found lurking in the invisible interstices of water?

This lively fancy was not at all understood in Arezzo and went down positively badly in Pisa, Siena and Florence. It was scarcely ten years since Darwin had published his own genealogy of the human race, and that had been impious enough in its proposal of a scurrilous ancestry that vastly pre-dated the Book of Genesis. Now here came this vagabond—an Italian no less—who was just as godless but even bleaker, to suggest that the frame made in God's image was composed of nothing but chemicals after all, regardless of its lineage. The Bishop of Lucca referred in a sermon to 'a fashionable, Satanic materialism that . . . reduces the sacrament of motherhood to the level of a factory or a workshop assembling puppets', a remark which some believe gave Carlo Collodi the germ of his fable *Pinocchio*, which was published a decade later in 1883.

Forbici, leathery and reclusive in his Aretine library, gave not a fig for the Bishop of Lucca. 'I look in the mirror and see— nothing,' he wrote exuberantly. 'I look through the casement at the people who, from the sound of their voices, I judge are in the courtyard below but who seem today not as visible as they should be. Our bodies—what are they? Diffuse clouds of whirling atoms held together by some clotting or electric propensity. Why should this appear so miraculous? How can we ever embrace? It is our brilliant *fluidity* that provokes me to love whatever our poor shadows extend. We pontificate and preen, we survive childbirth and shipwreck with all the corporeality of a cloud. The sky-cities we saw above Pacific horizons have long since returned to the ocean, and so shall we. What is it about this process that makes one confident and affectionate? Cradles full of clouds. Coffins full of clouds. Shaving-mirrors full of clouds. Books full of clouds.'

This retired traveller then went on to meditate—at too great a length, maybe—on water. He returned to the relationship between dilution and concentration. Was it possible for a stone [*un nocciolo*] to be dilute and still remain an essence? Can a concentration be said to exist even when dispersed among extraneous things? It is hard for today's readers to address such questions with Forbici's tirelessness. His staunchest admirers are obliged to admit that in his later, landlocked years, the great Justus Forfex became obsessive about water, bodies, the oceans, ink and so forth, returning to them in essay after essay. He never did manage to pull them (or himself) together into a single philosophical proposition. Instead, they flow in and out of his thoughts and writings like busy *animalcula* crossing a microscope slide. Cholynesia had taken its toll.

His earlier monograph on sea burial, though, showed him at his best. It is a lively volume full of arcane and jolting details, still widely consulted by anthropologists, scholars and ghouls. It lists with great attention to detail the classical or ancient practices as well as those he had personally witnessed in the southern archipelagos. And yet even this essay lacks a central thought as to what it might mean to be returned to water, as opposed to the magic benefits accruing to survivors for burying a body in the sea. 'Returned to water' is the significant phrase, one which might not have occurred to him then because this little book antedated his final and most traumatic shipwreck. He had not yet formulated his thesis that all bodies are by nature oceanic and that earth-burial, urn-burial, cremation etc. are merely forms of postponement. And, of course, he was unable to end his monograph with the highly pertinent story of how he had finally been rescued from his atoll with its dwindling ink supply.

Forbici dealt with all this in his so-called 'Parergo', a 'by-work' or corollary to the rest of his writings. When Marcello Vanni came to produce the collected edition in 1907, he judiciously printed the 'Parergo' twice, inserting it as an appendix to *Viaticum* (where it forms a neat climax to his author's adventures) and again as an addendum to the monograph on sea burial, *Talassotafia*. In this position it augments the list with one last strange example, while the autobiographical element gives it an immediacy which is irresistible.

Over the long weeks of isolation on the atoll he had undoubtedly entered an extreme world. There were times when all his shipwrecks and misfortunes collapsed together and he knew he had been living on the islet for centuries, slowly wading through its leeward shallows in a constant quest for food. He had reached the stage where the finding of a single overlooked sea urchin became the high point of the day. Using probes of antler coral he would prise open the friable shell, trembling, so as to leave the inside undamaged. Then, having reluctantly discarded the animal's rudimentary digestive tract (which only made him vomit ink), he greedily ran his thumbnail around the shell's interior, scraping up a tiny mound of gonads, which tasted to him like the rarest caviar. The ghost crabs which lived in burrows in the coral sand and danced in and out of the rippling wavelets at dusk were still plentiful but difficult to catch. When by guile (blocking up its bolt-holes) he did succeed in catching one, he triumphantly ate it whole, crunching up claws and carapace even as the translucent kicking legs scrabbled at his lower lip.

He had tried and failed to catch fish, even the tiniest fry that hung like flakes of brilliant metal about the coral outcrops. No net, no line, no hook. The scholar was reduced to dropping boulders into the shallows where the fish flickered in the hope of stunning one. The turbulence subsided, the water cleared; nothing had changed except the new naked rock lying there with the braver fish already nosing around it. Forbici did find one place on the atoll that looked promising, a pool among the rocks on the windward side. Roughly circular and about four yards across, its ragged sides fell vertically for several fathoms, forming a kind of porous shaft. Over many centuries some freak of the current must have scoured it out of the dead coral formations of which the islet was built. By lying at its lip and putting his face close to the water's surface he could see, beyond his own ragged castaway's visage, a dark bottom strewn with broken coral: white chunks and lengths among which bulky parrotfish moved lazily.

For long hours he pondered a way of trapping these succulent creatures. With some damage to his hands he managed to break off several wands of the tough little bush which had become his shelter. These he tried to weave into a trap of sorts; but no sooner had he dipped this crude, lopsided construction into the water than it began to unravel. Besides, as he realized too late in an outburst of rage, he had no cord with which to lower it, and nothing tempting with which to bait it. He gave up and went back to eating titbits of weed and mollusc he found beneath the rocks in the lagoon.

Otherwise the days passed unrecordably, and the listless view from beneath the macrophyllum repeated itself at the mesmeric pace of evolution itself. It is not difficult, even well over a century later, to be confident of what Forbici saw. On the atoll's windward side the craggy foreground hides the water's edge. Impelled by the long Pacific swell, occasional tufts of sea leap up among the coral rocks into the dazzled air. A marine heartbeat thuds underfoot and trapped air sighs gustily in vents and fissures. The water in the pool rises and then sinks. This is land no solider than a petrified sponge, with the sea passing continuously through its roots. Small crustacea move on the lunar surface; the isopod *Ligea* scurries everywhere into cracks like a littoral woodlouse. It is a fossil scene.

At night, according to Forbici, a cool breeze sprang out of nowhere. In an act of self-burial which he hoped might bring him a little warmth, he would heap up the detritus of a billion dead creatures over his legs, for he was sick and shivery. He had nothing to do but lie on his back and stare at the universe. Forbici's cosmos was entirely classical: Greek and Roman and Arab. Apart from his training as a scholar, years of voyaging had left him with a good knowledge of the heavens. The pictures he saw were familiar: an archer, a herdsman, Hercules; a plough and a lyre and Berenice's Hair. To stop himself falling forever upwards into the radiant silverpoint overhead (for the tropical night sky sucks the soul away from its human moorings and dissolves it in oceans of eternity) he would retell himself the stories he could remember. He believed it was Tycho Brahe, the Danish astronomer and Kepler's teacher, who had introduced Coma Berenices (which in fact was only faintly visible from Cholynesia's latitudes). Instead of choosing a story from Scandinavian mythology, or else making some contemporary allusion, Brahe had instinctively gone back to the classics. The devoted Queen Berenice vowed that if her husband Ptolemy returned safely from war with Assyria she would cut off all her hair and present it to Venus. When Ptolemy duly returned in triumph she remained true to her promise. Jupiter, awed by this sign of human devotion, retrieved the pledge from the temple and hung her shining tresses in tribute among the spring stars. By such means Forbici did his best to cling to his culture, his identity, his memories. But that had been in the earlier part of his marooning.

Nights on the atoll were severing one by one the threads that still attached him to a previous life somewhere beyond the flickering horizon. To rest one ear on his gravel pillow was to hear the ocean on all sides of the atoll, rinsing and clucking and mewing. But it was also to hear it thrumming below in deep gasps like those of a labouring beast as it turns and turns a creaking watermill. These sounds filled Forbici with terror. Trapped between the starry ocean overhead and that which surrounded and undermined him, he knew himself about to be engulfed. He awoke from hectic dreams of typhoons, of tsunami-like waves big enough to sweep the atoll bare or else tear it loose like a twirling stone raft. The whole weight of the universe pressed down on him until he felt himself trodden beneath the waves, buried by immensity, sinking through ever-blackening layers, a miserable fragment of mind lost among the ocean's roots. In still other dreams he found himself trudging across waterless orange deserts, maybe on Mars or in some Arabian wilderness, in driven search for the oasis where all yearnings would be quenched. Mirages floated up in the trembling air and flowed together until they formed a rim of palms that encircled his whole horizon. It no longer mattered in which direction he urged his stumbling feet: there was nothing but the mockery of endless recession. Here he would awake in black tears. Lying exhausted, beached on dawn's calm and lapped by undrinkable ocean, he forced his parched mouth to repeat the tales he knew, declensions of Greek verbs, multiplication tables, the names of relatives.

It seems that one day Forbici, delirious with ink, sun and hunger, was sitting semi-comatose beneath his macrophyllum when two heavy wooden craft appeared off the atoll. Long in the waterline like war canoes, with outriggers and thatched cabins, they were evidently dugouts hewn from monster tree trunks. Besides blood-coloured sails, eight oarsmen apiece propelled them, whose polished brown backs glistened with sweat and spray. Each craft had at its prow a striking device: one an enormous fish with gaping mouth and counterbalanced, swivelling eyes, the other a great wicker bird with streaming raffia plumes dyed red, green and yellow.

The two boats hove-to within fifty yards of shore. Forbici made no move, having taken them for one more hallucination. He thought this diagnosis confirmed when the fish and the bird began uttering shrill cries, the one rolling its eyes and the other flapping its gaudy wings. He wondered if they were talking between themselves or interrogating the islet to see whether it was propitious to land. After a long while the creatures fell silent. Then a hinged flap fell open beneath each, and a child crawled out backwards and fell into the boat; whereupon a drum took up a deep, lugubrious pounding from the shrouded cabin.

These heavy drumbeats began with both drums in unison, slow and regular, appearing to Forbici as the thudding of his own blood in his ears. Little by little the two drummers drifted out of synchrony, becoming increasingly independent and setting up ever-changing syncopations. This went on for some considerable time. At length the drummers must have reversed the process, for their rhythms gradually approached one another until the two were finally in unison once more. In his account Forbici observed that it represented a feat of rhythmic control and musicianship that would far exceed the abilities of even the best European orchestral players. At the time, though, nothing seemed to him more miraculous than anything else: the boundary between a world dominated by ink and one of pure delirium was vague indeed.

As he watched the two strange boats run their keels up the dazzling beach, the state of his head could be described as fugal with assorted wisps of story. The men jumping into the shallows not forty yards away could as easily have been Ulysses and his crew as archipelagic gypsies on the other side of the world. Not knowing whether he was watching events taking place inside or outside his skull, he sat where he was and made no move. At any rate the disembarking men gave no sign of having noticed the presence of a half-cracked European on the islet. They were too much taken up with handing out, from one of the curtained cabins, a life-sized statue carved in ebony. This was carried reverently and shoulder-high beyond the surf in a procession which was brought up by the two little boys (who swam the first few yards), two men carrying the fish and bird figureheads, and lastly the drummers with their turtleshell instruments.

When the two parties were assembled on the beach, Forbici could see that everyone with the exception of the children was masked. Plain hoods of dark material were drawn over their heads, featureless but for eyeholes.

This procession now walked purposefully across the islet, passing within twenty yards of the observer as he lay beneath his bush. Nobody spoke. The drummers drummed softly, the little boys held hands. The ebony statue was borne above the party's heads at the full stretch of glistening brown arms. They disappeared among the rocks in the direction of the coral pool. It was, as Forbici himself remarked, a measure of his weak and incurious state that he had not the slightest inclination to follow them. In a little while the sound of the distant drumbeats ceased, and all that came to his ears was the sea's familiar stirring. Whether or not all this was a delirious fantasy, it had brought with it a peculiar melancholic charge. The sudden interruption of his long isolation—which he could easily believe had already lasted several years—had imposed a trivial human dimension on what was becoming a grandly geological scene. So far had Forbici turned into a mere component, a kind of sentient rock, that it never occurred to him to announce his presence, to caper with pathetic joy at the sight of fellow-humans, or otherwise to greet his rescuers. The waves now spoke to him more familiarly than any human voice. Even when he came to write of this day, he was unable to say whether the sadness that had descended so abruptly had to do with the solemnities of the ritual or with his sense of being dragged away from an impending private destiny.

Those gull-like cries—were they, too, a property of the moving water that surrounded him? Such mournful screams blurred with surf! He wondered whether he had ever seen a seabird land on this atoll. He could not remember for certain. Long ago he had dreamed of turkey-like birds so tame he could catch them with his hands before roasting and devouring their succulent steaks . . . Mere dreams of hunger based on Galapagos tales: that trusting tameness which ought to pose any human being a moral dilemma but which never seemed to. Once broken, the rules of Eden fell in tatters before the rules of self-interest or commerce. Had he not lately read of British entrepreneurs in Antarctic lands? Protestant flint-hearts so weary from clubbing penguins to death that they had taken to driving their victims up walkways, so that they fell living into the huge cauldrons in which they were rendered down for oil? Again the far-off cries reached him, and afterwards a great outburst of drumming.

It may be that Forbici fell into a doze at this point. He next became aware of the scuff of footsteps passing behind his bush towards the beached craft. The masked figures maintained their silence, the turtleshell drums were mute. The ebony statue was missing, likewise the figureheads and the children. Once embarked, they pushed off. The boats were rowed a few hundred yards offshore before pausing, the one alongside the other as though in discussion. It suddenly mattered to him to know whether or not he was dreaming. He dragged himself from beneath his bush and tottered down to the coral pool on the islet's windward side. There, invisible from the boats, he knelt and peered into the water.

When his eyes had adjusted he could see very clearly the ebony statue lying on the bottom of the shaft among the white pipes of coral. Nearby lay the two figureheads: the great wicker bird with its plumes trailing in the gentle current, the wicker fish with one eye staring fixedly up through the fathoms of pellucid water, mouth agape as though for air. The immense fish he had once thought to trap were bumping at the wicker and ebony with inquisitive snouts.

Forbici crawled back to his shade and discovered that the boats had also returned. The natives had surely not failed to notice his presence even if they had elected not to interrupt their ritual. He never did learn whether the now-unmasked men had come back to rescue him or to salvage the glass carboys, which would have represented valuable storage containers. As they approached the macrophyllum they certainly fell on the empty flasks with excited shouts before greeting this blackened scarecrow of a human with a certain matter-of-factness. Their language was not wholly opaque to him, for the archipelago's dialects overlapped in such a way as to leave audible beneath the surface a framework common to all. He heard *'Aa'*, which he knew to be 'man'. He heard *'bangsa saddi'*, which he interpreted as 'other race'. They half carried him to one of the boats and gave him musky water from a gourd. It tasted like nectar.

The 'Parergo' describes at some length the weeks he spent

aboard a succession of boats as his wandering rescuers went about their maritime business and allowed him to regain his health. They often saw land but seldom went ashore. They did so for fresh water and, on two occasions, for wild pig. But they were clearly not at home there, venturing only fearfully into the jungle, which began almost at the high-tide mark. The endless sea was where they felt most secure, and they knew its ways with respectful intimacy. Their fishing abilities were extraordinary, as was their navigation. Out of nowhere, towards dusk, identical boats would appear and moor alongside each other. Sometimes as many as twenty craft congregated in mid-ocean, a family to each, to celebrate a birthday or a wedding. For a while they formed a floating hamlet or random village. Then, at dawn, or after a few days, sails would be hoisted and the houses would scatter away again over the horizon.

As time passed and language became less of a problem, Forbici was less than ever inclined to return to what and where he had been. This congenial way of living, bounded and dictated by nothing but water, was a transcendent version of the sterile and terminal existence his shipwreck had recently thrust upon him. But the time came when a port was nervously approached and they stood out in the roads until he could be trans-shipped into a schooner. This was bound for Makassar and the unsought curiosity and attention of his own kind. What comes off these last pages of 'Parergo' is regret. Yet as if Forbici himself could never make his mind up, it is unclear whether this was regret at leaving his rescuers, for their having rescued him in the first place, or even for something yet larger and vaguer he had perceived but could not write. At some point during his mid-ocean stranding on the atoll he had ceased to be a European, and yet he had not become a true sea-gypsy. Maybe that was the source of regret? Maybe, too, he knew he must either lose the sea for ever or else become it for ever by diving in and omitting to surface again. Hence Arezzo, and the grumpy discourse of his later years.

Meanwhile, he learned that the ebony statue had been the body of one of their princes, wrapped mummy-like in a single length of sharkskin flayed on the bias in the manner of a peeled orange. Once tightly bound, this skin was given many thick coats of a shellac made from boiled carrageen or similar seaweed mixed with a mucilage extracted from turtle bones and tree sap. This treatment produced the smooth, dully shining black surface he had so easily mistaken for carved wood. The care and ritual the natives had lavished on their chieftain's body was proper to the awe in which they held the sea and their duty to return their own bodies to its dissolving embrace. To lie buried on land was unthinkable. As he understood more and more, Forbici appreciated the irony of having been cast up in a marine cemetery. Not snapped-off flutes of coral, then, but countless gypsy bones had strewn the bottom of the pool. From time to time he heard again the small, gull-like cries among the sound of the waves, and saw the fat fish sniffing around the wicker figureheads lying companionably near the mummy. Had the children known their fate even as they shrilly begged the island's spirits for permission to land, rolling their eyes and flapping their wings? He never found out. Or if he did, he never confided it to his 'Parergo', with its mood of grieving for unnamed things.

6

The last pair of divers brought their baskets of lobsters to the surface at around three-thirty in the morning. The gullies both south and north of the Madonna had been worked out, but there were many crevasses yet to be explored. A couple of empty ice chests were left over when the others had been filled.

'That's enough,' the captain said.

'There's another good hour's darkness left,' somebody objected.

An electrical storm far out to sea gave silent glimpses of cloud banks low on one horizon, snapshots of a bruised pearl-and-ginger colour. Otherwise the night was lit only by constellations. Little Turtle's river of tears, known elsewhere as the Milky Way, flowed across the sky as though grief were the universe's most prominent feature. It outshone the other playlets, yet the starlight faded as it fell to earth. The ocean mopped up its dazzle as with thick cloth. In the darkness surrounding the

Medevina little ambient detail was visible. The coastguard's patrol boats were evidently in another patch of territorial water tonight.

'We shouldn't push our luck.'

The boat's name was a composite of those of captain Nicomedes and his wife Divina, though the craft was jointly owned by four people who worked it as a cooperative. Medes's decision to call a halt might have been challenged by any of his three companions who thought it wasteful not to profit by an extra hour and fill the last boxes. Yet nobody argued. It was as though everyone aboard was mindful of the dead fisherman we had left afloat so many hours ago, of the vengeance his spirit might wreak if given the provocation. (You will not have forgotten that when the trip was nearly over, and a familiar coastline was once more off the bow, one of the divers confessed he wouldn't have felt easy that night working any new beds further away from the Madonna, whose chalky lump had given its blessing to our poaching activities.) Spell and counter-spell.

So the air hoses were coiled and stowed; the engine was stopped and reconnected to the propeller shaft; weak, sweet coffee was passed around in the ringing silence. Cigarette ends glowed in relief. An offshore breeze brought distant beach smells of wrack and drying caves. The tension that had preceded the diving had gone, the omens were forgotten. Quiet laughter rose from murmured talk. We were not going to be arrested this trip.

The engine was started and we took up a homeward course. The starlight fell yet more faintly. An overcast was creeping from the east, extinguishing the Octopus's suckers one by one, then the Brazier, and finally blotting Little Turtle's tears. The night grew deeper. Though there was scarcely any wind, the sea became suddenly choppier and from this we knew we had left the shelter of the invisible headland and would soon be out of enemy waters. An hour later we had a tiny running light aloft, dawn seemed no nearer and the chop was sending smacks of spray from the bows to rattle aft against a hunching of plastic raincoats. This was no threatening change in the weather, though; just the patchy moodiness of the sea as it was strained through the archipelago, bounced between land masses, alternately heated and cooled, convected and churned between abyssal currents and shallow races. Soon the coffee's warmth was long gone and everyone had retreated into himself, wrapped in wet plastic, staring at the same patch of planking or tackle, waiting for the return of daylight and calm water and the heat of the rising sun.

The cold end of a working night, the hypnotic blare of the engine: it must have been these which explained the lack of attention. With a crash the boat suddenly reared and flung everyone sprawling in the bilges. Cries went up and the captain cut the engine. The first thought was of having run aground at full throttle, the constant fear in coral seas where hidden reefs can rise to within inches of the surface. But the bottom was still in the boat and we were not yet floundering in the dark ocean. The captain and the mate hurried forward with torches. According to their curses we had rammed a drifting log, a common hazard in these parts.

'If ever a trip was jinxed . . . '

Lights were flashed astern to see what we had overrun. Sure enough, something was rolling in our dispersing wake. The captain was on his knees in the bows, examining the damage. We were holed on the waterline: not a crippling wound, but several square inches of marine ply were stove in. A strong smell of petrol was stealing over the boat. More shouts. A cigarette end was flung judiciously overboard. A spare polythene container of fuel stowed in the bows had been holed by the impact and several gallons had run into the bilges before the two men extricated the crushed container.

You will not have forgotten how everyone set to bailing with every available mug and bowl. The boat's rocking dead in the water was accompanied by crunchings and creakings from the darkness where the port outrigger lay. Light beams focused on it. Tangled up in our paired bamboo floats were the tilted spars of a small boat.

'We hit a boat!'

'It wasn't a log!'

'Jesus, Mary and Joseph! This whole damned ocean's full of abandoned boats tonight.'

'It was a log! Look, you can see it behind us.'

But beneath the vaporous smell of petrol another, familiar

41

stench was filling the air. A single voice cried out, 'Oh my God, it's *him!*' and a select chill went through us all. The more trembling beams converged on the torpid object in the sea astern, the more clearly they revealed it as the body we had abandoned some eight hours earlier.

If, as claimed, there is in the human mind a gambling instinct, a constant assessment of odds, moments of shock reveal it as being definitely more reliant on superstition than on statistics. There was nobody aboard, yourself included, who did not become caught up in demanding what were the chances of hitting the same boat . . . ? And coming up with the predetermined answer: 'Astronomical!' Afterwards, though, on dry land and with a couple of nights' sleep separating the event from its memory, anyone might soberly have reassessed those chances. The fisherman had been drifting with the current; our captain always went with the current as far as possible. It was the act of a seaman who knows how to lean on nature and save fuel whenever he can. Our collision was unlikely enough, surely, but not so incredible as to make it seem—as it did in the dark, with water and petrol bubbling around our bare feet—fated, ordained, even Justice catching up with us. Nobody who lives off the sea remains a rationalist for long. Those of the crew who earlier had consoled their consciences with defiant cries of 'No time!' now began planning the truce they would enact with the dead man before his unappeased spirit might ruin us entirely.

The boat was paddled backwards until the body drifted under the counter. The curious crowded back to view it, thereby making the captain's repairs easier by lifting the hole in the bows clear of the water. The stink of fuel and decay rolled over us. Nobody dared light a cigarette to make breathing easier. Torn-up rags were tied over faces so we became the masked crew of a plague barge. A rope was belayed around one of the fisherman's swollen calves. The noose's friction soon began to slough the skin off and it seemed likely that his little boat had itself been leaking so that his lower body had steeped in sea water for several hours.

The hatless corpse had swollen greatly since the moment we had last glimpsed him like a lone King Arthur faring forth to Avalon. His back was now as wide and flat as a slab. The T-shirt stretched across it advertising a brand of paint was already going in ovals at the seams. His shorts were likewise cracking as though the buttocks beneath were plumped with silicone. Pathos no longer attached itself to this body, wallowing inert as a bolster. His statuesque silence and exaltation had vanished. Only his hair, the liveliest part, floated and streamed in puffs of current as it once had on windy days.

'This time he must be buried.'

'For certain. I don't care if he committed suicide. We're risking our lives until he's given a Christian burial.'

'Oh don't start that again, Mots. We don't know his religion.'

'It's all one God,' the dogged voice said. 'We'll give him a Christian burial because it's the only one we know.'

'You know it, do you? The proper service like Father Deme knows?'

'Even Father Demetrio doesn't know it. He *reads* it.'

The talk went on. It revealed nothing but a universal refusal to touch the decaying body, to turn it face up, to have anything further to do with it other than piously to wish it gone.

The two boys crawled out on the struts and freed the remains of the fisherman's boat. Without support the little hulk filled and sank until nothing but the outline of its own bamboo outrigger was visible. Since it was too small for an engine it had never been registered and there was no identifying number painted on its bow. Nor was there any way of towing it. The captain ordered it to be cast adrift and it soon vanished.

All this time dawn was slowly breaking above the cloud cover, sending down a stealing greyness as through a suspended sheet of ground glass. Our world took on shape. A swirl of water became visible from just beyond an outrigger.

'Oy pating, pating!' someone shouted, and the additional fear of sharks found a perch next to the other dread spirits already crowding our boat's superstructure. There was no question now of doing anything with the body except sinking it as hastily as possible. The longer it stayed tied to us, the longer we ourselves would remain bait.

Meanwhile, the captain and the mate had jury-rigged a repair. The patch was not quite watertight but with luck would hold at reduced speed provided we kept our weight in the stern. They now decided what they might sacrifice to send the dead man to the bottom. The spare anchor could go, and so could the rusty acetylene cylinder used as a reserve air tank when a third diver was deployed. A discussion broke out as to how much weight was needed to take the corpse down, inflated with gas as it was. The men decided to err on the side of excess. Nobody wanted to see this man ever again, although he was probably destined to bob up in many a dream. Now, respectfully, and with the sacrifice of many dollars' worth of equipment, he was being asked to leave us alone.

The assorted weights were firmly tied to the end of the rope attached to his leg. At a suggestion, some people took amulets and crosses from their own necks and wound them around the iron. The captain said: 'I don't know this service. Let's say the *Ama Namin* for the poor fellow, and God give him and us rest.' Out on the dawning ocean the Lord's Prayer rose raggedly towards the ground-glass ceiling. The sea was calmer now and the boat merely wallowed slightly in the swell. Had the sun been up we would no doubt have been revealed once more as surrounded by an iridescent membrane of fuel clawed here and there into holes by cat's-paws of wind. Swaying on a few planks above unknown fathoms of water the crew muttered while the grey bowl of air around us began to fill with the sensation of lifting, as though the remaining darkness were rising like helium to dissolve in the sky. Barely waiting for the various murmurs of 'Amen' and *'Siya nawa'*, the captain began unhitching the cord that secured his precious boat to its albatross. With a series of loud splashes the weights followed each other into the sea.

The length of line gave the iron a second or two in which to sink and take up the slack between it and the dead man's ankle. Then—and how quickly it happened!—the corpse gave a start, a half twist and a sweep of one arm like that of an engrossed snorkeller jerking up for air. For a shutter's click his face turned towards us, a swollen and eroded Buddha, before he vanished. A collective sigh was heaved; nobody spoke. We continued, mesmerized, to watch the water as though expecting him to reappear.

So we stood in the lightening dawn and stared at the sea.

Hardly any of us doubted the unknown fisherman's power to haunt. If meeting him once had seemed fated, his finding us again had been uncanny. Nobody would have been much surprised, though petrified, had he miraculously started up out of the waves, pointed a dripping finger and cursed us all. But a long minute passed and nothing more menacing occurred than a couple of abrupt disturbances in the water some way off to suggest the restless prowling of predators. Then the entire boat was enveloped in a reek of corruption that made everyone clap his hands across his cloth-wound mouth. It was so intense it suggested a physical presence, as though the deceased had secretly joined us again, his identity concealed by a mask. On an inspiration a bottle of rum was passed around, the liquor liberally splashed on the cloth protecting mouth and nose. Pulling himself from this collective trance of disgust, the captain tried to start the engine. On the third attempt it caught; and in the welcome blare of machinery we moved slowly from under the primitive cloud and set a course for home.

As soon as the masks were ripped off and lungs were filling with morning air, a discussion broke out between those who believed the appalling stench was the manifestation of an evil spirit and others who thought that when the corpse had reached a sufficient depth, pressure would have ruptured its decomposing tissues and released the pent-up gases in one stinking bubble. Either that, or a shark had attacked it, which would have produced the same result. This debate was still going on when there were fresh cries from the stern and once again the engine was cut.

It seemed that even now the dead man was not finished with us. Someone had noticed that the pile of polystyrene cool boxes containing the lobsters had become shrunken and lopsided beneath its protective shroud of tarpaulin. On investigation it was found that the leaked petrol had melted the bottoms of the two lowest boxes and that all the lobsters in them were dead or contaminated by fumes. One by one the mate began throwing them over the side. Each small splash represented wasted time, wasted danger, wasted effort and diminishing pay for everyone aboard. Finally the last of the spilt fuel was mopped up and the surviving boxes restacked on a base of boards scrounged from elsewhere in the boat. The two bottomless and soggy boxes were balefully thrown overboard where, light as they were, they drifted cantedly astern as we resumed our course. They remained visible a long while, brilliantly white in the rising sun, like children's coffins floating in our wake.

7

Do you remember this?

Uneasy weather. Beneath blusters of warm wind, the empty metallic ringing of crickets. Uneasy place, too. A little coastline familiar in its every indentation, recently condemned to death, or at least to transfiguration. (The toad developers. Restlessly they gobble up beaches and excrete hotels, restlessly they move on.) You were in a doze, half watching the never-settling terns pick morsels out of the surf, when you thought the dead fisherman walked out of the sea and stood in front of the sun. He was bones but he wore the same recognizable clothes and had even found his conical straw hat. The T-shirt was faded, the Boysen paint ad. illegible. It was huge now, draped across his clavicles as though on a hanger. The baggy shorts hung off his hip bones. Yet when he began his harangue he enunciated clearly even though his tongue was missing. He was neither maledictory nor exalted, but sneering.

'Easy—it's so *easy*, isn't it? The mellifluous prose? An ear for cadence and some good, heartwarming ethnic action—us brown fisherfolk doing our thing. Add to that the old chestnut, Death, guaranteed to bestow solemnity on the emptiest writing.

'So here we are in the South Seas, near enough, which despite everything still carries a feeble voltage of the exotic for your sort. They will ask: *Was it true? Did that story really happen about the dead guy sitting in his boat? Did you actually . . . ?* And there's no answer. That's the splendid thing about writing: it's neither true nor untrue, fact nor fiction. What it is, is words on a page ordered more or less skilfully. You might have witnessed these marine dramas scores of times or never once—there's no knowing.

'How easy, too, to drop in some delicious little games: bogus scholarship, cryptic parables, fake cosmogony . . . Are you telling me that stuff about fishes' spirits and Little Turtle and shipwrecked scholars was *genuine*?

'No—don't interrupt. How is it you foreigners feel so free to come half across the world to load us with your fantasies and anxieties and well-earned guilt when God knows we're laden enough as it is? "Idyll"—that's the word you're always using to describe our workplace. That and "paradise". Look at me,' (and here the figure raised his arms, bones greenish in the sun). 'Do I look like someone who has recently passed through paradise? Do *you*? Besides, what's wrong with cement hotels? There's more of a future in them than in stick villages. We'd all like the chance of a job in one. Waiter, pool attendant, bellboy, chef, maid. Toiling away, maybe, but toiling away in air-conditioning and for a regular wage. Myself, I quite fancy croupier. Raking in cash has the edge over hauling in fish.'

You will remember that it was being able to see the terns again, still not settling at the surf's edge but constantly making as though to alight, that woke you to his sudden absence. The fisherman had gone. Nothing now stood between you and the sun, and in its light the cantankerous and ungrateful old fool's arguments became as shadowy as he.

When the terns had gone and sunset's massive city was heaped on the horizon in cinnabar and madder, you will remember that the dead fisherman (even then puffing through your lungs and coursing in your blood) had not had it entirely his own way. Before he faded you had got a word in, sharp with the triumphalism of the living. You told him there might once have been a pathetic resonance in the suggestion that he had committed suicide, but there was no further need to be respectful towards a distress that would have vanished at the moment of death. You told him his arguments were nothing, vapour, just the constant opening of blind conversational alleyways which were as constantly closed off again, conceptual clouds. You informed him that you would use him entirely as you saw fit, together with his compatriots, the scenery, diverting cosmogonies, smells, sounds and words. The reason was simple. For as long as you were alive it was your world and your ocean.

8

You will remember how puzzled you were as a child to discover that an event is more like itself when anticipated or recalled than when it is happening. The sea's deep discovery must also speak of things other than itself to ring on in the mind, the sonar pulses of enquiry bouncing back from hidden apprehensions. In like fashion, and according to taste, death needs stars and ocean for it to be real, to acquire proper echoes. Cut off from its grand inklings and sprawling starfields it is wispish. Without playlets it has no weight. Without a little solemnity death is a kind of failure, recasting the handful of days as trivial and forecasting only a savage void. Yet as long as Little Turtle can see it and weep, the fatal life is acknowledged, safe in its moment. The ocean wraps the planet like a caul. Flinging grave, the mind's capacious habitat: we are its children. Provided the sea takes us back, the bloat and decay are acceptable even if the deal remains raw.

Slowly you grew accustomed to this idea that the mind must always falsify things before they can become true. Otherwise, a gap opens between facts and the need to make them private. So you once wrote that even as you were seventeen, you yearned to be seventeen, a fancy that seemed perverse until you found it echoed in Basho's haiku:

> Even in Kyoto, hearing the cuckoo's cry,
> I long for Kyoto.

All the unresting melancholy that the now announces—through its cuckoos, its breaking waves, its playground voices, the idea of Kyoto—pushes thought aside. Sitting at night alone on the ocean in a small boat ought to pare things right down. It does; but never to that point of inhuman Buddhistic virtue where one embarks on an immaculate passage into nothingness. The details of survival, of the sea itself, beguile; the playlets captivate. Not being fish we mourn things, the present especially. The now is as irretrievably shut to fishermen as to poets. It is less accessible even than the past, peopled as that is with ancestors and our lost companions. We are filled with homesickness for no identifiable home: for the Kyoto in which we are writing which is not quite the Kyoto we long to be writing in; for the birthday we passed through but never quite achieved; for the sunlit embrace of an end that will heal us from itself. Playing with time, we embellish the bonework of existence to our solitary taste.

One morning in early spring, at an open casement in Arezzo, we catch an impossible whiff of ocean. A figure in battered clothes steps out of the front door below carrying a single strapped bag. It is Giusto Forbici. He has the air of someone who will not return.

Those cries on a lift of wind from beyond the railway station are the sound of gulls and surf, or maybe of children foreseeing their deaths. That is not snow but petals drifting past the window, the cherries returned to gauntness and waiting for leaf.　　□

A journey at the edge of the world

PHILIP MARSDEN

AUTHOR OF **THE BRONSKI HOUSE**

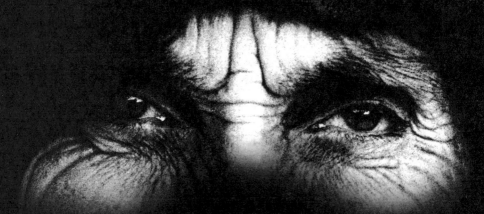

THE
SPIRIT-WRESTLERS
A RUSSIAN JOURNEY

The most penetrating account of Russian life since
the Soviet Union's collapse made travel possible again

'Marsden has a dazzling gift for poetic evocation'
JOHN FOWLES, *Spectator*

HarperCollinsPublishers

IAN JACK
SERENDIP

SS Nuddea, 7,928 gross tons, 1919-1936   DUNCAN HAWS

The people of Sri Lanka (or Ceylon as it was then known) first saw the power of steam in ships, and then the railways came. Much later, in 1981, I met a madman on the platform of Colombo railway station, the narrow-gauge side. The Tamil war on the island was just beginning. I was working for a Sunday newspaper in London at the time and had filed my copy for the week. Now, on a Sunday afternoon, I could relax. I decided to take a look at the little branch line, rumoured to be still worked by steam locomotives, which runs up from the capital to the town of Ratnapura and the tea and rubber estates in the foothills. That was how I met Mr Goonawardene.

No trains were expected. The station was deserted. He must have been watching me for some time from his position behind the pillar. He may even have seen in my behaviour a kindred spirit; the way, for example, I walked up and down the platform peering over the edge for tell-tale signs of locomotive cinders on the tracks—what could that be but derangement? His approach was startlingly direct.

'Sir, sir, allow me to introduce myself. My name is Goonawardene and I am a racialist.'

He was a thin man in grubby white clothes and black lacing shoes which lacked shoelaces. He wanted to tell me his theory of the world, how it had developed and where it had gone wrong.

The guilty party, he said, was Western science. Out of science had come industry and medicine. The industrial countries of the West had enormous appetites for raw materials—cotton, tea, sugar, rubber, oil—and to feed these appetites they had behaved like capricious gods, plucking people from one country and dumping them in another without a thought for tomorrow. Think of it! Africans dispatched by sea to the Caribbean to cut sugar; Indians exported by sea to Africa to build railways; and here, in Sri Lanka, Tamilians shipped by ferry from India to pick tea. Then Western medicine had come along with its bag of tricks and permitted all these black and brown people to multiply; 'to breed like microbes', was how Mr Goonawardene put it.

He shaped a globe with his hands and waggled his fingers to show it pulsating. I imagined a round Dutch cheese alive with grubs. 'A mess, a most terrible mess. Blacks, whites, browns, yellows, all mixed up. They must be sent back to where they came from and then we shall have some peace.' His fingers stopped moving. The globe was now calm and orderly. 'That is why I call myself a racialist.'

I was anxious to get away. 'Well,' I said, 'no trains to Ratnapura today. I should be getting back to the hotel.'

But it was not so easy. 'No, no, train is coming soon. A little train, lots of smoke. You'll like it.' He dusted a station bench with his sleeve. 'Sit, please sir, sit.'

We sat. Mr Goonawardene leaned forward, as though he had noticed me for the first time as a person as well as an audience. 'Which is your country?'

'Britain.'

He broke into a broad smile. 'Ah, then you are the guilty-party-in-chief. Step forward into the dock. I shall be the prosecutor. Now tell me, Mr Britisher, who perfected the steam engine?'

'James Watt.'

'Correct. A Scotchman, born I believe in the seaport of Greenock. A great man. It may be that he and Isaac Newton are the only two British scientists of what we may call world class, at least until the atomic age. Now give me the place and date of the first railway in the world.'

'Stockton and Darlington. Was it in 1825?'

'Very correct. George Stephenson was the engineer. Imagine! A boy who worked at a coal mine, who could neither read nor write by the age of eighteen, and yet he built the world's first really successful steam locomotives. But I can see you know everything, your knowledge is A1.'

We sat together like a schoolmaster and his successful pupil. Then Mr Goonawardene winked and became playful. Could I tell him who had perfected the internal-combustion engine? I fumbled; not Henry Ford?

'No, no. Herr Rudolph Diesel, 1897. And Diesel was a native of which country?'

I guessed Germany and Mr Goonawardene said that was right, though in fact Herr Diesel had been born in Paris. The inventor died in mysterious circumstances, vanishing from the deck of a cross-channel steamer in the year before the outbreak of the First World War. Mr Goonawardene suspected suicide. 'Like many great men he may have suffered mania and depression. I am also suffering from the same condition and I have been tempted by the same fate. But do you see what I am trying to tell you?'

His arms went out to make a see-saw. 'Britishers invent the steam engine. Britain goes up. Germans invent the petrol engine. Germans and their cousins the Americans go up. Britain comes down.' These days, he said, only backward places such as Colombo ever saw a steam locomotive and even here they were rare.

The afternoon wore on. It was a grey day in the tropics. A curtain of rain swept in from the Indian Ocean and hammered on the station roof. Mr Goonawardene began to shiver.

'When is the train coming, Mr Goonawardene?'

'Soon, soon.'

A lie; but he couldn't let me go, our quiz was too delightful a conversational form. What tune had the band played when the Titanic went down? Who was the most powerful man in Stalinist Russia? ('Stalin?' Tsk, tsk! 'Beria, the head of the secret police?' Tsk, tsk again. No, it was Maxim Litvinov, the Soviet ambassador in London and Washington, though I can't now remember why.) And then he named three prominent Britons: a journalist, a peer and a politician. Did I know these people? I said I knew of them. Then would I write to them on his behalf?

'I want them to set up a commission of enquiry, to come to Colombo and establish my sanity.' For the past twenty years he had lived in the Angoda lunatic asylum—it was, he said, 'a fine three-storey building of the British period'—but he had never believed, because he knew so much, that he could really be insane. 'And you must admit,' he said finally, 'that I am knowing a pretty damn lot, isn't it?'

No train ever came, at least on the narrow-gauge side. My companion went home to his asylum and I returned to my room overlooking the ocean at the Galle Face Hotel. There were ships on the horizon, their shapes occasionally blurred by the rain which came and went in squalls and dark patches which moved across the sea. They were square shapes. I imagined a flat hull loaded with containers and not the raked funnels and curving sterns of my childhood. That night, remembering Mr Goonawardene and the ships, I wrote to my father, who was dying.

It was not a good letter. Nobody had told my father he hadn't long to live, though perhaps in his conscious moments he understood this well enough. My letter was part of a cheerful pretence. I knew that more than fifty years before he had sailed into Colombo as a junior engineer on a cargo steamer, the SS *Nuddea*, and so I described Colombo: how a lighthouse still stood in the main street, how the tea now went by containers, how some people still remembered the British India Steam Navigation Company, the line which had owned the *Nuddea*, though the puritanical black-and-white funnels of its ships no longer popped up above the dock's high walls. In my father's time it had been one of the biggest shipping companies in the world. I made a few jokes—cheerfulness, that was the thing—and hoped that he was feeling better.

He died a couple of months later. For most of his life he had worked as a steam mechanic, a fitter, one of the men who were on the downswinging end of Mr Goonawardene's see-saw. One of Watt's children; I had never heard him mention Herr Diesel, though the German had perfected his engine five years before my father was born. The saddest change in him, my mother said, was the way that, long before the end, he had completely lost interest in the world. He had read a few sentences of my letter from Colombo and then laid it down on the bedspread and said nothing. 'And you know what your father was like,' my mother said, 'he was always so interested in things.' I remembered a saying of his, spoken from the heart of a man who had grown up among the gossip of a small Scottish town: 'Stupid folk talk about other folk. Intelligent folk talk about things.'

Five years later I came back to Sri Lanka. The Tamil war was now in full swing. Tamil guerrillas had beaten back the Sri Lankan army in the north of the island. Troops were regularly ambushed or blown up by landmines, and the Sinhalese in the south were frightened and angry. Bombs went off in Colombo, while in the countryside entire villages were rounded up and massacred, Sinhalese by the Tamils and Tamils by the Sinhalese. Tourists and businessmen no longer came. Colombo's hotels were empty. At the Galle Face they said I could have any room—even the Royal Scandinavian Suite—for less than half the listed price.

Mr Goonawardene's diagnosis looked in the case of his own country to have been right. Ethnic differences within the same nation had exploded into savagery (though science and the West could hardly be blamed; Sri Lanka's Tamil separatists were not those Tamils imported from India by the British to pick tea; they had arrived long before European colonization). But where was Mr Goonawardene? Now, on another Sunday with another newspaper story safely filed, I went down to the railway station again. Nobody in the stationmaster's office had seen him. What kind of man was I looking for?

'Thin and old,' I said, 'and slightly mad, but he knows a lot. He said he came here often in the afternoons—the platforms on the narrow-gauge side.'

'We have seen no such person.'

Sitting alone in the wide open spaces of the Royal Scandinavian Suite and listening to the sea, I began to think I'd made him up. The next day, I asked at the British Council library. The women behind the counter said she thought she knew who I meant. He had died a year back. 'He came here every morning to read the *Encyclopaedia Britannica* and the London newspapers. He wrote a lot in his notebook. He was interested in everything, all kinds of facts.'

That was all she remembered: Mr Goonawardene as a heap of facts who was locked up every night in the Angoda asylum. He had left no other trace of personality. An old version of Europe— the Europe of Watt and the British India Steam Navigation Company, the Europe of curiosity and enquiry—had sailed to Sri Lanka and planted seeds in him. And the seeds had sprouted to cover his personality like bindweed. His was a seaborne disease. □

GEORGE ROSIE
NORTHERN LIGHT

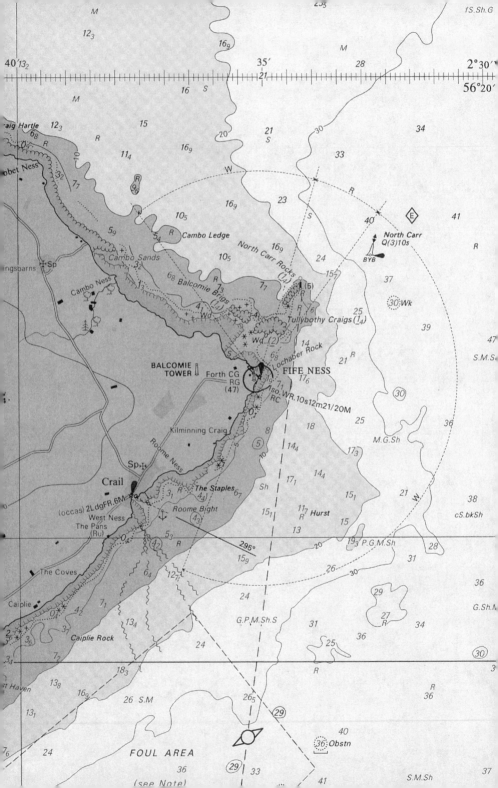

Trying to catch sight of the place where my father used to work, I drove along the dull, straight road that runs from the little town of Crail to the headland called Fife Ness. The road ran across flat farmland, attached to farms with names such as Sauchope, Foulhugger and Balcomie, and then through the derelict hangars and barracks of what used to be the Royal Naval Air Station, Crail, before it petered out in the car park of the Crail Golfing Society. I parked the car and walked down the track that led to the lighthouse and the coastguard station. At the foot of the lighthouse, I took out my binoculars and focused them on the sea to the north-east, but the tide was high and there was hardly anything to see. The remains of an ancient iron beacon stuck out from the water, which, some distance behind the beacon, took on a slight turbulence, a chop and a swirl. I knew from my map that this rougher patch marked the eastern extremity of a series of fourteen sandstone rocks. My map gave each a name: Englishman's Skelly, Knee Stone, Tullybothy Craigs, Lochaber Rock, Mary's Skelly. Collectively, they are known as the Carr Briggs or the North Carr rocks. Beside them lie wrecks: the schooner *Louise*, the trawlers *James Ross* and *Festing Grindall*, the tanker *Vildfugl*, the brig *Andreas*, the paddle steamer *Commodore*, the coaster *Island Magee*, the cargo steamers *Einar Jarl* and *Bjornhaug*. The Carr Briggs stand at the entrance to the Firth of Forth and have been wrecking ships since ships first sailed in the North Sea.

I walked among the rocks, sand and coarse grass of Fife Ness and looked again at the slight roughening out to sea. I had never been to this place before, and yet I had known it all my life. For almost forty years my father had manned the North Carr lightship, first as a seaman, then as mate, and finally as skipper. From the time he first climbed up the side of the *North Carr* in the autumn of 1932 until the autumn of 1969, the rocks off Fife Ness had been at the centre of his life. Guarding the rocks had given him a skill and a wage. They had dictated how we lived and where.

My father is ninety-two now and nearly blind, a short, stocky man, often smiling, who has never lost the half-Gaelic, half-Scots accent of Caithness, his birthplace in the far north of Scotland. He followed his father into the Caithness fishing trade, and when, in 1932, he made the 300-mile journey south to Edinburgh he came clutching references from an assortment of shipowners and skippers. 'A good and competent hand', wrote the owner of the motor vessel *Burrayness*. 'Very satisfactory . . . a young man of excellent character', was the opinion of the skipper of the herring drifter *Mayberry*. The master of the steamship *Helder* regarded him as 'a steady, sober and industrious worker'.

The letters impressed the Northern Lighthouse Board, which assigned him as a seaman to the North Carr lightship. With a steady job—none of the fickleness and uncertainty of seagoing—he decided to marry and sent to Caithness for my mother, who was then working in Wick in the steam and heat of the John O'Groats Laundry. In Edinburgh, my parents settled into a small, well-defined world. They moved only once: from a two-roomed flat (in an 1890s tenement) with a view of Granton harbour to a four-roomed flat (in a 1930s tenement) with a view of Granton harbour. The second had a bathroom; the first did not. The distance between the two houses was about a mile. We were happy in both. We lived to the rhythms of my father's work, with his two weeks of every month at sea and the other two weeks ashore.

He loved his ship from the beginning. The third (and last) North Carr lightship came new from her builders on the Clyde a year after he had joined the service, replacing her ungainly, Victorian predecessor. ('An old scow of a thing,' my father told me. 'She sat so low in the water that her decks were always awash. Your seaboots were never off your feet. And the only way up to the light was up a rope ladder in the rigging. No joke on a rough night.') The new *North Carr* was a hundred feet long and weighed 250 tons, with a forty-foot-high light tower placed in the middle of her superstructure. She was kept on station by a main anchor weighing three tons and many fathoms of steel anchor chain. Her light signal was two quick flashes every thirty seconds; her fog signal two blasts every ninety seconds. She had her problems. In a north-easterly sea she proved too lively for comfort and had to have twenty tons of ballast added. The mizzen-sail that was supposed to keep the ship's head into the wind proved to be more trouble than it was worth. But to my father, she was, as he often said, a palace.

We got to see her every two years, when she was towed up the Firth of Forth and into dry dock in the port of Leith for overhaul. Her anchors and chains would be inspected, her diesel generators, compressors and electrical systems checked. There would be repainting—the words NORTH CARR were picked out in large white letters on either side of her red hull—and something like six tons of barnacles, mussels and assorted gastropods would be scraped from her. During this time, we'd visit the ship as a family every Sunday. My younger brother and I were put into our best clothes and then took the tram two miles along the shore to Leith.

My mother did not enjoy these visits—she loathed everything to do with the sea and ships—but my brother and I never wearied of clambering into every corner: the engine room, the chain lockers, the galley, the crew's quarters, the wireless room, the watch room, my father's 'saloon'. The big event was being allowed into the lamp room. It was like climbing into a rainbow. The sunlight that streamed in through the windows struck the facets of the four big lenses, separated, and danced around the room. I can still see the way the fragments of colour played across my father's face as he gently unhinged the lenses and tried to explain the mystery.

This is what he told me: the concentric circles of ground glass that made up the lenses magnified the light from a 250-watt bulb hundreds of thousands of times. The lenses took that light, focused it into a narrow beam, and threw the beam out for more than ten miles. A motor in the engine room turned the apparatus so that it gave two quick flashes every thirty seconds. That signal told every ship entering or leaving the Firth of Forth exactly where the Carr rocks lurked, and to steer well clear.

No smear of grease was allowed to impede the progress of the light. Every morning at the end of the four-to-eight 'dog' watch, the crew would clean the lamp-room windows inside and out, and polish the ground glass of the lenses until every facet shone. In my father's kingdom, the light was everything. Tending it was his career. He was promoted from seaman to mate (the junior master) in time for the Second World War, when the *North Carr*, newly armed with anti-aircraft guns, was towed from the east to the west coast of Scotland and anchored at the mouth of the Clyde estuary, where she marked the mine-free channel used

by the convoys that crossed the North Atlantic. There, at five
minutes to midnight on 5 October 1944, she was hit by the Cunard
liner *Franconia*, outward bound for America and sailing at speed
to avoid U-boats. 'What a bang that was,' my father would say.
'It was only a sideways swipe on the starboard bow but she damn
near did for us. Nor did she stop to see what had happened, or
whether she could help. She probably never noticed.'

In 1945, the *North Carr* went back to her old station. In
1946, my father became the skipper, the senior master. I was five
years old then. Gradually I got to know him, in an Edinburgh
and way of life that has almost ceased to exist.

Edinburgh was then a maritime city, even though it always
seemed half-ashamed of the fact, too grand for it. Nautical
enterprises of all kinds flourished on the three miles of the
city's shore between Granton harbour and Leith docks. There
were four fleets of trawlers, there were seine-netters, cargo ships,
shipbuilding yards, boat repairers, one factory that made fishing
nets and another that made wire for ropes, and a wide range of
ships' chandlers, shipping agents and marine insurance brokers.
Edinburgh Zoo had, and has still, the finest stock of penguins in
Europe because the Leith whaling ships brought the birds back
from the Antarctic.

But seagoing jobs were chancy. The coastal lines hired on a
trip-by-trip basis. The whaling industry was on its way out. The
Edinburgh-based 'deep-sea' firms demanded all kinds of
certificates. Wages from the fishing depended on how good your
skipper was at finding the fish. Jobs on the tug and pilot boats
were few and poorly paid. Very few Edinburgh seamen had the
kind of job security that my father had. And so a procession of
hopefuls used to turn up at our door looking for 'Captain Rosie'.
Most of them were ex-trawlermen, some had been in prison. My
father would always invite the man in, sit him down and question
him, while my mother made them both tea. She liked to form her
own impressions. 'She was a better judge of character than I was,'
my father said after she died. 'She was usually right about who
would last and who wouldn't. If she told me that I'd be sorry for
hiring a man, I usually was.'

I was loyal to the *North Carr*, but as I grew up her engineless condition bothered me; I dearly wished that she could sail under her own power like the grey warships that slipped up and down the Firth of Forth to Rosyth, or the tough little trawlers and coasters that sailed out of Granton and Leith. One of my friends, a boy called Billy Alexander, had a father who was reputed to be one of the finest trawler skippers ever to sail out of Edinburgh. One day Billy goaded me: the *North Carr* wasn't a real ship because it didn't have an engine. He was two years older than me, and a lot bigger, but I let fly. He hit back, and I ended up with a loose tooth and a fat lip. Later, after the tears had been dried and the blood mopped up, his father took me aside. He told me that there was nothing trickier than steering into the Firth of Forth on a 'dirty night' and that if it wasn't for the *North Carr*, trawlermen like himself would be in trouble, if not dead. I remember his words. 'Your dad's ship is the most important ship in the Firth. And that makes him the most important skipper in Edinburgh.'

The idea that he planted in my head—that my dad's boat kept everybody else's dads alive—stuck with me. It was a good thought, and it grew. I began to see my father in a light that would have startled him. He became the heroic leader of a heroic crew, a grim figure guarding the jagged Carr rocks in storms which had the ships of other people's fathers scuttling for safety. Then, some years later, when I was thirteen, it turned from a comforting thought into an uncomfortable reality. In the early hours of 27 November 1954, the lightship *South Goodwin*, stationed in the English Channel, broke her anchor chain in an eighty mile an hour gale and was swept on to the sands, where she capsized. The master and his six-man crew died. The only survivor, a twenty-two-year-old scientist studying bird migration, had been plucked off the ship by an American helicopter. Lifeboats, as well as a warship and lightship tender, had sailed to the lightship's rescue but could do nothing.

When frogmen eventually cut their way through the hull they found no one. The inquiry decided that the crew had probably been swept away trying to abandon the ship.

I can still remember how I felt as I studied the picture of the overturned lightship in our copy of the *Scottish Daily Express*. It

63

was an aerial photograph. The ship was lying on her side on the sand with the seas breaking around her. She looked almost identical to the *North Carr*. I had a sudden, terrifying picture of my father's body being tumbled along the sandbanks of the English Channel.

My mother did her best. She told me that the *North Carr* was a better-built ship than the *South Goodwin*, and that the English Channel was, somehow, more dangerous than the Firth of Forth. The waves were bigger, the swell stronger and the Goodwin Sands more exposed than the Carr rocks. She tried hard, but I was not convinced. I could see the fear in her eyes, and I could hear it in her voice when she mentioned 'those poor women' of Kent and Sussex who had lost their menfolk. There had been calamities much closer to home. Her own brother David was lost at sea. In the winter gales of 1950, the Granton trawler *Margaret Paton* had disappeared, taking with her my father's cousin, James Watt, and several men who had previously crewed the *North Carr*. My mother knew them all; James Watt's sister was her good friend. But the fate of the South Goodwin lightship haunted her in a way that the loss of other ships and other men did not.

Still, my unease faded. My mother stopped fretting, my father's routine went on uninterrupted. Every two weeks a lighthouse tender—smart little ships with yellow funnels—would take him out to or back from the *North Carr*. It was humdrum, regular. At sea, after they had kept their watch, there was little for him or his crew to do. They fished a bit, and made things: wooden toys (garages, forts, yachts), belts woven from string. My father's speciality was rope. He wove indestructible rope doormats and rope slippers (I still have a pair), which he would bring back along with treats given to him by other light keepers, who were often Northmen like himself. We got white cheeses from Orkney, the whey we called 'crowdie', thick lumps of cooking chocolate, and gulls' eggs gathered from the Bass Rock or the May Island. They were dun-coloured and brown-speckled and they tasted pungently of fish. My mother would crack them into a bowl of flour and make scones.

It was a way of life that now seems more interesting to write than it was to live.

Inevitably, I began to nurse ideas of going to sea myself. These were gently, but firmly, undermined by my mother. She knew what made a seaman and it was not me. My father was not too keen either. They wanted something better. Some of my friends (Billy Alexander, for example) joined Edinburgh shipping lines as deck apprentices, but I became a student at the Edinburgh College of Art.

I still lived at home in the Granton tenement with the bathroom. I was there when, in the early hours of 8 December 1959, a gale roaring outside, my mother got a telephone call from my father's Edinburgh headquarters, the Northern Lighthouse Board. The *North Carr*'s anchor chain had severed and the ship was adrift in heavy seas off Fife Ness. The wind was from the south-east and it was pushing her towards the rocks. My mother made a wonderful fist of being calm. I wanted to stay at home with her, but she made me promise to attend my lectures. Everything would be all right. Nothing would happen to the *North Carr* so long as my father was in command.

Then, later that morning, I phoned her from the college and she was crying. A terrible thing had happened. The Fife Coastguard had called out the Broughty Ferry lifeboat to take my father and his crew off their drifting ship. In the howling darkness of the early morning the lifeboat had foundered at the mouth of the Tay. All eight men aboard had died. And the *North Carr* was still adrift, closer than before to the rocks of Fife.

For the next two days we lived, I think, in a suspended state of fear and shock. The telephone would ring. There was good news, or news that was not so good, and often no news at all but newspaper reporters looking for it. How did we feel? What did we think? How old would the sons in the family be? What were their father's favourite hobbies? Could they collect a family snap? My mother fielded the calls with remarkable grace and patience. I kept seeing the photograph of five years before, of the South Goodwin lightship lying on her side on the sandbank, and somehow I remembered the name of her drowned master: Tom Skipp. I had no idea what Tom Skipp looked like. I saw him only as my father, who was now a newspaper story himself.

What happened to him during those two days, however, is

best written in his own terse and sometimes ungrammatical account, which was submitted to the Northern Lighthouse Board within a few days of the event. His main anchor cable had parted at 02.02 on Tuesday 8 December. Immediately he put the port 'bower' (auxiliary) anchor over the side along with ninety fathoms of cable. At 06.30 that too had parted; 'with the result we were adrift again driving in a northwesterly direction'. Fifteen minutes later, and only 900 yards off the coast, he had tried again. He got the starboard bower anchor over the side along with 240 fathoms of cable 'to help hold the ship and also to lighten her head and make it easier for her to ride the heavy seas that were running'. It worked. The starboard bower anchor and the fathoms of cable held. (How I wished, again, that he had a ship with engines.)

Meanwhile, the lighthouse tender *Pharos* and the Navy tug *Earner* were steaming down the Firth of Forth towards his stricken ship. They arrived early in the afternoon and began a long struggle to get a line on board. For more than four hours, they fired rocket after rocket with lines which broke as quickly as they were secured. Eventually my father and Jim Hunter, the master of the *Pharos*, decided it might be safer for the lightship crew to stay aboard and ride out the storm in the hope that the weather would improve. But at daybreak on the Wednesday the wind and sea were worse than ever. More attempts were made to get a line aboard. All failed. At 11.30 the *Earner* radioed the naval base at Rosyth and asked for helicopters. An hour later, two hovered above the *North Carr*. To avoid the danger of their lines snagging on the mizzen-mast, my father ordered for it to be chopped down and heaved over the side. The first man was lifted off the roof of the watch room at 13.00. My father was the last to be picked up, at 13.45.

A newspaper photograph shows him being hustled out of the helicopter, still dapper in his brass-buttoned uniform and peaked cap. Another has him with a pint of beer at a hotel bar. He reported: 'After having a meal at the Golf Hotel, Crail, we left for home (by taxi) at 15.20 and arrived in Edinburgh at 18.00.' He ends his report with a tribute to his men who ' . . . in face of all this danger, never showed any sign of panic and carried out every order promptly and efficiently'.

That evening I pushed my way through the reporters who

had gathered outside our tenement. I found my father coming out of the bathroom. He was stripped to his vest, and there was shaving foam on his cheeks. He looked haggard, but he grinned when he saw me. He said: 'Hello, sonny boy.'

Two days later he was scrambling up a rope ladder on the *North Carr* to bring the ship into harbour for repair. He spent another nine years on her, fortnights on and off, but he was never quite the same. A few days after seeing the *North Carr* into Leith docks he went to bed: a chest infection, followed by angina and high blood pressure. He was too ill to attend the memorial service for the lifeboat crew in the ugly little Victorian church across the street from the lifeboat shed in Broughty Ferry, but every now and then he would talk about those men; forty years later, he still does. His guess is that the lifeboat turned south too soon, just before she had cleared the sandbar at the mouth of the Tay, and ran on to the sand and rolled over. 'Or maybe the sand had shifted,' he will say. 'It does that. We'll never know. But it's a hell of a thing to live with. The thought that good men died trying to help you. A hell of a thing.'

My mother, even after that time, never so far as I know complained or suggested he look for a job ashore. She was pleased for him when in 1961 he was awarded a British Empire Medal (an order now abolished; it was too obviously given to the lower ranks) and was disappointed only that the Minister of Transport officiated at the ceremony; she thought he had done enough to merit the Queen.

When he realized that she might have cancer, he wanted to take early retirement. But she would have none of it. He would be bored. He would get under her feet. He would miss his crew, his ship, the sea. But when the cancer came on, he retired anyway. He was sixty-three and soon widowed.

Many years after my mother died, I found a scrap of poetry scribbled in the flyleaf of one of the pre-war romantic novels she liked to read. It was from 'The Dry Salvages' by T. S. Eliot. I can't think where she'd come across it: Eliot was not on the syllabus of the John O'Groats steam laundry, and I had never heard her mention his name. But the words seem to have struck home:

Pray for all those who are in ships, those
Whose business has to do with fish, and
Those concerned with every lawful traffic
And those who conduct them.

Also pray for those who were in ships, and
Ended their voyage on the sand, in the sea's lips
Or in the dark throat which will not reject them
Or wherever cannot reach them the sound of the sea bell's
Perpetual angelus.

The *North Carr* herself was retired in 1975 and now, as part of Scotland's 'maritime heritage', lies moored in Dundee docks. Earlier, before this final resting place, she was berthed in a harbour on the Fife coast. One Sunday, I took my father to see her there. He was eighty-seven, frail and already almost blind. It was the last time he set foot on her. He went up steep stairways, down passages and through the hatches with a sudden, extraordinary agility. He remembered everything.

I thought of that other afternoon as I sat on the rocks at Fife Ness. It was now dusk, a haar was creeping in, and the wind was chill off the sea. But I waited until I saw it: three quick flashes of bright light, then ten seconds later another three flashes. It was the signal of the 'East Cardinal' buoy that now sits where the *North Carr* and my father sat for so long—at 56 degrees 18 minutes North, 02 degrees 32 minutes West. All I could see was the light. But I knew from the Northern Lighthouse Board that the light came from a buoy which is just under ten feet in diameter and just over eight feet high. The light is powered by solar batteries which charge during the day. My father, when he came to hear of it, quite liked the notion that he and his crew had been replaced by sunshine. □

ORHAN PAMUK
THE BOY WHO WATCHED
THE SHIPS GO BY

For the last thirty years I've been keeping track of the ships that sail through the Bosporus. Romanian tankers, Soviet cruisers, small single-masted fishing boats from Trabzon, Bulgarian passenger ships, Turkish Maritime's Black Sea liners, Soviet meteorological survey vessels, snazzy Italian transatlantics, coal freighters, peeling, unkempt and rusty coasters registered in Varna, dark ships with indeterminable flags and ports of origin. I don't keep an account of all the water traffic. I don't pay any special attention to the water buses that go back and forth across the Bosporus carrying office workers to their jobs and housewives to the market; I ignore the ferryboats on which dazed and forlorn passengers smoke and drink tea from one end of Istanbul to the other; and the American cruise liners full of apprehensive tourists who sail up the coast to take a quick, wary look at the Black Sea.

I can't tell you with any certainty why I notice some vessels and discount others. All I know is that I began spotting ships in the early Sixties, when my parents and I lived in a small flat in Jihangir that had a view of the sea. I was in my last year at primary school: I must have been eleven. Once a month, before I went to bed, I used to set the alarm clock to wake me several hours before sunrise when it was still dark and quiet. Since I wasn't yet able to light the stove that had been turned off for the night, I would dive into the spare bed in the spare room where the maid sometimes stayed, where I tried to keep myself from chattering with the cold in the dark of winter. My Turkish textbook in my hand, I would furiously repeat the poem that had to be memorized before going to school.

> Flag, oh glorious flag,
> Fluttering in the sky!

Anyone who's had to commit something to memory knows that when we are busy etching the words on our minds, memorizing a text, a prayer or a poem, we pay little attention to what we see. While we're learning something by heart, our eyes gaze on the world as if entirely for their own pleasure, independent of our minds. On those dark winter mornings, shivering with the cold and memorizing poems, I'd look out the window into the darkness where the Bosporus was barely visible.

Although the water could ordinarily be seen over the roofs and chimneys of old wooden houses and behind the minarets of the Jihangir mosque, it would appear utterly black at this hour, too early even for the ferryboats to start lighting the water with their headlights. Sometimes the pitch darkness would be relieved by the lights from the cranes working at the docks across the water on the Asian shore in Haydarpasha, or the lights on a freighter sailing by quietly, or a solitary powerboat, or the wan light of the moon. But mostly the sea remained dark and mysterious. Even when apartment buildings and graveyard cypresses became visible on the Asian shore, long before the sun rose behind the hills, the Bosporus was still black. Often when my head was busy with mysterious mnemonic games, repeating and memorizing, my eyes would be fixed on something sailing slowly against the current. Although I didn't pay any mind to what I was observing, my eyes would follow the object out of habit, as if the vessel had permission to pass only after I confirmed that it was routine and unexceptional: Oh, yes, it's a freighter; a dark fishing vessel; yes, there goes the water bus ferrying the first load of passengers across to Asia; and, yes, there's a Soviet coaster under way to some remote harbour.

On such a morning, I was curled under the quilt memorizing my poem when my eyes were suddenly riveted in astonishment on something they had never seen before. I remember being transfixed, completely forgetful of the book in my hand. It was as if some sort of giant craft were rising out of the water, growing larger as it approached. An enormous drifting fort that floated out of the fog and darkness as if from a story book. A Soviet warship! The engines were cut way down, but even so their quiet rumble sent small shivers through our house. The window sill and the wooden floors creaked, the fire tongs on the stove and the pots and pans in the kitchen rattled. So the gossip that went around Istanbul was true after all! Soviet warships really did slip through the Bosporus at night.

For a moment I was gripped by a sense that I was the only one who had witnessed the apparition. I felt sure that this terrifying Soviet vessel must be on some sinister mission. It was up to me to wake Istanbul and warn the world! It reminded me of

71

the derring-do in children's stories, which had boy heroes who roused sleeping cities to save them from floods, fires or enemy invasion. But I also had no intention of leaving the quilt I had warmed with such great difficulty.

I worried. But I solved the dilemma by doing something that became a habit from then on: I impressed each passing Soviet vessel on my mind with all the attentiveness of a boy learning a text by heart. Just like the legendary American spies who supposedly photographed all the communist vessels that passed through the Bosporus, I recorded in my mind the salient features of these ships. By registering a warship in my mind, I fancied that I could domesticate it. I had a notion that whatever could not be recognized, whatever was left unregistered, would be the harbinger of disaster. So I began tracking not only the Soviet navy but all the other water craft 'worthy of note', in an effort to keep the world under my supervision. We had been taught all through school that the Bosporus was the key to world domination, which was the reason so many powers, especially the Russians, were always trying to seize our beautiful straits. I began keeping track of the sea lane outside my window, not only to ease my own anxieties, but also for the sake of world peace and order.

More than thirty years later, the Bosporus is still my geographical centre of happiness and disaster. I feel I must stay near it. When I have to go away, I always come back as soon as I can, to stand guard over the channel. I make sure I live on a hill with a view of the Bosporus, even if from a distance and in between domes, tall blocks of offices and flats, and bluffs. Like my fellow Istanbulites, I also like to look out of my window and watch the street and notice maybe an American-make car, or a beribboned little girl on her way to buy bread at the grocery store, or a white horse pulling a produce cart. We look to the street for diversion. We look further off to the water for something larger—to reassure ourselves that all is right with the world. The view, no matter how distant, takes on a spiritual meaning. The window which looks on to the Bosporus becomes an altar (*mihrab* in mosques, *teva* in synagogues); the chairs, sofas and dining tables in the living room are all arranged to face the sea. The result is that many thousands of greedy windows cross-watch each other. Windows on the ships watch Istanbul, while windows on the shore watch the ships.

I came to understand that I wasn't alone in my ship-spotting habit and its accompanying anxiety when I eventually told other Istanbulites about my thirty-three-year-old secret. Quite a few of them turned out to share it. Quite a few also go on glancing out of the window, keeping track of ships on the Bosporus day to day, in an effort to figure out if great reversals, catastrophe and death are at hand. Behind the impulse to keep track of the traffic on the Bosporus there is, of course, the fear and pleasure—and the pleasurable fear—that this narrow, dark and fast-flowing body of water provides for us.

Disaster is the true state of being; joy is the absence of disaster; so let me begin with disaster. I was only eight and hadn't yet begun keeping track of sea traffic when one night there was a great explosion, and dark smoke obscured the starlit sky; apparently, two oil tankers had collided halfway through the Bosporus. Sometime later, a family friend called with the news that oil storage tanks in the area had also gone up and the Bosporus was on fire. As happens with all great fires, someone in the house had seen the flames and the smoke, then heard a false rumour or two, and despite all the opposition from aunts and mothers, a few of us were unable to resist going to see for ourselves.

My uncle woke us up quickly and piled us into his car and took us to the hills of Tarabya. I remember the excitement and disappointment of seeing police roadblocks where a grand hotel was being built on the shoreway. I was envious to hear the next day in school that one of my classmates had been allowed through, thanks to his father, who had flashed his card with a swagger, announcing himself, 'Press!' That night, in the autumn of 1960, hours before daybreak, it was with exuberance that I watched the Bosporus burn, standing in a crowd of curious Istanbulites who were observing the fire in their nightgowns and pyjamas, or in trousers that had been hurriedly pulled on, their feet in slippers, babies in their arms, bags and satchels in their hands. Many years later, during other magnificent Bosporus fires involving waterside mansions, boats, and the sea itself, I observed all kinds of salesmen

who appeared out of nowhere and began working the crowd, hawking their wafer candies, rings of crisp sesame *simits*, bottled water or roasted pumpkin seeds.

As it turned out, a Yugoslavia-bound tanker named *Peter Zoranich* (according to the papers it was travelling off course through the straits carrying 11,000 tons of oil and 10,000 tons of gas, which it had loaded in the Soviet port of Tuapse) had collided with a Greek oil tanker called *World Harmony*, which was on its way to the USSR. In a couple of minutes, the oil that spilled from the Yugoslavian tanker caught fire with an explosion that was heard all over Istanbul. The crew on both the tankers had instantly burnt to death even as they tried abandoning ship; without anyone at the helm, both vessels were running around out of control, dragged every which way by the heavy and unfathomable currents and whirlpools of the Bosporus, bursting into fireballs that threatened the suburbs on both shores, the tea gardens of Emirgân, the mansions in Yeniköy, the district of Kanlıca, the oil and gas depots in Çubuklu, and the shores of Beykoz lined with their old weathered-wood houses.

On whichever shore the two burning tankers were drawn towards, people abandoned their homes and, carrying their quilts and children, tried to get away from the sea. The Yugoslavian tanker drifted to the European side and slammed into the passenger ship *Tarsus,* which soon caught fire. When the burning vessels closed in on Beykoz, people began to flee up the bluffs and into the hills beyond. The sea was ablaze, and the water looked intensely yellow. The ships had turned into infernal masses of metal; the funnels, the masts, the captain's bridges had melted and collapsed. The sky was lit by a red light that seemed to come from the bowels of the ships. Explosions went off at intervals, and shards of sheet iron the size of blankets fell into the sea like burning sheets of paper; screams and cries rose up from the hills and the beaches; the loud crying of babies could be heard after each eruption.

What can be more instructive than witnessing hills alive with tearful human beings who have escaped their homes in their nightclothes? These hills under an inflamed sky, surrounded by explosions and fire, were the same hills where one took one's ease smelling the spring flowers and the perfume of Judas trees and honeysuckles, where one treated oneself to heavenly naps under the mulberry trees, and on summer nights, where one entertained metaphysical thoughts while watching the silken light of the moon on the waters of the Bosporus. Disaster had happened here, it came to me later, because I had not stood guard. I had not been keeping track of the passing ships.

The other lesson I learned through this glimpse of catastrophe was the astonishing fact that misery is always more spectacular than happiness. Only an old lady on her last legs would want to witness a contented family leading a paradisical existence in an old wooden seaside mansion on the Bosporus. But should that mansion go up in flames some night, curious crowds would gather on either shore to watch the spectacle, and those who must see everything for themselves would get up close to the inferno in small boats.

In my early youth, my cronies would call each other up to report such fires, and we would pile into cars and go, say, to Emirgân and park alongside each other. Listening to pop music on the tape deck, we would watch in awe and delight as a mansion burnt down on the Asian shore opposite, while we ate toasted cheese sandwiches and had soft drinks brought to us from a tea house nearby. We would tell stories of old Istanbul fires when white-hot nails were known to fly from the walls of blazing buildings and out across the Bosporus, sending a house on the opposite shore up in flames. We would also gossip about who was in love with whom, politics, soccer games, and the stupidity of parents. But the thing was, if a dark tanker happened to pass by the mansion burning on the shore, nobody paid it any attention. Disaster had already struck. When the fire was at its most intense and calamity was upon the place in its most awful guise, my friends in the car would fall silent, which made me sense that by watching the flames each of us was imagining our own private disasters.

Sometimes, in Istanbul, we are awakened between midnight and daybreak by the hooting of a ship, a deep and powerful sound in the still of the night that reverberates around the hills, telling us that the water is under a shroud of fog. In the meantime the foghorn at the Ahırkapı lighthouse also blares out its forlorn sound. Between sleep and wakefulness we picture in our minds the phantom of a great ship trying to find its way in the fog and the strong current. What flag is it sailing under? What freight does it carry? What is troubling the harbour pilot on the bridge and his helpers? Are they caught in a cross current? Have they sensed a dark shadow approaching in the fog? Have they gone off course? Half awake in bed, listening to a horn that seems more plaintive and hopeless each time it sounds, the Istanbulite veers between a bad dream and the dread of a real and awful event out there on the water. Whenever there was a big storm, my mother used to say, 'God help those who are out at sea in this weather!'

On the other hand, the apprehension of some terrible catastrophe is the best way of going back to sleep. The half-awake Istanbulite falls asleep wrapped in his quilt while keeping track of the blasts of horns, perhaps dreaming of being on the fogged-in boat and close to peril. In the morning, he forgets he was awakened by the foghorns in the night, just as he mostly forgets his dreams when he wakes. Only children remember. Next day, going through our daily routines like waiting in line at the post office or having lunch, we overhear someone say, 'I was awakened by ship horns last night.' That's when we know that six or seven million people who live on the straits of Bosporus had the same dream the night before.

The closer people live to the water, the scarier their dreams. On one particular foggy night, 4 September 1963 to be precise, at four o'clock in the morning, a 5,500 gross ton freighter called *Arhangelsk*, carrying military equipment from Russia to Cuba, was heading down the straits when it went aground at Balta harbour, destroying two houses and killing three people inside.

'We woke to a horrifying noise,' one of the survivors later testified. 'For a moment we imagined our home had been hit by lightning, but then the building cracked in two. As luck would have it, we were in the wing that didn't collapse. When we regained our presence of mind enough to see what had happened, we came face to face with a huge freighter sticking its prow into the third-floor living room.'

Along with similar accounts, the papers had printed a photograph of the freighter wedged into the living room. On the wall was a portrait of an ancestor in military uniform; bunches of grapes were sitting in a dish on the sideboard; part of the rug was blowing in the breeze like a curtain because half the floor was gone. The snout of the ship had pushed its way into familiar furniture, the same kind of chairs, tables, sofas we had in our own homes. Looking through the bound newspapers from thirty years ago once again, I remembered that all Istanbul had discussed the mishap for days: how the pretty high-school girl who had died in the accident had recently become engaged; what had been said in the conversations between victims and the survivors, the now dead and the still living, on the night before; how the boy next door had discovered his lovely fiancée dead in the rubble.

Back then, only one million rather than ten million souls lived in the city, and a story could travel around the neighbourhoods by word of mouth and attain the proportions of a legend. At that time, about two dozen ships went through the straits every day. People who keep count report that these days the number of ships averages 120. Many of them are tankers, ten times larger than those in my childhood, carrying oil, petroleum by-products and nuclear waste. Today, accidents on the Bosporus are lost among all the daily disasters of a city teeming with people. When I talk to my friends about such matters, I'm astonished to find that we all cling to the memories of old catastrophes with dewy eyes, as if we are talking with nostalgia about the good old days.

Do I remember, they say, the time when an excursion boat sank somewhere between Yeniköy and Beykoz with the members of the Turkish-German Association on board? Sometime in the July of 1966, I believe. It ran into a barge carrying lumber down the Bosporus to Marmara. Thirteen people were lost. Remember?

Or that time when a Romanian tanker called *Ploiesti* just barely touched a fishing boat and, in the blink of an eye, the fishing boat went down in two pieces. Remember?

Or some years later (remember?) that Romanian tanker (*Independenta*) and another boat (the Greek freighter *Euryali*) collided in front of Kadıköy (no, out in front of Haydarpasha). And then the seepage of fuel oil caught fire and both ships (no,

79

only one) exploded with a horrible noise that woke us all up. (Yes, I do remember that. Although our flat was miles from the accident, half the windows in our neighbourhood burst into smithereens with the force of the explosion, and the streets were covered with shards of glass.)

And then there was that boat that went down with the sheep. Remember? It was on 15 November 1991. A cattle boat sailing under Lebanese colours was going through the Bosporus with over 20,000 sheep it had loaded in Romania; it collided with the freighter *Madonna Lily* registered in the Philippines, carrying wheat from New Orleans to Russia, and sank with its live cargo. A few of the sheep managed to jump ship and swim ashore, where they were rescued by Istanbulites who a minute before had been reading their newspapers in tea houses along the Bosporus; the rest of the hapless creatures are still waiting for their rescuers at the bottom of the sea.

I should tell you that this accident happened directly below the second bridge built over the Bosporus, known as the Fatih Bridge, but I shan't explore that bridge's main reason for fame, which is that people jump off it, a habit that has become popular in Istanbul over the past twenty-five years. After all, suicide is an individual misfortune. Our subject here is public disaster, and its attendant pleasures. As I consult my own memory, or the newspaper files which brim with stories of wrecks, or elderly friends who consider the Bosporus to be just this side of paradise, I realize that most people don't like divulging their joyful moments. It is so much easier to talk of misfortunes and catastrophes in this corner of the world.

There are so many theories on how nations, tribes and communities come about: shared history, shared language, shared dreams. As I review the years I've kept track of ships, I have a sense that it must be shared calamities that create this feeling of belonging. And some calamities—calamities at sea—have a timeless quality. They happen so often and so easily. Here is an Istanbul newspaper report dated 3 November 1997:

> A car, carrying nine persons on their way back from a wedding and bound for Tellibaba to make an offering to the saint, plunged into the sea in Tarabya when the driver who was

intoxicated lost control. A mother of two was drowned in the accident.

How many cars and their occupants over the years have plunged into the Bosporus and gone down into the deep from where there is no return? All those cars! They've carried screaming children, quarrelling lovers, bantering drunks, absent-minded drivers, suicidal melancholics, husbands hurrying home, old fellows with poor night vision, adolescents testing the brakes, distracted drivers who shift into forward instead of reverse, people who have no clue how the incident happened, the retired director of finance and his good-looking secretary, the preoccupied policeman, the proud husband and his family out for the day in the company car, a hosiery manufacturer who knew a distant relative of mine, a famous Beyoglu hood and his moll, that poor family from Konya taking their first look at the Bosporus Bridge. They don't sink like stones, either: for a moment these cars seem to float on the water. If there's enough light, those of us on the shore can almost see the horror on the faces of those who are unwillingly going down as their car is slowly buried in the dark currents.

Once a car descends into these depths, water pressure will no longer allow the doors to be opened. During a particularly busy period for this sort of accident, one assiduous Istanbul newspaper provided its readers with instructive advice on this matter.

HOW TO EXIT A VEHICLE SINKING INTO THE BOSPORUS:

1. Don't panic. Roll up the windows and wait for the water to fill the vehicle. Make sure the doors are unlocked. Don't move around.

2. If the vehicle continues to descend, put on the handbrake.

3. Just as the water level rises almost to the top, breathe deeply the remaining air, completely filling your lungs, open the doors quietly, and exit the vehicle without alarm.

I'd like to add an extra step: 4. Good luck! Try not to get your raincoat caught in the handbrake. If you can swim, and if you make it to the top, and if the season is summer, then you will instantly see that life and the Bosporus are beautiful.

81

Orhan Pamuk

I am still keeping track of ships, up in my office in Jihangir,
which has a better view of the Bosporus than my parent's flat,
where I first saw the Soviet warship thirty-three years ago.
Although the new place is quite close to the water, I am up in a
tall building on a steep hill, and from my desk, I can see ships
miles and miles away, but also the movements of the cranes on
the Asian shore. I can see fishermen in their boats bobbing on the
water close by, and, if they're leaping joyfully into the air, the
dolphins whose presence in the waters of the Bosporus has been
constant since my childhood. I can also see, just below me on the
European shore, an old and inconspicuous vessel being loaded
with Turkish-made plastic bags in different colours, the car ferry
that transports trucks from one shore to the other, and the sea
foam churning in the wake of the ferryboats and crowded water
buses. Whenever the water traffic is heavy, when, for example,
hundreds of small fishing vessels clog the traffic lanes, the huge
oil tankers blow their horns as persistently as they do when the
fog is in. Before daybreak, when the city is still fast asleep, the
great ships still slip through the mist like silent phantoms. I try to
keep track.   □

Translation by GÜNELI GÜN

82

HUNTERS
JEAN GAUMY

Jean Gaumy, the photographer and film-maker, grew
up close to the Bay of Biscay and now lives in
Fecamp, the port from where France's cod fleet once
set out for the Newfoundland fishing grounds. He
has sailed with several fishing fleets. His pictures on
the following pages come from two voyages: here,
and on the eight pages beginning overleaf, with a
Spanish crew line-fishing for tuna; on subsequent
pages, aboard another Spanish boat trawling in
the Atlantic and the North Sea.

JUSTIN WEBSTER
LOS PIRATAS

Day one

It is six o'clock in the late afternoon, 16 April 1997. I am standing on the poop deck of a Spanish fishing boat, the *Beti Zorionak*, as she leaves the Galician port of Burela. She's a *palangrero*—a long-liner—bound for an area of the North Atlantic known as the Irish Box. As the captain—Angel—wheels her over to salute the white statue of the Virgin and Child perched high on the vast grey breakwater, the boat see-saws in the swell. My stomach lurches. Last night, I dropped my loose change into the collection box beside that madonna, hoping she would watch over me during the weeks ahead. But now I am nervous.

The deck tilts as we plunge out to sea, heading north-west. It heaves and rolls as the eastern fringe of the Atlantic comes at us from the side. I hang on to the bow rail by the wheelhouse, trying to keep my eye on the horizon. The mist on the hills shines in the early evening sunshine. Angel leans out of the doorway and points out some factory chimneys down the coast. I can't reply.

Day two

I am ill, and have no idea how long it will last. Days? Weeks? On one side of the bridge someone has bolted a garden chair, with one of those thick cushions that reach down to your ankles. I don't ask any questions—I just slump into it. As night falls, other crew members congregate on the bridge to listen to the football on the ship's radio. They talk loudly in Galician. I doze but my thoughts, like snatches of tuneless songs, make me feel worse.

I ought to have been grateful. Only later did I realize that the garden recliner had been put there purely for my benefit. I owed a great deal to Angel. Until he stepped in, I couldn't find a boat that would have me aboard. I thought I knew why. The London newspapers were full of angry comments about Spain's insatiable fishing fleet, mainly from bitter British fishermen bewildered by the loss of their own livelihoods. Was it true that Spain had launched a new generation of brigands on the high seas? As an Englishman married to a Spanish woman and living in Spain, I wanted to see for myself.

'They don't care about you being a writer,' someone told me before I embarked. 'They're worried that you're a spy.' I had fallen in with the British skippers working the 'flagships', the old British-registered boats bought by Spaniards to fish the British quota. Even they were cagey. One told me: 'A-am not talkin to no-a fockin journalist whu's gonna fockin twist ma fockin werds.'

His name was Peter. He had just picked up his second British court summons in three trips, having been more than four times over his monthly hake quota in Irish waters. The Irish inspectors were cracking down, he said. The fines—once laughable—had shot up. Peter had been working out of La Coruña for sixteen years since South Shields shut down. In the modern fishing conflict he's a mercenary, and the Spanish company he worked for was going to the wall because of the fines. The atmosphere was ugly.

What drives them all on is Spain's hunger for fish. The Spanish eat more seafood per head than any European nation except the Portuguese. It is a poor man's protein in a country with a long coastline and fragile agriculture; in the chaos that followed the Civil War, fishing kept many people from starvation. But it is also a sublime delicacy—hake, monkfish, prawns and shellfish are the crowning glory of their national cuisine.

To feed this hunger, the Spanish fishing fleet has become by far the largest in Europe—it supplies a third of the total shipping tonnage in the European Union. But Spanish waters are not well stocked: the Atlantic drops sharply to unfishable depths, and the Mediterranean holds neither the volume nor the variety of fish that a Spanish menu demands. So the Spanish fleet, based in La Coruña, Vigo and Burela, explores more distant seas, with predictable consequences. At home, its fishermen are venerated as pioneers; abroad, they are branded pirates. They are the front line in a fishing war which escalated two decades ago, when countries started to claim more extensive ownership of the seas around them, an act which has led to many squabbles over who owns the wild, dumb animals that swim beneath the waves.

In 1995, in the so-called Halibut War, four bursts of gunfire from a Canadian gunboat stopped the *Estai*, a freezer ship from Vigo, and the captain was arrested for using illegally fine-meshed nets. In the previous year, French gunboats fired rubber bullets at boats from Burela in a high-seas brawl which became known as the Tuna War. The famous 'quota-hoppers', the Spanish-owned British 'flagships' in La Coruña, were bought precisely to acquire extra fishing rights. Each country in the European Union is given a strict quota, which it divides between the registered boats that fly its flag. But the boats can be owned by anyone, and many Spanish companies have bought British boats in order to acquire their rights to hake and monkfish, for which there is no serious market in the UK. These flagships are run and crewed by Spaniards, but catch British quota. They sail from the harbours of northern Spain flying the Union Jack—a resonant symbol of Spain's determination to catch other people's fish.

British skippers such as Peter are refugees from the first and most serious of these fish wars: the Cod War. In 1976, the EEC recommended that its members impose 200-mile limits on their coastal waters. Iceland and Norway responded by setting their own limits and defending them fiercely. This effectively sabotaged British fishing, which was based squarely on cod from far-off waters. Spanish shipowners reacted swiftly, snapping up cheap British boats and—most importantly—their precious licenses.

Day three

I manage a light lunch of tuna salad. The mess-deck is small for sixteen of us—backs against the wall round an L-shaped table. I sit on the edge. 'Do we have a seaman yet?' asks Angel. I nod. I borrow a cigarette from Antonio, Angel's number two, smoke it inquisitively and feel fine; it is the first time that smoking has seemed a symptom of good health. At dinner I even drink wine. There are cartons lying on the table, but no glasses. You have to hold the carton and squirt a jet into your open mouth. The others are watching, as if it is a test. Moreno, the cook, is delighted.

'That's right! You've got to *xarear*!' he booms, tipping up an imaginary bottle to show me how. He is a big, meaty extrovert.

The crew argue over the brandy supply. Moreno is in charge of provisions—the crew pays for food and drink. Cartagena, the oldest man on board, eyes a young hand across the table as he fills his steel mug with *calimocho*—a mixture of Coca-Cola and red

From left: Cartagena, Antonio, Manolo and Traile

wine. There is an edge to the conversation, which grinds on until Angel steps in: 'There are only three fundamental things . . . ' He pauses until everyone is listening: 'Potatoes, oil and bread.'

The *Beti Zorionak* is spacious below deck. A corridor below the bridge connects the mess-deck and the galley—a steel kitchen and larder—to the cabins; one for Xuxo, the chief mechanic, one I share with Moreno and Eldelmiro (the cook and the second mechanic) and two dormitories for the ten deckhands. There is a cramped washroom with basins, lavatories—wall bars help you balance while you squat—and showers. The corridor skirts around the engine room and the relentless groan of its 680-horsepower motor. The boat was built thirty years ago along simple, solid lines. The pipes in the engine room are painted yellow, red, green or blue—for diesel, oil, fresh and salt water. Polished tools line the walls, brightly lit as if in a window display. On the bridge, Antonio takes a reading from the Global Positioning System to transmit to Cork and Madrid. The water is still too deep for the seabed to register on the scanner, which sounds to 600 fathoms.

The Spanish world service radio's daily programme *Spaniards at Sea* leads with news of the crew of a Spanish ship in court in

Bantry after colliding with and sinking an Irish boat off Dursey Island. The Irish boats are small and wooden-hulled, and the Irish skipper—a popular local figure—was killed. He was buried with a naval guard of honour. Ireland's Minister of the Marine attended. The Spanish were charged with negligence, which Irish fishermen considered an understatement. According to Spain's embassy in Dublin, this is what lies behind the recent crackdown on Spanish boats in the Box. So far this year, the number of boardings is up by a quarter. The Irish are marshalling £40 million a year and 1,000 Navy personnel to guard their waters. Of the fifteen boats in Irish courts at the moment, ten are Spanish-owned.

We have entered, I realize, the field of conflict.

Day four

We steam past a group of seven Spanish long-liners. Angel fences with them over the radio in his drawling *gallego*. '*Me cago en dios!*—I shit on God!' are the only words in Spanish, but they pepper every transmission. Among Spanish fishermen, the Galicians are the pioneers. Even when they sailed wooden-hulled boats they had to look beyond their own waters. So this thick, butch *gallego* can be heard on seas all over the world.

The trawler *Pitufo* passes by, on her way back to La Coruña, where she is famous. The day we set sail, Galician papers reported that Irish inspectors had ordered *Pitufo* to port on suspicion of catching undersized fish. She was released, but her skipper says he nearly had a heart attack. The fines, the catch, the crew's wages—everything was at stake. The other skippers call him on the radio, laughing, listening, wishing him well. He is a returning hero. I ask Angel what is so special about him. He doesn't answer. He has become tense and quiet as we get closer to the grounds. Finally he grunts: 'He always comes back with more than anyone else.'

Through his binoculars Angel identifies a Dutch freezer ship, probably fishing for mackerel. He is on the lookout for inspectors, and thought it was a patrol boat. The inspectors infuriate him: he claims that they are breaking the rules. They board without warning at night, when boats are under way. 'If one of them falls in,' he says, 'then he'll be under the propeller in seconds and we'll be blamed. We're not against inspections. They should inspect, but not like this.' He says that in Scotland, where they had recently spent thirty-six days, the inspectors would call to notify boats of inspection and ask them to lower their ladders.

I tell him what I had heard in La Coruña. That the monkfish stocks in Scottish waters have been destroyed by the flagships. That some captains only fill out the logbook when they are inspected, leaving them free (if they escape inspection) to enter fewer fish than they have actually caught. That some skippers do not hesitate to boast about overfishing. That everyone jeers at the inspectors. One skipper said: 'A rich man used to put his son in the church, now he makes him a fishing inspector. They're thick.' I tell him that none of the other shipowners in La Coruña would let me aboard, and that I can guess why not.

Angel is calm. 'I've nothing to hide,' he says. 'The problem with the flagships is that they have a very small quota.'

Down below, on the quarterdeck, the crew are tying hooks. It looks like a sweatshop: each man has to tie 2,000 hooks a day. Sheaves of line hang like hair above the working tables. I talk to Casimiro. He barely looks down as he makes a loop at the end of a line, holds a silver shining hook beside it with thumb and forefinger, winds the line round four times, pulls tight and cuts the end with a knife. The skin of his hands is thick and yellowed with salt water. He's only been on the *Beti* a year. Most of the others have been with Angel since he bought the boat eight years ago. But Casimiro has been at sea for twenty years, most of them fishing for swordfish around the Canary Islands.

'This is the number one boat in Burela,' he says. It has a stable crew—a sign that it makes money (profits are shared). Casimiro has had bad luck in the past. He once returned from a two-month trip and was paid nothing. It is not unheard of for crews to end up *owing* money. But if all goes well on this trip, and the captain does a good job, he could make £1,000.

Burela is a small town, but it has become one of the leading bases from which the Spanish *Gran Sol* fleet—the Spanish-owned and registered vessels—sails to French, British and Irish waters (with the relevant permits). In 1994, when it was at the centre of the Tuna War, the Spanish fleet of liners massed in Burela attacked the French for using illegally long nets. They rammed French boats, lobbed Molotov cocktails, and even towed the *Gabrielle* back to Burela as a prize. Angel doesn't want to talk about it except to say that it was Asturians and not Galicians who did the kidnapping. He pauses, then adds: 'The thing about fishing is it makes you very envious. You get hotter and hotter under the collar until . . . ' Silence again.

He is toying with his options. Either we stay in the Box—so called because it is the rectangle formed by the waters round Ireland, including the Irish Sea—and go to El Coral. Or we steam to a bank called 'Porcupine'. If we stay in El Coral it will be the first time the *Beti* has fished in the Box. Spanish vessels were banned from it until 1996. The Spanish government boasted that getting its boats into the Box was a political achievement, but according to Angel most of the *cofradias* (fishermens' associations) were against it. 'We said it would be better if no one fished there. We know that if the fish are left to breed in the Box, then they'll come to the grounds outside.' The government paid no attention. The *Beti* stayed outside the Box last year, but for hake fishermen the Box means El Coral, and El Coral is rich for only three months of the year, from April to June. This is when the fish are spawning.

There are obvious questions here about the long-term damage to fish stocks. But they are not pressing ones for a captain with a crew on a profit-share and a break-even of around £15,000 per trip. 'We are not going to be idiots,' says Angel. 'If there are other boats fishing there, then we will too . . . '

Hundreds of birds are following us. We even have a pair of migrating swallows resting on the gunwale. Storm petrels flit like black butterflies above the waves, and flights of herring gulls, fulmars and kittiwakes follow our wake. The sun is sending shafts of light through the clouds to the west, which form a strip of silver where they meet the sea. Apart from the birds, there is not a thing all the way round the horizon.

Day five

Hunched like a chess player, Angel reaches his decision. He opts for El Coral. But there is a problem. The permit for the

Beti to fish within the Box starts on 22 April. We will have to wait for two days without fishing. It seems extraordinary that out of sight of anyone, in the middle of a vast expanse of water, the regulations have any binding force. I wonder if he will really wait.

We pull into El Coral in the middle of the night. It's like arriving late at a party. There are already ten boats, all brightly lit and long-lining for hake. Angel is glued to the radio, making notes on scraps of paper, drawing diagrams in a notebook and writing names, which he is constantly rubbing out and moving to new positions. The radar shows a bunch of orange blips and a few stragglers: *José Luisa y Mary, Greenland, Sylvanna, Hermanos Garcia, Madre Querida, Ayr Quin*. There are five Spanish-registered boats, four British and one French. But every single one is Spanish-owned, and all the *pescas*—the skippers—are Galicians. Angel knows them by their voices. The bridge fills up with crew.

'How's it looking?' I ask when the radio chat has subsided. He turns his gaze towards me as if he is returning from another world.

'Fucked.' He laughs.

We stare out of the windows at the distant blaze of deck lights jiggling around in the dark. Then we hear one of the British captains speaking Spanish. At night the navigation captain, or *costa*, is usually on duty. These *costas* are often British, and I think I recognize a voice from La Coruña.

'You should try and learn English, it's in your interest. My captain's certificate is recognized in more places than yours . . .'

'I don't care . . . no way, no way,' moans a Spanish *costa*. 'I'm taking pills for depression. I don't want to think about it.'

Angel hands the receiver to Cartagena, who shouts down the line, telling the *costa* to get on with his job and mind his own business. The airwaves erupt (*'Me cago en dios!'*) with laughter.

'He's sharp,' says Xuxo, nodding at Angel. *'Muy fino.'*

Day seven

Slack-faced and bleary, the deckhands shuffle into the kitchen and take coffee from the thermos at two in the morning. After a week at sea, and a two-day pause waiting for our permit to become valid, this is the first day of fishing. The mate, Traile, is in charge. A few years younger than Cartagena, he has an intelligent tanned face, a moustache and a crest of unruly hair.

The hands open a hatch in the passageway and start hauling up wooden boxes of frozen sardines. Antonio comes down to supervise; everyone else puts on oilskins. The sardines are dragged to the quarterdeck with long iron hooks and hosed down. In a few moments, when they have thawed, the hands pull out boxes full of flattened coils of thick line, with hooks attached by thinner lines. They bait each hook with a sardine, and restack the boxes.

Word comes down from Angel to bait up 110 boxes, or *aparejos*. This means that 8,800 hooks have to be baited. With eleven men it will take only a couple of hours. Traile seems happy. In fact they all seem relieved to have started.

At five-thirty they shoot the gear. Angel manoeuvres the boat to the exact position he's chosen as part of the complex etiquette of long-lining, parallel with the other boats and on the outside of the formation. Eldelmiro recharges the battery of one of the buoy's homing devices, and with the boat motoring slowly, the deckhands lug it over the side, followed by four hefty granite blocks which whip out a safety rope from the deck as they sink to the bottom.

As the boat leaves the buoy, the *palangre*—the 'fleet' of long lines and hooks—begins to pay out. Five boxes of baited hooks are lined up on the conveyor-belt-like tray on the quarterdeck. Traile is at the mouth of the hatch. He watches as the line and the sardines are plucked from the first box, then tosses a small float overboard and shouts to the others working behind him; he shoves a new box into position and pulls the empty box inside. After every five boxes he signals for a granite weight. When the fleet is finished he has more weights thrown, and another buoy.

What is left on the seabed is a strange, fragile contraption twelve kilometres long: a huge zigzag line held up by floats and pulled down by granite, inconspicuous enough to present the hake with nothing more than a row of sardines floating in the current.

I go to bed just before dawn, exhausted. The others will carry on until eight-thirty. I haven't been sleeping well because of the noise, and because I haven't yet hit on a way of lying still. But this time I find the engine's roar almost musical. I curl up in a foetal position, my knees against one side of the bunk, my back against the other. As we steam to drop the second fleet, the boat moves at a lolloping canter. For the first time, I fall into a sweet sleep.

Day eight

I wake in the afternoon to the smell of fish. Antonio and Xuxo, looking sour, are busy transferring lines from big black plastic baskets to crates in a flurry of movement. They nod greetings to me. I sense that I am welcome, that I can lend a hand.

Everyone except Angel helps to unravel the fleets when they start to come in. In the fo'c'sle I find a sedate, orderly scene. Traile, in yellow oilskins, hair still stuck up like a cockerel, smiles crookedly from his place by the winch where he watches the line come in. The sea is gunmetal grey. The *palangre* comes on to the deck, bare hooks jumping like flies. Casimiro lays it in tangled circles in a black basket, sinking the hooks into the foam rubber round the lip. The others are untangling the used sets of tackle.

'Where are the fish?' I ask. Chapa, the young hand in charge of gutting, shows me the dark, slimy backs of five fish, about half a metre long, in a single white plastic tray. Their eyes bulge like marbles. He motions to me over the noise of the winch. The new arrivals slither down from the platform where they land, with a smack, for the hook to be pulled out. They have bright silvery flanks, bloated bodies, and what looks like an inflated tongue in their jaws. Chapa gaffs one deftly, holds it by the gills and slices into the white stomach, cutting upwards. He digs his fingers into the cut and pulls out what looks like a pair of white lungs. He chucks them into a tray.

'Eggs,' he says. 'There'd have been even more a few weeks ago.' We stare at the pregnant fish for a moment, knowing what this means. I say nothing. Even the crew seems uncomfortable.

The tongue-like thing is in fact the fish's stomach, blown out by the decompression of being dragged up from 300 fathoms. Along with the rest of the guts, the remains of sardines and a small by-catch of unwanted fish, it is sent down a shute into the sea. The gutted fish go into a steel tank full of clean sea water.

They have been at it for less than an hour. Already the

113

rhythm is relentless. The boat has become a small, cramped factory. After lunch, the night shift joins in; now, a dozen men grapple with the incoming lines. They work steadily, in silence. The fish seem almost an afterthought in some mysterious manufacturing process, passers-by caught in a web woven and unwoven every day.

Day nine

On the bridge Angel tells me that a nearby Irish gunboat has already boarded six boats. I say that I hope it inspects the *Beti*. Angel thinks it quite likely. I go on to the upper deck to take a look. The gunboat is steaming around the other fishing boats about three miles away, close to the horizon. I expect an official-looking launch, and am surprised to see a miniature battleship, complete with a gun turret. It changes shape as it steams in circles in the distance, sometimes looking as if it is heading in our direction. Then it turns and disappears over the horizon.

Angel beckons me into the wheelhouse, hands me the radio and explains that he wants me to make an announcement on the open channel. I take the microphone, and try for an official voice.

'Attention! All those boats inspected this morning are under arrest. Please proceed to port.'

Then we sit back and listen to the responses.

'It was this afternoon, not this morning. *Me cago en dios!*'

'That's just what we need.'

'*Me cago en la Virgen!*'

Angel chuckles. Between *pescas,* the radio is a continual game of poker. No one reveals what they are really catching—unless they are from the same family, and then they scramble the channel. Some, like Angel, never talk about fish at all.

Day eleven

We are on the edge of the continental shelf, at 348 fathoms, on the western side of the ground. Angel didn't have much room to manoeuvre, but had to choose whether to fish on the 'wet' or the 'dry' side of the other boats. He opted for the 'wet', the deeper side. El Coral is named after a coral bed which makes it inaccessible to trawlers, whose nets would snag on the coral, though gill-netters, the bane of the long-line fisherman, can fish there with their static nets. One gill-netter, *White Sands*, comes quite close, but for now the zone is covered by liners. We have to wait for some of the other boats to turn for home; then the *Beti* can move closer to the middle, where the fishing is usually best.

I ask Angel what counts as a good day's fishing.

'Thirty, forty boxes,' he says. 'Sixty is a lot. But it depends on the price. If everyone is fishing a lot the price drops. Sometimes you don't fish as much and make more money. At Christmas, when the price goes up, it can reach one thousand six hundred pesetas a kilo [£8]. Then in the summer, when there are lots of fish, it falls to seven hundred pesetas or less. Depends on the size too— bigger fish are worth more.'

'What about the fish we've caught so far?'

'They're a good size. But you don't get the really big ones any more, six kilos or so. In the summer, when we go to the beach . . . '

'The beach?'

'Seventy, eighty fathoms. Here.' Angel spreads a map in the wood-panelled hallway between the bridge and the cabins.

'In the summer the fish are smaller.'

I pore over the maps. The main banks and particular spots— some official names, others known only to fishermen—are marked on the spiralling contours of the seabed. Angel points out the places, such as El Coral, which all the *pescas* know: Pistol, Swimming Pool, Penicillin, The Jungle, Knife, Head of a Dog, Anton's Avenue, Marisol's Tits. Some are named after the shape of the contours, others from some now-forgotten incident. On another map the fishing grounds are marked in red, blue and green symbols according to the species they hold. A neat group of green triangles—hake—is marked El Coral, about sixty-five miles due west of the south-western tip of Ireland. The map is dated 1976.

'This is still valid?' I ask.

'More or less,' says Angel. A *pesca* not knowing this map would be like a lorry driver not knowing cities and motorways.

Angel has decided I have much to learn. He pulls out books from the drawers and cupboards on the bridge, darting back to check on Traile and the line coming on to the platform. He inundates me with data, showing me the fishing regulations drawn up by the northern Galician *cofradías* in 1994 (since dropped because they were ignored by the boats in La Coruña). He shows me the logbooks and an almanac of the Spanish fleet. I struggle to concentrate on the pages of print. Outside, the fish are hauled in.

Day twelve

Chapa shows me how to repack the line, feeding it out of its bowl and into the crate, coiling it and sticking the hooks into a strip of foam on the edge. The bowls spin on metal spokes, and the line inside is twisted. It comes alive as soon as I pick it up.

'Just send it the way the line asks you to,' says Chapa. The line's angry loops ease into flat coils. Then it seems just to scuttle into the crate. It is all done with the fingertips, without forcing.

I try, but it is like getting a snake to lie down. The boat is pitching, and the hooks on the smaller lines snag me when I try to untangle them. I find myself flailing. My gaze rests enviously for a moment on my neighbour's tidy bowl.

My first box takes three hours, with help from several hands, who have taken about half an hour on theirs.

I grab Traile's oilskinned arm and, raising my voice above the winch, ask him what I can do. He smiles. 'What am I going to tell you? You watch and then join in. Wherever you like.'

Eldelmiro tries to talk me out of it. I'll get wet. But when I persist, he lends me a set of oilskins and boots and I am greeted in the fo'c'sle with amused encouragement.

'Be careful, they bite,' calls out Littbarski. Most of the men go by nicknames: Littbarski is named after a German footballer.

I pick fish out of the tank and lay them head to tail in white plastic trays. 'You have to pamper fish,' says Chapa, repeating a phrase I have heard Angel say. Sorting them here on board means that the fish will be handled as little as possible on land.

Hake are ugly brutes, like fat eels with big heads, but once the effects of decompression subside—the eyes returning to their sockets—they have a certain sleekness. Any fish with a cut in the flesh, or that has lost a few scales, is put in a discount box. The

Beti has a reputation to maintain. Angel says that Burela's hake sells for a few hundred pesetas more per kilo than La Coruña's.

Later, Chapa broods for a while when I ask what lured him to sea, as if trying to compress different things into his answer. He looks healthier than when we set sail—he has already told me that he sleeps even less at home than in the boat, so as not to waste time when he could be enjoying himself.

He did badly at school, and his father, a seaman, said: 'At least he'll do for the sea.' To scare him. Everyone knows that life at sea is hard. But he saw friends coming back from fishing with lots of cash, buying nice cars and motorbikes. 'Now it's difficult to get out,' he says. 'What kind of job could I find on land, at my age?' At thirty, he is one of the younger deckhands. He has been on the *Beti* for eight years.

He is meticulous about his job, a useful side effect of the profit-sharing system, so I too am careful to be gentle with the hake. While we are talking I see the end of a hook in the gills of a fish I have just boxed. It is flapping about, as hake often do even after they've been gutted, so I reach in to stop the hook damaging the other fish. A pain like an electric shock makes me jerk my hand back. I must have cried out because the others are smiling. I have been bitten by a hake. Chapa advises: 'I know it's difficult, but it's best not to pull your hand away when that happens. It makes the cut worse.'

The hake's teeth have sliced clean through my rubber glove. When I take it off, I find my hand covered in blood and two neat razor slits in the tip of my finger. Hake bites bleed so much that they don't swell up like other wounds at sea. But my new-found concern for hake conservation suffers a momentary dip.

Day fourteen

Routine has taken a grip of the boat. 'Always the same,' the crew say as I poke around looking for unexplored corners. I go down into the refrigerated hold, where Traile and another deckhand are stowing the fish. Swirls of mist come off the ice between the wooden bulkheads. It is strangely peaceful below the waterline. The rocking of the boat is gentler.

At dawn, as we steam to drop the first fleet of the day, I am huddling in the lee of the wheelhouse with Cartagena, Casimiro, Chapa, and Manolo, an energetic new hand who is deaf. The sun is rising slowly, spreading a yellow light over the heavy sea. The *Beti* crashes down from the crests of the waves. Feeling sick again, I concentrate on a gannet skimming the surface; it often seems about to plough into a bank of water, but the water always falls away at the last moment. I notice the others watching too. 'Not a single mistake,' says Manolo admiringly.

I have surprising dreams aboard the *Beti,* ones that take me back to people and places in the past I thought I had forgotten. Many leave me with a feeling of regret, of not having done or said something, of not knowing then what I know now. It's a common enough sensation, but at sea such dreams seem unnaturally clear. I wake in my bunk and can recall everything, even adding extra touches, fresh details of rooms and people at certain moments.

I tell some of the crew, and they listen sympathetically. They agree that it is easy to get mixed up in stupid thoughts at sea. Eldelmiro says there are two thoughts in particular you have to hold at bay, fears about your family—because only in very serious cases involving the immediate family will you get a message from home—and regret over things you have said or done.

This badly hidden side to their bravado, this strategy for forgetting, is something which seems to shape the fishermen as much as the constant physical tussle with the sea and the cold.

Day fifteen

I am losing track of the days. We must be over halfway through the voyage, but there is no date set for our return. I think back to my local market near Barcelona. On Saturdays the aisles between the fishmongers are jammed with stout *señoras*. Hake goes so fast a porter is constantly emptying two- or three-kilo boxes of *palangre* on to the ice: if they are line-caught they are marked *palangre*, and if they are trawled they are just called *merluza* or hake. The *señoras* will pay more for *palangre,* because it is better quality. It's been pulled out of the sea on a hook, not mashed up with a mass of other fish in a net.

Before my voyage, I had called up Carlos Roberto Jones—Charlie the Fish to his English friends—an international fish broker. He took me down to Barcelona's wholesale fish market, one of the biggest in Europe, at five in the morning. Charlie, half-English, half-Argentine, grew up in Madrid and went to university in Oxford. His father persuaded him to go for 'a proper job' in the City. He ended up broking fish.

He moved to Barcelona four years ago to be closer to the buyers. He's big in prawns, especially Australian kings. He's a force in Nile perch, a delicious freshwater fish from Lake Victoria which is served up all over Spain as grouper. He dabbles in lots of fresh fish—he doesn't do frozen—and has developed a good line in South African hake. He can switch from Oxford English to fish market argot, and does the same in Spanish, as comfortable in his black leather jacket fingering a consignment of Mexican octopus as he is hobnobbing with smart clients in Santander.

He's been complaining for a while that a once-sophisticated market is in decline. Every species—and there are five or six of hake (*merlusius merlusius*, the British-Irish one, being the real McCoy)—used to have its own price. That suited his taste for intricacies. The Spanish eat 38.4 kilos of fish per head per year, more than twice the British or Irish consumption and three times the German. As significant, seventy per cent of the roughly £1 billion they spend on fish a year is spent on fresh fish.

This requires a culture of standing in line at the fishmonger. But that is slowly dying. Today, price sets the agenda: it comes down to what supermarkets can sell for under 1,000 pesetas a kilo.

'It's a levelling process I absolutely hate,' says Charlie. He is fiercely snobbish about one thing: the classification of fish.

Day sixteen

Up on the bridge during the night, I talk to Antonio. He is more militant than Angel about the *palangreros,* preaching the superiority of long-lining over other methods. Gill-nets are too efficient and indiscriminate, he thinks. Spanish boats have never been allowed to use them outside their own waters—and there are only a few licenses for coastal waters—but British and

Justin Webster

Irish boats are keen on them. One gill-netter, a British flagship, caught seven tonnes of hake in one day a month ago. Antonio despises such catches. 'You know the fish we put aside to sell off cheap? Their fish is all like that.' Liners catch only hake, and only hake big enough to eat a fairly large sardine. The only significant by-catch are a few beautiful red bream with eyes like golden paperweights.

Antonio says all this in a friendly way, but he is bitter about the Irish inspectors, and pessimistic about the future. 'This way of fishing is coming to an end,' he says. 'We depend too much on other countries, England, Ireland, Portugal, Namibia, Morocco. We're the ones who pillage and rob. It's always been the same.'

We smoke our cigarettes together. The fishing has stalled. Only nineteen boxes today. Hours pass with not a single hake coming up.

Traile throws me a live metre-long hound shark to have a look at. It has an amazingly bright emerald-green eye. I feel the rasping touch of its skin as I hold it, very carefully, by the tail. It sinks suddenly, quite unlike a fish, when I lob it overboard. Seeing my interest, Nicolás, the neatest crew member, presents me with his own typed notes on marine fauna.

It is becoming obvious that, given a choice, none of the crew would think twice about taking a job on land. 'This is not a life,' says Nicolás. Antonio, the deckhand opposite, agrees. He is waiting another year, trying to save enough to start a business—a bar or shop—with his wife. They have it all planned. 'She's a wonder, my wife,' he says. 'She fixes everything at home. A great reader, too. You should see our living room. It's like a library.'

Later, we are chatting with the chief mechanic, Xuxo, in the mess-deck, at around eleven p.m. Xuxo is tall and lanky, with a pale face and thick, pointed lips; when he speaks he sits sideways on the bench, hangs his head and shuffles restlessly like a child.

'I am upset. Very, very upset,' he sighs. 'There's a saying: the night is for foxes and the sea for fishes. Out of choice no one comes out here. No one.' His two-and-a-half-year-old son came down to the docks to see him off this time and called out to him. If there were other jobs going there wouldn't be anyone left on the boat, he says. Xuxo is one of the luckier ones: for every two

120

trips at sea, he spends one on land, unlike the deckhands.

Nicolás tells me how his son, when he had just learned to talk, asked him where he was going.

'To the sea.'

'Don't go, Daddy, don't go.'

'But I have to go, to earn money to buy clothes and sweets.'

'I've got money,' said the boy, and went to fetch some toy coins he'd been saving. 'Here you are. Now you can stay.'

I suddenly see the *Beti Zorionak* in a very simple light, as I sit missing my own daughter. It is a ship of absent fathers.

Day seventeen

A ngel comes into the galley while I am waking up over a cup of coffee. 'The gunboat was here last night,' he says casually.

'But they didn't come aboard,' I say.

'Oh yes, they came aboard.'

I let out an angry whine. 'And nobody woke me up?'

'*Tranquilo*, they didn't come aboard this boat.'

Angel is relieved. Inspections are risky. The *Beti* has twice been arrested and escorted to port. Once it was justified: Angel and Antonio were caught fishing in Zone VII, where they did not have a permit. The other time, though, they were arrested for not having an identification number on the buoys—a technicality, since the buoys did carry the boat's name in large letters.

The Irish inspectors had tried to surprise their targets. To evade radar, they dropped their launch six miles away from the fishing boats, at three a.m., and approached through a thick mist. The first boat they boarded, the *Madre Asunción*, was a Spanish-registered vessel. They gave it a formal warning for not having the logbook correctly filled out. The day's fishing has to end at midnight and the log be filled out for the day, even though for a liner the day does not really end until the last fish have been pulled aboard in the early hours of the morning. It was only a technical infraction, but it was punishable. The inspectors checked the fish in the hold, using the plans of the boat to ensure there were no secret compartments.

Over the radio, the *Madre Asunción* told everyone to get their logs filled out fast. The inspectors boarded five more boats, but found everything in order.

Day eighteen

We know now that we will stop fishing on the evening of 4 May. The *Beti* is booked in to sell its catch in Burela three days later. Cartagena calculates that he has to shoot the gear only one more time. Moreno serves *pulpo a la gallega*, octopus with oil, red pepper and potatoes, to celebrate. The faces around the table look exhausted. Littbarski's eyes are squashed; Chapa's are swimming. Cartagena is hunched; Nicolás is grey.

I go to the fo'c'sle, where the evening sun comes through the winch door like a slab of butter. The walls are plastered with pictures from porn magazines: contorted nudes, huddles of bodies frozen in climactic moments. 'Now we're heading home,' explains a deckhand, 'we have to get in the mood.'

Angel is locked into a lengthy debate on the radio. The *Beti* is about to leave El Coral, and he has to allocate new positions for the other boats, writing and rubbing out names on a list again. Even over the radio, his voice has an edge sharp enough to cut through arguments. He has not once been down to the fo'c'sle. His only orders have been about the tackle boxes before the first day's fishing. I have seen him lose his temper only once, when a few fish fell off their hooks before coming aboard and had to be retrieved with a long gaff.

But now he cracks. We are about to finish the last fleet and turn for home. I am in the mess-deck, reading. Angel appears.

'. . . *dios!*'

He snatches open a cupboard above my head and flicks a bank of switches down. All the lights go out, except the one in the kitchen. Moreno comes to the doorway. Some kind of emergency?

'What's up?' I ask.

Moreno shrugs. 'When a Galician loses it . . . '

I take a look down the passageway to the fo'c'sle. I hear only the sloshing of the bilge water and hushed voices in the dark.

Xuxo comes up from the engine room. I follow him up to the bridge. There is nobody there, but I can see three deckhands struggling with a buoy up by the prow. Looking back, I glimpse Angel in his cabin with his feet up. He mutters to Xuxo.

The lights come on. Everyone asks quietly what happened, and then cottons on. The last *palangre* got entangled with the next-door boat's, often a messy problem. This time it was easily solved. But Angel flipped. Fatigue, the pressure of maintaining the right tone on the boat, the fear of arrest, the financial and navigational worries—everything came to a head. 'He hardly knows what he's doing when he's like this,' says Xuxo, shaking his head. The incident is over quickly. Nobody mentions it again.

Day twenty

I have been trying to find the right moment to ask Antonio about something Angel has told me. Last year the *Beti* lost a man. Antonio was in charge when it happened.

We are on the bridge, in the dark early hours of the morning. 'What happened?'

Antonio looks straight ahead, out to sea. 'It was on the second or third of July. When we set off it was clear Iaki wasn't well. He was cramped and ill, but he was always like that for the first four or five days. Then he cut his thumb with a hook. On his last day he didn't have any lunch. We were still a few hours from reaching Porcupine where we were going to fish. The crew woke me up at about five in the afternoon. We're missing Iaki, they said. We searched the boat from top to bottom. Someone found his slippers on the poop deck. I put the boat into the search routine. We steamed up and down along parallel courses. Nothing. There was a force eight gale blowing. So we turned back to Burela to report it to the Guardia Civil.'

Iaki was twenty-seven. His family said he had problems with drugs, though none of the crew ever saw him take anything.

'How did the crew handle it?' I ask.

'That day you suffer. I didn't eat. I smoked three packets of cigarettes. And on the way back . . . but then you get over it.'

He turns round and stares at me.

'This life is shit. Do you call this living?'

Day twenty-one

We have been lucky with the weather, and no one is more grateful than me. Now it seems our luck is about to change. As we head for home, the printout from the meteorological office in Bracknell, England, shows a depression coming up from the south. The BBC is forecasting gale force eight.

The wind strikes, but it comes bang on the stern. So it just pushes us on faster. We ride the waves like a surfer, the prow hanging over a trough for a moment before sliding back with a motion that would have had me retching three weeks ago. The deck tips into extreme, almost vertical positions, as we roll off sideways—but gently, in slow motion. At the bottom of each trough I look up at walls of water ahead and steep hills surging up behind. On the crests, the horizon bursts into view. On any other course we would be in danger. On the radio we hear that Spanish boats on the north coast are confined to port. Those on an outward course will have to turn back or point their bows into the wind and sit it out. But for us the wind is a godsend. We're making eleven knots, instead of the usual nine and a half. 'When the wind is behind,' says Angel, 'all the saints help.'

Day twenty-two

Traile is tying hooks alone in the fo'c'sle, dressed like a jogger in an old sea-green tracksuit with a hood. I ask him how he became a fisherman. He stops smiling for a moment. Puts his head on one side. Finishes a hook.

'Money,' he says finally. 'I was a painter, working for myself. I painted my uncle's flat. He was in the Guardia Civil. May he rest in peace, he's dead now. And we were in a bar drinking wine and there were fishermen who had just come back from a trip talking about how much they had earned. My uncle said that if I wanted he'd find me a place. The first time I went out we sailed from La Coruña to Ferrol, and at Ferrol I asked the shipowner to let me go, I was really sick. But he encouraged me to stay.'

A pause; he finishes another hook.

'You know how to recognize a fisherman ashore? He can't

converse. He doesn't know what's going on. Football, politics, anything. I find it even with my children. We're illiterate. We know how to read and write, but we're illiterate.'

Xuxo joins us. He too earned more in the past. These days, the boat has heavier expenses, and the owners have recently increased their cut of the revenue from fifty per cent to sixty per cent, to cover the new, higher social-security payments.

'What about the disputes with Britain and Ireland?'

'I think there should be more inspections and limits, or a biological rest period like they have in Morocco. Then prices would go up. We'd earn more and so would the owners. The more we fish, the more fish there seem to be, and the price is lower.'

'The owners in Burela tried to have a month with no work,' says Traile. 'But they gave up when they saw others fishing.'

For our last dinner, someone produces a bottle of whiskey. We have Irish coffee.

Day twenty-three

On the bridge at two in the morning. I see the light from the land from twenty miles out and then the shape of the breakwater becoming clearer with every sweep on the radar.

We slip into the quiet harbour. I've picked up something—I hope it is only flu—on board, so when I step ashore I feel almost as bad as when I set out. The crew unload 780 boxes—fourteen tonnes—of hake, the ten boxes of eggs, and a few crates of conger eels and bream. The sorters, pillar-like women in green oilskins, rearrange the boxes, rapidly weighing and counting. The chilled fish gives off a strange, unfishy acrid smell. Angel stands by and makes a methodical map of the expanse of boxes, stacked two high and spread out to cover half the warehouse.

The auction begins at eight. It starts with the freshest, smallest fish and works up in size. The auctioneer, a neckless man in glasses, stands on the edge of a box and sings what sounds like a single, many-syllabled word; then he stops dead as if someone has flicked a switch. Thirty or forty buyers with mobile phones follow him, balancing on the rims of crates without ever slipping into the precious merchandise beneath their feet. The price starts at 1,180 pesetas a kilo and holds steady. It has been a successful trip. The deckhands will clear close to 250,000 pesetas (£1,000).

It is time for goodbyes, but there is still work to be done. The ship has to be cleaned, boxes have to be stacked. And in any case there is little to say. Back on land I have quickly ceased to be part of the crew. And they leave too often to make much of farewells.

Three days later

Back at my home near Barcelona, there are strange new adjustments to make. Not having to hold my plate when I eat. Clean clothes. Opening the front door and going for a walk.

I am telling friends about the trip, trying to explain what I have learned. But it is hard to summarize, apart from saying that humans are almost supernaturally adaptable. Most people want to know how blatantly the Spanish fishermen are flouting the regulations. I can only say that the *Beti* is a successful, legitimate boat; some are not. It doesn't take much to see that thirty-metre boats with three-tonne monthly hake quotas are either losing money or overfishing. Or that while most Galician ports shun gill-netters and are campaigning to have them banned, in La Coruña some *palangreros* were being fitted with gill-nets. For a reduced fleet of Spanish-registered boats, the quota is accommodating enough to make rule-breaking unnecessary, but the rules themselves seem faulty. Conservation is wheeled out to mobilize public opinion; mixed with nationalism it is particularly potent. But it slips easily off the political agenda. Some fishermen *want* more regulations, as long as they are good ones. They, after all, are in the best position to feel how disastrous jealous rivalries can be.

I sense that my friends want a simpler answer. But what can I say? I guess I had expected to find greed and perhaps recklessness among the fishermen, a disregard for the future. Instead, I found hard-working men convinced that their way of life is doomed. Pirates? Even in a good month they earn only £1,000. I feel a brief fisherman's prickliness at not being understood.

I am struck by a strange feeling. I look at my watch. By now, Angel will be once more riding the heaving motion as his boat hits the swell. The men of the *Beti Zorionak* are at sea again. □

CHARLES NICHOLL
CONVERSATIONS WITH
A GIANT

Giants in Patagonia, 1764-5

DON'T MISS OUT ON MAJOR ISSUES

Granta publishes the most lively, original, entertaining and informative writing it can commission, inspire or find, four times a year. There are almost no boundaries. It can be fiction or non-fiction, short story or memoir, reportage or polemic. The only demand that *Granta* makes is that the writing illuminates not other literature but life—and that *Granta* publishes it first.

Subscribe now and you'll save up to 30% on the £7.99 bookshop price and get *Granta* delivered to your home!

'Essential reading'  **GRANTA**
Observer

DON'T MISS OUT ON MAJOR ISSUES

SAVE UP TO 30% (OR £28) WITH A **GRANTA** SUBSCRIPTION

Subscribe to *Granta* and you'll save money and get *Granta* delivered direct to your home, four times a year.

A subscription to *Granta* makes a great gift, too. See the form overleaf for details.

'The quality and variety of its contributors is stunning . . . *Granta* is, quite simply, the most impressive literary magazine of its time.'
Daily Telegraph

no stamp required if posted within the UK

GRANTA

FREEPOST
2/3 HANOVER YARD
NOEL ROAD
LONDON
N1 8BR

There are stories about giants in just about every language in the world, but this one is different. The earliest surviving version of it is found in manuscript copies, in both French and Italian, dating from about 1523. It begins as follows:

> One day, quite unexpectedly, we saw a giant. He was on the shore of the sea, completely naked, dancing and leaping and singing, and as he sang he poured sand and dust over his head. The Captain sent one of the sailors over to him. He told the sailor to sing and leap like the giant, so as to reassure him and show him friendship. This the sailor did, and presently led the giant to a little island where the Captain was waiting. When the giant stood before us he began to be astonished and afraid, and he raised one finger upwards, thinking that we came from heaven. He was so tall that the tallest of us only came up to his waist, and his body was very well built. He had a large face painted red all over, and his eyes were painted yellow, and there were two hearts painted on his cheeks. He had only a little hair on his head; this was painted white. When he came before the Captain he had clothed himself in the skin of a certain beast, very skilfully sewed. This creature has the head and ears of a mule, a neck and body like a camel's, the legs of a deer, and the tail of a horse. There is a great quantity of these creatures here. The giant's feet were also covered with the skin of this animal, made into shoes. The Captain had food and drink brought to the giant, and then the men showed him some things, among them a steel mirror. When the giant saw his likeness in it, he was greatly terrified, and leaped backwards, and in doing so knocked down three or four of our men.

There are further incidents, to which I will return, but perhaps certain details have already suggested what is special about this story, what makes it different from Odysseus' encounter with the Cyclops or Jack's adventures up the beanstalk. For this is not a legend or a fairy tale; it is an encounter that occurred at a specific time and place, and was witnessed by several people besides the narrator. It is, in other words, a piece of travel writing. It belongs to a genre that might be called—to borrow the title of another sixteenth-century travel book—'News from the New World'. This does not necessarily dispose us to believe the story. Travel writers often exaggerate and sometimes lie, and when they have been at sea for nearly a year they might be expected to do both. Meeting a giant would certainly come under the heading of 'good copy', perhaps suspiciously so.

What interests me is precisely the ambiguity of the story. It is a true report that sounds like a fairy tale; it is a fairy tale that real people have experienced.

The author of this account was a young Italian gentleman called Antonio Pigafetta: an unsung hero of early sea travel. He was a member of the expedition commanded by the Portuguese adventurer Fernão de Magalhães, better known as Magellan. The expedition became famous for achieving the first circumnavigation of the world.

The incident he was describing took place around the beginning of June 1520, on the coast of what is now Argentina. Magellan himself is the 'Captain' referred to in Pigafetta's account.

Little is known of Pigafetta's early life. He was born in the northern Italian town of Vicenza, probably in the year 1486. He may have seen some military service against the Turks—he compares the arrows of the 'giant' to Turkish arrows—but the first certain knowledge we have of him dates from early 1519, when he turned up in Barcelona in the service of another Vicentino, Monsignor Francesco Chiericati, a powerful churchman and politician who was then the *Protonotario* or Papal Ambassador to the court of the Spanish king, Charles V.

Here Pigafetta first learned of the 'small armada of five ships' being prepared by Magellan in Seville, and of its daring intention to sail not just to the New World of America, as others had done since the pioneering voyages of Columbus and Vespucci in the 1490s, but beyond it, in search of a new route to the spice-rich islands of the East Indies. He set off for Seville and signed up for the expedition.

He describes this decision with a mixture of awe and nonchalance: 'I knew the very great and awful things of the ocean, both from my reading of books and from conversing with certain learned and well-informed people who attended on my master the *Protonotario*. So now I determined to experiment, and to see with my own eyes some part of those things.'

In contemporary documents Pigafetta is described as *criado del capitán*: Magellan's aide or assistant. He is also described as a *sobresaliente*, or supernumerary. He was not, in other words, a regular member of the crew. He was not primarily a sailor at all, though he was a scholar of sorts, well grounded in the mathematics and astronomy of the day (among his extant writings is a treatise on the computation of longitude). He was also a political servant, and was careful to note that he joined Magellan's expedition 'with the favour' of both his master the *Protonotario* and the Spanish king.

What these terms and contexts add up to is this: that Pigafetta was, probably for the first time on a voyage of this sort, specifically there in order to write about it. He was the observer, the chronicler, the reporter. His 'desire', and that of his masters, was 'that it might be said I had performed this voyage, and had seen well with my own eyes the things hereafter written'. The account he produced—drily entitled, in the French manuscript from which I am quoting, 'Navigation et Découvrement de la Indie Supérieure'—is mostly a fulfilment of this aim. It is lucid, factual, and demonstrably based on a journal or logbook kept throughout the voyage.

If his meeting with the 'giant' seems to us an exaggeration or a lie, it might not have been intended to be so. Was it something more like a hallucination, something so powerfully imagined that it seemed to be real?

The mariner bound for the New World faced many dangers. There were the tempests and twenty-foot waves of the Atlantic; the diseases and brutalities of life aboard ship; the threat of piracy or enemy action. There were the man-eating fish with teeth like saws which the Spanish sailors called *tiburón*. There were the periods of privation when men ate sawdust and oxhide, and dead rats fetched half a ducat apiece.

These, perhaps, were some of the 'great and awful things' envisaged by Antonio Pigafetta as he boarded Magellan's flagship, the *Trinidad*, in August 1519. Most of them he would come to experience in the course of his three-year journey round the world.

But no less pressing were the dangers of the imagination, the tricks of the mind, the visions that came when darkness fell and the sea was calm and he lay in his little cabin with his nostrils filled with the bonfire smoke of *estrenque*, the faggots of dried grass they burned on the poop as a beacon to the other little vessels of the fleet, straggling along somewhere out there on the Ocean Sea.

For the ancient world, to which Pigafetta still partly belonged, the sea was a place peopled by apparitions: the sirens, mermaids, monsters and gods of classical mythology. In the Bible too the sea was associated with visions. 'They that go down to the sea in ships, that do business in great waters, these see the works of the Lord, and His wonders in the deep.'

These sea visions were elaborated into a darker idea of the 'deep' and its contents. St Augustine wrote: *'Mare saeculum est'*— the sea is the world, in other words, 'the element subject to the devil'. It is a 'gloomy abyss', the realm of power allotted to the devil and the demons after their fall. The impenetrable depths of the sea symbolize, indeed contain, the dark secrets of human sin. This is already some way towards the interpretations of modern psychoanalysis, in which the sea is thought of as a symbol or archetype of the unconscious. Jung refers to the visions associated with the sea as 'invasions by unconscious contents'.

To a man of learning like Pigafetta, this lent a magical dimension to that long and arduous sea-crossing, and some of it surfaced in his narrative. In the midst of a storm, he wrote:

> The body of St Anselm appeared to us in the form of a fire lighted at the summit of the mainmast, and remained there near two hours and a half, which comforted us greatly, for we were in tears only expecting the hour of our perishing. And when that holy light was going away from us, it gave out such brilliance in our eyes that for nearly a quarter of an hour we were like people blinded and calling for mercy. It is to be noted that whenever that light which represents St Anselm shows itself and descends on a vessel in a storm at sea, that vessel is never lost. Immediately this light departed, the sea grew calmer, and then we saw various kinds of birds among which were some that had no fundament.

This was not a hallucination—he was describing the electrical phenomenon known as St Elmo's Fire—but the language tends towards the visionary, and ends with the rather inexplicable seabird that lacked (though how did he know?) an anus.

One has a sense of mental disorder here. Already the strange but true—'There are also fish that fly'—begins to mingle indistinguishably with the strange but not quite true. The grasp on what is possible grows weaker. And then, on St Lucy's Day, 13 December 1519, after nearly four months at sea, the fleet touched land on the coast of Brazil, and they were in the New World, where just about anything was possible.

A t first, they were in territory already explored and marginally settled by Europeans. Some of the crew had been there before. They were careful to avoid the settlers, who were Portuguese (Magellan had deserted the Portuguese in favour of Spain, and his expedition was designed to break Portugal's monopoly of the East Indian spice-trade), but after the hazards of the crossing this was paradise. The climate was sweet, the land abundant, the natives amiable. They dined on tapir meat and 'a fruit named *battate* [sweet potato] which has the taste of chestnut and is the length of a shuttle'. A sense of relief and assurance is reflected in Pigafetta's text, which is at its most sober at this point.

But as they moved slowly south, away from 'the equinoctial line', or equator, in search of the desired passage to the Pacific Ocean, they began to enter the kind of unknown landscape which is the real stuff of the New World experience.

Hic finis chartae viaeque: here ends the map, here ends the known way.

By the end of March 1520, more than four months after their first landfall, the fleet was coasting down along the grey, wind-whipped tundra of what is now called Patagonia. They saw penguins, which Pigafetta called 'sea geese', and walrus ('sea wolves'). The weather was worsening, the companies were restless. Here, at a location which Pigafetta accurately estimated as 'forty nine degrees and a half in the Antarctic heavens' (i.e. 49 degrees 30 minutes South), they found shelter in a wide inlet which they christened Puerto San Julián, after the patron saint of hospitable welcome. They decided to winter here. For two months they saw

133

no one at all. Then one day, around the beginning of June, 'quite unexpectedly', they met the giant.

L et us try and separate the elements of truth and fable in this encounter.

The 'giant' was almost certainly a Tehuelche or Tcheulchi, a member of one of the nomadic tribes of Patagonia. They were, and are, a very tall race. Bruce Chatwin described them as 'copper-skinned hunters whose size, strength and deafening voices belied their docile character'. And that extraordinary hybrid creature of the region whose skins the giant wore—described by Pigafetta as part mule, part camel, part deer, and part horse—is also real. It is recognizably enough a guanaco, a smaller cousin of the llama still found in the area.

This much is true. The difficulty arises precisely with the use of the word 'giant'. This is not just a loose description, since Pigafetta specifically says that the tallest of the Europeans 'only came up to his waist'. Other members of the tribe are similarly perceived: they are all described as giants, and indeed giantesses— the latter's huge pendulous breasts are especially noted by Pigafetta. Nor is he alone in his perception of them. A fragmentary logbook kept by an unnamed Genoese mariner on the voyage says: 'There were people like savages, and the men were from nine to ten spans high.' A span, the width of an outstretched hand, is generally taken as nine inches: the giants were therefore reckoned by this observer to be as much as seven and a half feet tall.

This is certainly an overstatement, as later travellers were relieved but disappointed to find. In 1698 a French explorer, François Froger, wrote of 'the famous Patagons': 'Some authors avouch [them] to be eight or ten feet high. However, the tallest of them was not above six feet high.' *The Guinness Book of Records* states: 'The Tehuelche of Patagonia, long regarded as of gigantic stature (i.e. 7–8 ft), have in fact an average height (males) of 5 ft 10 in.'

It would be easy to say that Pigafetta and the Genoese pilot were exaggerating and leave it at that. But this would have been uncharacteristic of Pigafetta. I prefer to think of the exaggeration as something intrinsic to the occasion rather than as an effect supplied later for literary or personal vainglory. The magnification of the Tehuelche into a giant occurs right there and then, in the impact of that first meeting. The emptiness of the landscape, the lack of visual comparison, would also have been a factor.

Pigafetta really thought that he was dealing with a giant, really felt he was a waist-high pygmy beside him. That was how it seemed to him and to others. It was a kind of collective mirage conjured up out of the freezing deserts of Patagonia.

We have to imagine what it was like to deal with these experiences, thousands of miles away from all that was familiar. The sheer novelty of the New World—its people, its creatures, its flora—was challenging in a way we find hard to appreciate today, when so much is already prepared in our minds, already mapped out, the impact of difference softened to a pleasant notion of the picturesque.

How did the traveller deal with all this strangeness? He did so by finding some kind of precedent: an illusion, at least, of familiarity. And since there was often no actual precedent within his experience, he resorted to other sources—to the reservoir of travellers' tales, partly printed, partly oral; to the folk stories and legends of his European culture. Much of the 'discovery' of America involved the importing of images and ideas and indeed fantasies from Europe. Like the sea itself, *terra incognita* became a place of wonders, an 'invasion of unconscious contents'.

There are many instances of this in the writings of Columbus and Vespucci. Columbus's obsession with cannibals derives in part from his avid reading of early travel-writers such as Marco Polo and Sir John Mandeville, whose accounts abound in man-eaters, including cannibals. Columbus actually invented the word 'cannibal' himself—it was a mishearing of the tribal name 'Carib'—but it was inspired by an idea, a fear, he brought with him. He also reported the existence of a tribe of 'dog-faced men' inhabiting one of the Caribbean islands. These too are an echo of Marco Polo, who wrote of certain supposed inhabitants of the Andaman Islands: 'They have heads like dogs, and teeth and eyes like dogs; for I assure you that the whole aspect of their faces is that of big mastiffs.'

Another spectre conjured up by the New World was the Amazon. On his first voyage Columbus heard of certain female warriors inhabiting the island of Matinino (Martinique). As he understood it, they lived without men; they fought with bows and arrows; and they wore armour ('plates of copper'). He called them, naturally enough, 'Amazons' after the tribe of warrior women who in Greek mythology swept down from the hills of Scythia to occupy various Hellenic sites, notably the Isle of Lesbos. They shunned men, except once a year for the purposes of procreation; they killed male offspring; they cut off their right breasts to facilitate the pulling back of the bowstring (hence their name, from Greek *a mastos*, 'without breast'). These formidable women are to be found in all sorts of classical and medieval sources. They encode, not very opaquely, a whole range of male sexual fears and fantasies. Columbus himself gave a long and rather erotic gloss on the subject in his commentary on the *Historia Rerum* of Aeneas Sylvius. Later, on his first voyage, he imported them wholesale into the New World.

On his second voyage in 1496, Columbus actually encountered armed Carib women on the island of Guadeloupe. They were suitably fierce, but otherwise shared none of the characteristics of the classical Amazons. They did not live without men; they did not cut off their breasts. But by then the connection had been made, the legend was alive. It circulated, it gripped the imagination, and when, fifty years after Columbus, Francisco de Orellana encountered female warriors in the hinterlands of Peru, it was natural that he too should believe they were Amazons, and equally natural, in this nameless continent, that the river he was travelling down should thereafter be called the Amazon.

The cannibal, the dog-faced man, the Amazon dominatrix: these are some of the chimera that haunted the traveller in the New World. (The cannibal is not quite a chimera, of course, but the practice of cannibalism was certainly not rife in the Caribbean.) There are others. The reader of Amerigo Vespucci's *Lettera delle Isole Novamente Trovate*, meanwhile, would learn that there were also dragons in the New World. Vespucci had seen one being captured and cooked by Brazilian Indians:

Their feet are long and thick, and armed with big claws; they have a hard skin and are of various colours; they have the muzzle and aspect of a serpent, and from their snouts there rises a crest like a saw which runs along the middle of the back as far as the tip of the tail.

This dragon, whose 'appearance was so foul that we marvelled at its loathsomeness', was in reality an iguana.

There is a common thread to these New World prodigies. They seem to represent an unconscious fear of being devoured, swallowed up, a fear of disappearing into the mysterious otherness of the New World. The traditional giants of legend and fairy tale also have this devouring aspect: 'I'll grind his bones to make my bread.'

Like those earlier travellers, Antonio Pigafetta set off on his journey into the unknown with certain preconceptions about what he would find there. He knew of the 'great and awful things of the ocean'. We cannot be certain what he had read—the only text he actually mentions in his narrative is Aristotle's *De Coelo et Mundo*—but it is a reasonable assumption that he knew the writings of Amerigo Vespucci, the Florentine explorer who is commemorated in the name 'America' (largely on the basis of his spurious claim to have landed on the American mainland in 1497, a year before Columbus's arrival).

Vespucci was, like Pigafetta, a man of some cultivation and social standing—his sister Simonetta was the swan-necked beauty who was the model for Botticelli's *Birth of Venus* and for various other Renaissance painters including Piero di Cosimo. And his influential *Lettera delle Isole Novamente Trovate*, published in Florence in about 1505, could easily have been the source of Pigafetta's giants (in the sense that Polo was the source of Columbus's cannibals). Among its descriptions is an encounter with 'giants' on the island of Curaçao. Vespucci and his companions first saw five women 'so lofty in stature that we gazed at them in astonishment'. They were 'taller than a tall man'. The travellers were tempted to capture them, 'to carry them to Castille as a prodigy', but were scared off by the emergence of a group of men who were even bigger. These men 'went entirely naked'. They were 'so well-built that it was a famous sight to see them, but they put us into such uneasiness that we would much rather have been back in our ships'.

Vespucci concludes: 'I call that island the Isle of Giants, because of their great size.' The legend 'Gigantes' was duly appended to Curaçao in various early sixteenth-century maps. It is not hard to see Pigafetta's experiences in Patagonia as an echo, a confirmation of what he had read in Vespucci's *Lettera*. He had anticipated the presence of giants in the New World, and suddenly, with a lurch of fear in his stomach, he saw one.

There is another book to be considered, one that may hold a key to the name of the region, Patagonia. According to Pigafetta it was Magellan himself who coined this name ('The Captain named this kind of people Pataghom'). The customary interpretation of this is that patagon means 'big foot' (from Spanish *pata*, a foot or paw), and that it relates to the footwear of the natives: huge galoshes of guanaco hide packed with straw. An Argentinian scholar, Professor Gonzáles Díaz of Buenos Aires, suggests another derivation, which is that the 'giants' of the region reminded Magellan (or perhaps Pigafetta) of a creature that featured in a popular romance, *Primaleon of Greece*. The chivalric hero Primaleon sails to a faraway island where the natives eat raw flesh and wear animal skins. They live in fear of a huge half-human monster 'with a head like a dog' in the interior of the island. Primaleon heroically vanquishes it, and carries it back to his homeland, 'Polonia', where it is civilized by the kind attentions of good Princess Zephira.

A Spanish edition of *Primaleon* was published in 1512, seven years before Magellan's departure. Its imagery has a strong tinge of the New World about it. That monster with the bestial features is called the Great Patagon. Is this the source of Magellan's name for the giants of San Julián? Is this another of those precedents the early traveller reached for when faced with the extraordinary?

There was a period of nearly three months between the first sighting of the Tehuelche giant and the fleet's departure from San Julián. During this time Pigafetta came to know two of the giants quite well. They were baptized and given Christian names— Juan and Pablo—and were kept on board ship. In Pigafetta's text they continue to seem like fairy-tale giants: 'they ate a large basketful of biscuit, and rats without skinning them, and they drank half a bucket of water at one go', but they also begin to emerge as human characters. Of Juan, Pigafetta writes:

> He was a gracious and amiable person, who liked to dance and leap. When he leaped he made holes in the ground where he landed to the depth of a palm. He was a long time with us. This giant pronounced the name of Jesus, the Paternoster, the Ave Maria, and his own name as clearly as we did. But he had a terribly strong and loud voice.

Over the weeks and months of the bitter Patagonian winter Pigafetta observed them, conversed with them, and learned something of Tehuelche society and culture:

> They have no houses, but have huts made of the skins of the animals with which they clothe themselves, and they go hither and thither with these huts of theirs as the Egyptians [i.e. gypsies] do.
>
> When they go hunting they wear a cord of cotton around their heads from which they hang their arrows, and they tie up their members inside their bodies on account of the severe cold. They eat a certain white powder made of roots [probably a form of manioc]. Sometimes they eat thistles.
>
> When these giants have a stomach ache they do not take medicine, but put an arrow, about two foot long, down their throats, and then they vomit up a green bile mixed with blood. When they have a headache they make a cut across the forehead and also on the arms and legs, to draw blood from several parts of their bodies. One of the two who were in our ship told me that the blood did not choose to remain in the place of the body where the pain was felt.

Of their pagan religion he writes:

> He [Pablo] told us, by signs, that he had seen devils with two horns on their heads, and long hair down to their feet, who breathed fire out of their mouths and their rumps. The greatest of these devils is called in their language Setebos.

This in turn explains an earlier sentence about the giants: 'They began to be enraged, and to foam like bulls, crying out very loud,

Setebos.' This sentence was translated by the Elizabethan travel writer Richard Eden, who included an abbreviated English version of Pigafetta in his compilation, *The History of Travaile*, published in 1577. This in turn was read by Shakespeare, and used for his own version of the New World native, Caliban in *The Tempest*: 'O Setebos! These be brave spirits indeed.'

Thus Caliban, anagrammatically a cannibal, is also in some measure a Patagonian; and thus the reality of this encounter on the shores of Argentina merges back into the fictional world from which it partly arose.

Towards the end of Pigafetta's stay in San Julián there comes a moment of great poignancy, a reaching out across the huge cultural differences between Europe and the New World, across the curiously blurred frontier between the real and the fictional. The giant called Pablo fell sick. He was in a cabin of the ship. Pigafetta was there with him:

> He asked me for capac, or bread, for this is the name they give to that root which they use for bread; and for olla, or water. And when he saw me write these names down, and afterwards ask him for other names, he understood what I was doing with the pen in my hand.

At this point, the relationship between them seems at last to become whole. The point of view changes. Suddenly we see Pigafetta through the giant's eyes: a small, dark-eyed, rather earnest man with this curiously plumed implement poised above the paper.

This moment of illumination enabled Pigafetta to produce a brief but impressive dictionary entitled, in the French manuscript, *Vocables des Géants Pathagoniens*. This is a list of ninety-one words and phrases in 'Patagonian'—a lexicon quite unprecedented in the European literature on the New World at this date. About half of the words translated are parts of the body, always easy to establish on a rudimentary point-and-tell basis. After anatomy is exhausted the list moves on: to fire, smoke, ice, wind and stars; to fish, dog, wolf, goose (i.e. penguin) and oyster. Pigafetta notes the guttural tone of the language—the words are 'pronounced in the throat'—but perhaps the keynote of this lexicon is not the strangeness of the sounds but the communality of the world they describe: a sense of what is shared by these two men.

Pigafetta concludes: 'All these words were given to me by this giant,' and one is touched by his brusque acknowledgement of a debt, of a gift he has received from this monster who turned out, after all, to be a man not much different from himself.

There follow the maritime adventures which have earned this voyage its place in history—the discovery of the southern passage into the Pacific now called the Straits of Magellan; the long months of privation as they drifted on westwards towards the Spice Islands; the death of Magellan in a skirmish with natives in the Philippines; and, on 6 September 1522, the final return to Seville of a single ship, the *Victoria*, and just eighteen of the 240 men who had set out three years earlier.

Among the survivors was the resourceful reporter Antonio Pigafetta. At Valladolid he presented to the Spanish King 'neither gold nor silver, but things much more precious in the eyes of so great a sovereign'. Chief among these was 'a book written by my hand of all the things that had occurred day by day on our voyage'. This original journal does not seem to have survived. The manuscripts that do survive—three in French and one in Italian—are essentially a paraphrase of it: 'I have reduced into this small book the principal things, as well as I could.'

In 1523 he was fêted at a grand reception in Venice. He was also admitted into the Order of the Knights of Rhodes, and signed himself thereafter with a flourish: Antonio Pigafetta *Cavaliere*. The following year he received permission from the Venetian Senate to publish his account of the voyage, but he does not seem to have done so. He retired back to Vicenza, the town of his birth. The aftermath of his great adventure is obscure; one perhaps discerns a note of exhaustion.

On the front wall of his house, on the street that was then called Via dalla Luna and which is now called Via Pigafetta, he had a plaque put up. It is still there, beside the graceful Romanesque doorway, though the house itself is now the premises of a smart dress-shop. One might expect it to say something grand and triumphal about circumnavigation, about the great and awful

141

things of the ocean, about going to the uttermost ends of the earth and back again.

But all he chooses to say, in somewhat ungrammatical French, is: *'Il n'est rose sans épines.'* There is no rose without thorns. If there is some deeper resonance in this, it escapes me. Perhaps the resonance lies precisely in its simplicity: he had travelled so far to discover this small truth.

He died in Vicenza in 1535, not yet fifty years old.　　□

PAUL THEROUX
UNSPEAKABLE RITUALS

Paul Theroux

W henever people ask me about travel I always suspect they are buttonholing me, eager to relate amazing adventures of their own. That is how I felt when I met Professor Wallack. 'One of the excitements of your travelling,' he said, 'must have been the chance to become acquainted with bizarre customs.' He was smiling, and I had a sense that this was an oblique pick-up line. But he was a very old and untidy man. What made my heart sink was that he held a thick envelope—undoubtedly a manuscript.

'Unspeakable rituals,' Wallack said, licking his lips.

I told him that in my thirty-five years of wandering I had witnessed many encounters which had never been described, some uniquely unpleasant, others mirroring practices we believe to be peculiar to our own lives.

'I think I can say the same,' Wallack said. He weighed the envelope. 'I agree with Geertz, when he called Malinowski's diary a "backstage masterpiece of anthropology, our Double Helix".'

'You knew Clifford Geertz?'

'I knew Malinowski,' he said. 'He was my teacher at Yale. So, tell me a little of what you've seen. Anything bizarre?'

I told him about the Naulu people of Amboyn, who smoke their dead like kippers to preserve them.

'That's pretty normal,' Wallack said. 'I have a greater interest in the odd, the irrational, the truly monstrous. In people who have been either ignored or badly misrepresented in the standard anthropological studies.'

He went on: 'There is also the question of correctness—the desire not to shock or offend readers with revelations of brutality. But my only ambition is to be faithful to what I have seen, no matter how strange or sad. What else have you got?'

I told him of the Jon Frum Cargo Cult on Efate, in Vanuatu; the harvest bingeing on Three-Penis Wine in rural Shandong; the diet of lightly cooked caribou droppings among the Naskapi Indians; ritual fellation among the Asmat; wife-inheritance, or *Chokolo*, among the Sena people of the Lower Shire River in Malawi (and how the widow in question is required to engage in sexual intercourse with the male relative while the husband's corpse is adjacent). The Urine Ceremony of the Bachiga.

Wallack responded by quoting an acquaintance of his, who

wrote: 'In Mali, best friends throw excrement at each other, and comment loudly on the genitals of their respective parents—this is proof of the love of friends.'

'Rather lovely,' he said.

He claimed that oddities such as this were telling, arising as they did from the heart of a culture. 'What ought to interest us,' he said, 'is the enduring nature of custom and belief in people who remain isolated and wholly themselves.' He mentioned an Englishman who, wishing to be contemptuous, expressed a tolerance greater than he intended when he wrote of the Chinese, 'These people are unlike any others on earth and can therefore be judged from no known standpoint, and not even from their own, if it can be found.'

'Can I leave this with you?' he said. He held out the envelope. 'My address is inside, if you want to get in touch after you've read them. Let me know what you think.'

My instinct was to throw it away, but later that evening, having nothing better to do, I pulled out the pages and read *Unspeakable Rituals and Outlandish Beliefs* by Feliks Wallack. Rifling the pages I saw what looked like a collection of short stories. There was an Author's Note:

> With regard to the odder practices, I prefer not to disclose the extent of my own participation, though an old motivating memory of mine is the line in *Heart of Darkness* which speaks of how Mister Kurtz would 'preside at certain midnight dances ending with unspeakable rites'.
>
> I have kept a record of such customs because in general I wished to evaluate whether they bore any relation whatever, even metaphorically, to the way we live in these United States.

A selection of stories from the manuscript appears in the following pages. The more outlandish tales have been omitted.

1. The Mouse Missions of the Plashwits

Among the Plashwits, a pastoral people in Central Asian Turkestan, the ability to carry a live mouse in one's mouth for a great distance without harming the creature is regarded as an essential skill, acquired in the passage from boy to man.

A Plashwit boy becomes a warrior by feeding flesh from his own body to the mouse, and once the mouse is fattened in a way that impresses the commander of the Plashwit army, it is eaten.

The male organ in Plashwit is also known as a mouse. Plashwit women are forbidden to look at a mouse or even to utter the word.

2. The Smoke Sickness of the Balumbi

In order to prove their strength the Balumbi, who are the dominant pygmoid people of the Ituri Forest, on the lower slopes of the Mountains of the Moon, enter smoke houses where they remain for long periods, inhaling the smoke of a vine peculiar to their part of the forest. The Balumbi are well aware that the vine is noxious, that the priests who administer it are corrupt, and that far from being a proof of strength it is addictive and leads to a fatal condition known as 'smoke sickness'.

3. The Bowl Cult of Baojiang

What began in the antiquity of Baojiang as an annual feast to which bowls of food were brought has become a ceremony of display in which latterly the bowls alone take precedence.

Only women, known as Votaries, take part in the ritual of presentation. The Votary carries her bowl, always a clay pot, and shows it to the others, who sit in a circle.

What makes the cult especially unusual is the intervention of a master potter, and the fact that clay is unknown in the sandy Baojiang desert of Qinghai province. The potter supplies perfect bowls at great cost.

Baojiang is an area where famine is common, but this has far from diminished the Cult of the Bowl. It could be said to have enhanced the cult, since bowls, some of them very lovely, with a sort of scrimshaw worked into the cranial bone, are occasionally fashioned from the skulls of those who have died of starvation.

4. Body Sculpture among the Mongoni

The first Mongoni I saw I took to be the victim of a tragic accident. This was in the early 1960s, in an isolated district of Nyasaland, where I was taking a sabbatical. On closer acquaintance with these remote and deeply insecure people I learned that it was the result of deliberate mutilation. As one group will prize the accumulation of muscle and flesh, the Mongoni notion of beauty is skeletal: physical contours are the more beautiful for being unnatural.

The Mongoni cut all excess flesh from their bodies—chunks from their calves and buttocks, lumps from their cheeks and arms. Scars are prized. A merely thin person is far less attractive than one rendered thin through the flesh being carved from the body, the skin itself scraped so that the face is cadaverous.

To display their wounds and their lacerated bodies the Mongoni wear hardly any clothes, just a wraparound. No power is derived from this ordeal, only the notion of beauty. The chief of the Mongoni I remember as monstrous, his wife carved almost to bits. It was common also for the Mongoni to hack off their fingers and toes.

5. The Cat Totems of Moto Tiri

At one time, all over Oceania, dogs were raised and eaten; they still are in many places. Dogs are also found in the meat markets of South East Asia and throughout China. Instances of cat-eating are rarer, chiefly occurring in Alotau in Milne Bay in New Guinea, and in some outlying islands in the Philippines.

147

But in Moto Tiri cats are universally eaten, and every part of the cat is used—its meat forming a significant source of the islanders' protein, its fur used as decoration, its bones fashioned into needles and hair fasteners, its teeth into jewellery. The cats are wild. They feed on the island's dwindling bird population.

Butchered cats are displayed in the Moto Tiri markets—the legs, the haunches, the back meat; some are sold dressed or stuffed. They are coated with sauce, they are smoked, some are dried or salted. Cats are the essential ingredient in stews; they are fried, poached, baked; they are served *en croûte* with a taro crust.

I mentioned to a man in Moto Tiri that cats are house pets in much of the world. He laughed at such a novel concept; in Moto Tiri, pigs are the house pets. They always have names, they are petted and made a fuss of. Pigs are never eaten. On chilly nights, they are often taken to bed by the natives and embraced for warmth, a practice which has given rise to the affectionate name for the pig on the island; 'a Moto Tiri wife'.

6. The Living Stones of Hanga Atoll

Local legend has it that the stones swam to Hanga Atoll on their own from the distant land of Honua, which means stone. The Honua granite does match the stone, which is not found anywhere on Hanga.

The stones are the size of humans, but of course much heavier. Many have been hewn into rudimentary human shapes.

Each person on Hanga is responsible for one stone: the stone bears the name of that person. When the person dies the stone passes to the eldest child in the family and the name of the person changes to that of the stone. If there is no child the stone goes to the nearest living relative.

Some people have no stones; many have one; a number of people have many. Incidentally, one of the meanings of the Hanga word for stone is the same as that of the word 'stone' as it is used in the biblical Book of Deuteronomy, meaning testicle.

The stones represent wealth, but the predicament of the 'owned' (ownership is reversed—in effect it is the stone that owns the person) is to keep the stone moving, clockwise around the atoll. Someone with many stones will spend a great deal of time moving the stones, often most of the day, every day.

A stone may be 'killed' by moving it to a cliff at the south side of the island, but if a stone is disposed of a family member must go with it. That is a sad occasion, yet it is the stone that is mourned and remembered, not the person.

7. The First Night Colours of the Mulvatti

The Mulvatti live on a lozenge of land, about the size of Delaware, tucked in to the south-east border of Yakutsk, in Russia. Mulvatti men and women consummate their marriages in a distinctive 'first night ceremony'.

It is not the wedding night or anything like it. Months and sometimes years pass before the Mulvatti couple make love. There is no specific expression for sexual congress, only an ambiguous Mulvatti word meaning 'It is happening'.

Perhaps it is shame, perhaps it is their low sexual charge, or their instinctive puritanism. The Mulvatti have one of the lowest birth rates in the world, a minus figure.

The normal Mulvatti home is a tent of felt. Animals share the single room, peat and dung are burned in the fire, and the Mulvatti worship wolves, believing themselves descendants of the wolf. Mulvatti women are so lupine in aspect that this bizarre belief seems understandable.

The 'First Night Colours' refer to vegetable dyes that are painted on the private parts of the Mulvatti man and woman on the night they enjoy sexual congress for the first time. They present themselves on the night wearing aprons, and when these are removed and their painted parts displayed they lie down. Innocence is greatly valued among the Mulvatti. Any expression of surprise at the lurid colours—the purple penis, the green vulva—is taken to be an unmistakable sign of previous sexual experience. It can lead to the annulment of the marriage.

8. The Elephant Protocols of the Shan States

In Upper Burma the Shans, a hill people, live adjacent to the Marins, who are traditionally the mahouts, or keepers, of the Shan elephants. But the Marins have degenerated into an isolated folk without animals or income, living precariously as subsistence farmers. Still they revere the elephants, and retain a memory of having managed these majestic creatures. They hold that the creator of the earth was an elephant and that the earth itself is the interior of an elephant's body—that we all live within an elephant, the First Elephant, and that the curved dome of the sky is the elephant's body cavity.

In the Marin belief-system, humans are nothing but an insignificant aspect of the elephant. This reverence is ritualized every four years when the Marin raid the haunts of the elephant and steal their great muffins of dung, removing this excrement to their villages where it is baked into their wheels of bread known as 'protocols'. These are consumed on a certain day, specified by the Marin priests. There is no word for dung in Marin. A clod of elephant dung is universally known as a record of a transaction, or a 'protocol'. I have almost no clue as to the significance of any of this.

A Marin woman told me that the elephant was a symbol of unity, prosperity and fertility. 'The elephant head is male,' she said—meaning it resembled a penis—'and the elephant hind-quarters are female'—meaning they resembled a pudendum. She was amused when I told her that in my culture an elephant was merely an animal with a long memory.

9. The Feasting Donkeys of Quevalo

In a time of great antiquity in Quevalo, in eastern Ecuador, a group of people, lost and starving, heard the braying of a donkey and were rescued. The Feasting Ceremony conducted every four years commemorates that deliverance.

All the donkeys of Quevalo are rounded up and herded into the village and ritually bathed. They are washed and brushed, carefully groomed, their tails and manes braided, their hooves painted. Each is brought to a hut and fed cakes and titbits prepared especially for the occasion. Money in the form of notes of high denominations is sometimes baked into the cakes the animals are urged to devour. The donkeys are fed all sorts of delicacies; they live in the house, and their members are stroked by the Quevalo women until they are tumescent. An old woman told me bluntly that ejaculation occurs.

The fine food seldom agrees with the donkeys. It is so much richer than the normal diet of grass that the donkeys swell with gas, break wind, cramp, bellow with discomfort. Yet the attentions are unceasing; the donkey is fed and stroked until it is stuffed and nauseated and excited. Finally, it vomits copiously, and the entire family feeds on the vomit.

In the event that the donkey does not vomit the family pokes a stick into its gullet, forcing the creature to regurgitate. This, too, is gratefully eaten, as it was by the lost family of Quevalo, long ago.

10. The Memory Priest of the Creech People

One person alone, always a man, serves as the memory for all the dates and names and events of the Creech, the hill-dwelling aboriginals of south-central Sumatra. (The word is also written Crik, Krich, Kreetch, and so on.) This person possesses an entire history of the people and may spend as much as a week, day and night, reciting the various genealogies.

This Memory Priest reminds the Creech of who they are and what they have done. He is their entertainment and their historian, their memory and mind and imagination. He keeps the Creech amused and informed. The Creech have no chief or headman. The Memory Priest serves as the sole authority.

The Memory Priest is awarded his title at birth. As soon as he is able to talk he is given to understand that he is the repository of all the Creech lore.

His is not an easy career. He must memorize great lists of family names and must be able to recite all the events that took place from the moment of his birth.

The Creech are mostly placid, though they are subject to odd fits of violence. Biting themselves in order to show remorse is not unknown, and clawing their own faces is common. They are also untruthful and unreliable, prone to thieving, gossiping, gambling and sudden spasms of the most aggressive behaviour.

What the Memory Priest knows, the immensity of his storehouse of facts, is nothing compared to the one fact that he does not know, a secret that is withheld from him. After thirty years have passed, and he is old by Creech standards (possibly toothless, almost certainly wrinkled and shrunken), a meeting is convened. He recites the Creech history, and at the conclusion of this he is put to death. He is finally roasted and eaten by every member of the Creech, in a ritual known as the Ceremony of Purification.

The next male child born to a Creech woman is designated Memory Priest, and elevated; history begins once again. Nothing that has taken place before his birth has any reality, all quarrels are settled, all debts nullified.

So the Memory Priest, now an infant, soon a man, learns his role, believing that history begins with him and never aware that at a specified moment his life will end. Yet it is the death of the Memory Priest that the Creech people live for and whisper about, the wiping out of all debts, all crimes, all shame and failure. They eagerly anticipate the amnesia his death will bring. Throughout his life, though he is unaware of it, he is less a supreme authority than a convenient receptacle into which all the ill-assorted details of the Creech are tossed. Secretly, he is mocked for not knowing that it will all end in oblivion, at the time of his certain death.

11. The Ornaments of the Wahooli

The Wahooli people of the Rumi river in north-west New Guinea made first contact with outsiders only in 1973 and after that they vanished—moved deeper into the forest, which was odd and perhaps inconvenient, since they were a fishing community. But they had their reasons.

The Wahooli do not write. That is not remarkable—the world is full of people who have not found any need for written language. But the Wahooli are unusual in having no pictures, or symbols, absolutely no decoration of any kind. In fact, all ornamentation is derided as suspect and wicked and anyone found in possession of any decoration is punished severely. The Wahooli believe that all such designs are meant to cast spells. Only the devil—in Wahooli cosmology an elaborately costumed demon—would approve of such designs.

The Wahooli go utterly naked. They feel no shame. Clothes are pomp, feathers a vice, even a skirt of dead leaves is vain. In every encounter, the Wahooli make a practice of peering very closely at each other's bodies; and their ritual greeting is a snorting or a sniffing. Even the odours of flowers or any perfumes are a despised form of ornamentation.

The Wahooli carry only the simplest spears and daggers, the most straightforward nets and fishing tackle. Much of their fishing is accomplished by damming various rivers and streams and making fish ponds in which the fish are easily caught by hand.

The Wahooli sleep in trees on roofless sleeping platforms, in family groups, one to each shelf. Although they have names, they use them with great reluctance. They have no words for please or thank you, no equivalent of good morning or farewell. No colours are recognized, and to all intents the Wahooli world is achromatic. Their language is almost without adjectives, although 'useful' and 'harmful' are two of their chief categories; 'edible' and 'inedible' form another. The word for stranger is 'inedible', while enemy is 'edible'.

The Wahooli are noted for their silences. They eat what they kill. Nothing is kept overnight, nor is anything stored. They do not use feathers or shells. It is a people without texture or design.

They have no leadership, and hardly any social organization. Women are equal to men, and though the infant mortality rate is enormous even children have specified rights in the Wahooli code. But then so do animals and birds and even fish, all of whom the Wahooli communicate with, often holding lengthy conversations.

All this I learned on my first visit. On my second visit I found that the Wahooli had fled even deeper into the interior.

12. The Rat Rooms of Rondok

The Rondok people of the Aru Sea inhabit the almost inaccessible heights on their island and have thoroughly resisted any attempt at integration by neighbouring Indonesia. Indeed, to save face—because the island has repelled all invaders—the Indonesians leave Rondok off their maps. Melville wrote of Rokovoko, Queequeg's island, 'It is not down on any map—true places never are.' As is the case with many people who have remained steadfast in their beliefs, the Rondok people are fierce and well-governed. Neither missionaries nor soldiers have made any lasting impression upon them.

It is a tradition that no outsider has survived a single night on the island; anyone who has not departed by sundown vanishes in the darkness, is 'swallowed'—literally, so I was assured in the short time I spent there, just a matter of hours.

From a Rondok fisherman who had wandered to the edge of the lagoon I learned two facts.

The first was the one I have just mentioned, the disappearance of anyone who remains on the island overnight (there were not many instances, owing to the obscurity of the island).

The second was the manner in which the Rondok people conduct elections to their highest office. Anyone may be a candidate, any number of volunteers are invited. In the initial caucus, various tests of strength are given, and they involve both mental and physical ability—running, jumping, feats of memory, repeating poems and songs, floating in the lagoon with arms and legs tied ('drown-proofing'), throwing heavy objects. Rondok women are not excluded.

The volunteer cannot withdraw, but must persevere in the tests until he or she is either eliminated or attains the level of Candidate. This may take months. When there are about a dozen candidates remaining they are individually locked into cylindrical pits called Rat Rooms, like shallow manholes sealed with heavy covers or lids.

Each candidate shares his or her small underground space with thirty or forty furious squealing rats. There is no light in the Rat Room, no bed, and because of the low ceiling the candidate cannot stand (and would not want to sit). There is water, but it is in a basin, at floor level, in what is known as The Tank, available to the rats and the candidate alike.

Some candidates, already exhausted by the selection process, and undone by the sheer misery of the situation, fall to the floor and are gnawed to death. These candidates are mourned. Another category comprises those who, starved and imprisoned, eat the rats. On their release they are put to death. The successful candidate is the one who emerges unscathed, who has neither been bitten nor has eaten any of the rats, who has found a degree of harmony in the Rat Room. This person is made head of the people, given the title of Rat Chief, and when he or she dies the tedious selection process begins again. □

GRANTA

JULIA BLACKBURN
THE MERMAID

The man was still there poised in indecision and staring at the thing which lay heaped at his feet. I saw then that it was not a human corpse, or the trunk of a tree, or a bundle of sail that he had found, but a mermaid. She was lying face down, her body twisted into a loose curl, her hair matted with scraps of seaweed.

The year was fourteen hundred and ten and it was very early in the morning with the sun pushing its way gently through a covering of mist that floated aimlessly over the land and the water.

The man had never seen a mermaid before except for the one carved in stone above the east door of the church. She had very pointed teeth and a double tail like two soft and tapering legs, while this one had a single tail which could have belonged to a large halibut or a cod.

The man stepped forward and squatted down beside her. The pattern of her interlinking scales glinted with an oily light. He stroked them along the direction in which they lay and they were wet and slippery leaving a coating of slime on his palm. But when his hand moved over the pale skin of her back it was as rough as a cat's tongue and very dry and cold.

He lifted a hank of dark hair, feeling its weight. Little transparent shrimps were tangled within its mesh and struggling to free themselves. A yellow crab scuttled around the curve of the waist and dropped out of sight.

He hesitated for a moment but then he took hold of the mermaid's shoulders and rolled her over. The sand clung in patches on her body like the map of some forgotten country. Her nipples were as red as sea anemones. Her navel was deep and round. Her eyes were wide open and as blue as the sky could ever be. As he gazed at her a lopsided smile drifted over her face.

He had presumed that she was dead and with the shock of her being alive he let out a cry and jumped to his feet. He turned and began to run as fast as he could over the ridges of muddy sand and towards the village.

I watched as he trampled on the grey scrub of sea lavender and the low samphire bushes, their thin skins so easily broken. But he trod more carefully once he had reached the strip of pale stones littered with the sharp empty shells of clams and oysters, until with his heart thumping in his throat he was beside the fishing boats and the wooden hut battered out of shape by the north wind.

The old fisherman was sitting there just as before, singing to himself as he mended his nets with his legs stretched out stiffly in front of him and his bones aching. He made no response as the young man tried to explain what the sea had thrown on to the land; he didn't even raise his head to look at the speaker.

The young man ran on again until he had arrived at the first house of the village. The shoemaker's wife was standing by the door, her arms cradling a huge belly which seemed to be about to split open like a ripe fruit.

'There is a mermaid!' he said to her, but she was lost in thought and hardly heard him although her baby lurched violently inside her womb as if it was shocked by the news. She remembered that later.

The man went into the house and from a back room he fetched one of those narrow wooden spades that are used for digging lugworms. Then he returned the way he had come. He meant to bury the mermaid even if she was still alive and his task made him walk slowly now, with all the solemnity of an executioner.

He looked out across the expanse of sand shimmering like an ocean of calm water. He saw how a flock of gulls had settled in a noisy mass on the place where the mermaid was lying and as he drew closer they lifted, screaming and turning into the air.

But the mermaid had gone. Nothing remained of her except for a single lock of dark hair which resembled a ribbon of torn seaweed.

Nevertheless the man dug a hole as deep as a grave: the salty water seeping into it, the sides crumbling away and seeming to melt like snow. And as he dug the surface brightness of the sand was replaced by greasy layers of black and grey mud smelling of age and decay.

When the hole was ready he picked up the hair and dropped it in, covering it over quickly and stamping it down. He marked the place with a big black stone.

That evening he sat with the old fisherman drinking from a jug of beer and going over and over the story of what he had seen and what he had done. During the night his wife Sally shook him awake because she could hear the sound of a woman crying, desperate and inconsolable. On the following morning a cow died for no good reason and the shoemaker's wife gave birth to a baby with the head of a monstrous fish which only lived for a few hours.

Everyone agreed that this must be the mermaid's fault and they told the priest to do something. So the priest went with the man to where the hair was buried. He took a holy candle with him but it kept on going out in the wind, and he had a bottle of holy water to sprinkle over the sand. In his spidery handwriting he had copied three paternosters on to a piece of parchment and he tucked this under the black stone while reciting a prayer to protect them all from harm.

After that things were quiet again for a while but it was as if a lid had been clamped down on a pot that was bound to boil over sooner or later. The mermaid had disturbed the pattern of life in the village. People waited with growing apprehension for what might follow.

The priest had a dream in which she slithered over his body like a huge eel and wrapped her tail tight around his legs. He was crying when he woke up.

The man who had stroked her rough skin kept on stumbling against her image in a corner of his mind. Whenever he went out with his boat he would hope to find her glistening among the fish he had caught in his nets. Searching for her, he began to travel further and further from the shore. □

SEA PICTURES

WILLIAM SCAMMELL, BELLA BATHURST, NEAL ASCHERSON, N.A.M. RODGER AND WILL HOBSON

*Elia Kazan shoots
America, America, 1962*
COSTA MANOS/MAGNUM

SNAPPER ON BOARD
William Scammell

The Cunard's Queens, the Mary and Elizabeth, each carried two thousand passengers and almost as many crew. It was the British Empire afloat: First Class, Cabin Class and Steerage . . . No, no, it was called Tourist by then, but no one was going to lose any sleep over those people's welfare. Three vast restaurants. Two swimming pools. The Silver Grille for the crème de la crème, who wanted something more exclusive than First could offer. (Rock Hudson and Debbie Reynolds, Burton and Taylor, Coward, Fonteyn, Orson Welles, who was already a small liner himself.) Libraries, cocktail bars, saunas, gymnasia, shops, hairdressers, nurseries, cabarets, dance bands, cinemas. Bingo was called tombola, I seem to remember, or some American equivalent. There was even a ship's newspaper, printed daily somewhere down in the bowels of D or E deck, which carried snippets about the weather, the daily mileage, and the latest share prices in the City and on Wall Street.

There were grand staircases, all chromium handrails and discreet lighting, for the white and black tuxes and confected ball gowns. The men's cummerbunds were their only grace notes, ranging from sober black to scandalous plaid. The women floated along in expensive *déshabillé* with snowy or sunbaked shoulders, lacquered hair, tooled lipstick and Cleopatra eyes. You could tell at a glance whether they were still human, or had mutated into walking assets. The thicker the veneer, the happier they were to strike a pose for the lens.

Walnut, maple, mahogany everywhere you looked. Pillars and parquet floors. Intricate and tasteless marquetries. Big public rooms full of Balmoral furniture, miles and miles of wood-panelled corridors, staterooms to sleep or party in, above or below water, according to your purse. Grand-hotel dining rooms with carved ice swans, starched tablecloths, stiff napkins, bumper menus, wine waiters, crêpes waiters with gleaming trolleys and inflammatory manners, regiments of ordinary waiters in white tunics and brass buttons, pompous upholstered chairs, vast pillars, anodyne murals, enough cutlery per person to start up a small restaurant.

Passengers got waited on by dining room stewards, cabin stewards, lounge stewards, deck stewards, barmen, swimming pool and gymnasium attendants, nursery stewards and villeins of various sorts. Stewards, when they ate, got cooked for and waited on by lesser stewards. Chefs were looked after by under-chefs. Officers had their servants, their servants had servants in turn, right down to the boys who stood at the First Class restaurant doors and copped a fortune in tips at journey's end. Everybody got paid for their services, either directly by the 'bloods', as passengers were called, or indirectly by those who had access to them. It was trickledown economics long before that phrase got planted on Reagan's and Thatcher's equivocal lips. Somebody milked the cow and everybody got to take home something in their pail. Conversely nobody got owt for nowt, unless it was the deck sailors, simple souls who coiled ropes, scrubbed decks, and ate the bangers and mash we never could find on our elaborate menus.

There were policemen too, called masters-at-arms, who had the fishy eyes and punctilious manners characteristic of the species; all-purpose administrators called pursers who booked the cabins, fielded complaints, and ran the bingo, which was rumoured to net them a king's ransom; cabin stewards and stewardesses, the former mostly alcoholics, the latter refugees from boring marriages or broken engagements and lacerated hearts; hairdressers, beauticians, laundrymen, deckchair attendants, and the Lord knows what else. When the ship wasn't the Empire or the Grand Hotel it was Versailles, with the captain as Louis and the alphabetized decks leading down into a clamour of rude mechanicals and oily swains who kept the whole enterprise afloat.

I was the ship's third photographer. Once properly at sea the serious business began, loading up cameras and spare magazines like guns. Captain's receptions—at which everybody filed in in their finery, shook hands with the great man, and consumed their allotted portion of champagne and caviar. Then a shot of every table in all three dining rooms—a major undertaking this, where a table might have a dozen people round it, and an officer (uniforms always went down well), and the narrow spaces between were crammed with waiters, trolleys, pillars and other impedimenta. Often you had to spread them all out and then break up the seating arrangements, and the conversation, of another table nearby while you borrowed some important lady's chair, stood up on it like a clown in your dress suit, waved, shouted, conducted the front and back rows until you could see every face in your viewfinder. The flash was ready to go (sometimes it wasn't), the waiter wasn't wrecking your shot, the officer condescended to look your way . . . then presto! The opportunities for mayhem, chagrin, self-loathing, were immense. Sometimes half the table would be for you and half against and the whole dumbshow turn into a Pinter play. Sometimes you'd make a balls-up, double-expose or accidentally fog the film, and you'd have to go back and do it all over again. It took hours and inevitably soaked us in sweat. When I started out we used 5x4 cameras and separate negatives rather than rolled film, which meant juggling each neg inside a leather bag at the back of the camera. Later we used Rolleiflexes for a bit, which simplified things enormously. Later still we moved on to 35mm and colour, which meant that our processing had to be a lot less slapdash. Proofs were printed on board, two or three thousand of them in four and a half days flat.

Next we shot the passengers on the grand staircases, or stepping out of the lifts, before they got into the dining room. We shot them at bingo or roulette, up on deck drinking beef tea, tangoing to Geraldo and his band, or whatever. The big jobs we did as a team. Late at night we'd split up to work the bars and public rooms: number one to First, number two to Cabin, me to the cavernous gloom of Tourist, where the drinkers were getting on with their drinking and the young with their flirting. You could relax a bit then, have a beer and a smoke. Back at the darkroom we'd develop the night's work and hang the rolls of film up to dry in electrically heated cabinets, ready to print the next morning. Even that could bring disaster. There were times when somebody put on a light mid-process, or the developer was exhausted and the negs too light, or the wet rolls were left hanging too close and dried stuck together.

166

Cabin party on the Queen Elizabeth, 1960   ERICH HARTMANN/MAGNUM

All being well, however, work finished at one or two in the morning. I followed another photographer's habit of visiting the night chef on the way back down to my cabin. He would, for a consideration, cook you a plate of bacon and egg sandwiches, washed down with a glass of cold milk. We slept like babies. □

SEA-TOWERS
Bella Bathurst

The lighthouse is petrified in affectionate memory. Its image has been used so often—by charities, building societies, churches, fish-and-chip shops—that it has long since become a shorthand emblem of reassurance. It stands in our imagination as a pale remote tower, stuck in the middle of a featureless sea; or (a more homely, seaside scene) as a stone stump rooted to a headland, striped like candy and glinting aimlessly in the summer sunshine. Their keepers, too, seem like an old-fashioned ideal, tucked up in their tapering hermitage, devoting themselves to night watches and logbooks. Burly figures in thick jerseys, smelling of hand-rolled tobacco and fresh paint.

By the end of 1998, every one of Britain's 210 major lighthouses will have been automated. The lighthouse-keeping profession—which at one time provided employment for about 1,000 people—will be obsolete; the job will no longer exist. Each British lighthouse will have its own computerized sensors, feeding digital signals to the world outside. Instead of old-fashioned human watchfulness, there is remote control. As the various British lighthouse administrations have realized, it no longer takes three men to maintain an electric bulb. In any case, the lights have outlived their purpose; the most useful thing now about many lighthouses is not the light itself, but the racon beacon, with its signature radar pattern, on top. According to some sailors, you could switch off every lighthouse in Britain and it wouldn't make a blind bit of difference. Even the lighthouses which double up as weather stations don't need supervision any longer. The lenses

168

LIGHT HOUSE. — I

SECTIONAL VIEW OF SKERRYVORE LIGHTHOUSE.

A. Water Tanks
B. Coal Store
C. Workshops
D. Provison Store
E. Kitchen

F. Bedroom
G. Bedroom
H. Officers room
I. Oil Store
J. Light room

1st Course

19th Course

32nd Course

28th Course

84th Course

94th Course

High Water

Eng.d by Tho.s Dick.

Feet 10   5   0   10   20   30   40   50 Feet and clocks of the old lights are now on display in museums; the logbooks and records are stored in historical archives. The beam of light and the slow rhythm of the radio forecasts might give the impression of human reassurance; both have long ago been demanned.

Two hundred years ago, almost half of all British seamen died pursuing their trade, either killed by the punishing life on board ship or sacrificed to storms and drownings. Nearly everything which the modern mariner relies on—competent maps, accurate instruments, good communication—was either unreliable or uninvented. Mariners nosed along the coasts half blind, travelling hopefully in the direction of shelter, governed by the moods of the weather and the temper of the tide. The major sea lanes around Britain were crowded and collisions were frequent. What is now fixed and understood was then debatable; navigation was more an art than a science. Sailors depended on experience or luck. When they ran into trouble, there was no kindly lifeboat service ready to put to sea.

No single event marked the shift from callousness to compassion; there was no sudden discovery that preserving lives was better than wasting them. The impulse to save people from shipwreck had always existed, as had the equally strong urge to profit from the sea. But until the eighteenth century it was harder to assist victims than it was to collect the proceeds from wrecks. Legislation defended the salvagers, not the mariners, and no one gave much thought to the human consequences of nautical disaster. Most efforts were aimed at protecting cargo, not at ensuring that the crew returned home intact with the goods. Besides, the ocean was regarded by many as a greedy god, to be appeased with regular doses of sacrificial souls. Lives lost at sea were regarded in much of Europe as natural wastage. Such superstition was only an emotional response to an unpalatable truth: the sea did kill people in great numbers, year after year. Short of refusing to leave Britain's shores, there seemed little that anyone could do to change that fact.

The tide of thought turned gradually, helped by advances in technology and a growing reluctance to waste precious manpower.

By the beginning of the nineteenth century there were moves to establish a national lifeboat service, and wrecking turned from a murderous trade into a legalized salvage industry. Just as importantly, the sea was beginning to lose a little of its supernatural power. If, as was evident, it was possible to control and improve the land, it was also now possible to harness the ocean.

Lighthouses were hardly a new idea. They could trace their genealogy back to the third century and the Pharos of Alexandria. But the modern, archetypal lighthouse—on its lonely rock in a lonely sea—is largely a product of Scottish imagination and endeavour. By the late eighteenth century, lighting Scotland's broken coast had come to be seen as a pressing necessity in a country whose sea lanes grew busy with the trade of the Industrial Revolution. The technical challenge was formidable. To place a building—any building—on a rock in the Atlantic Ocean needed money, skill and self-confidence. The pressure of wind, wave, tide and weather on a lighthouse was exceptional; no other structure—not even a harbour—had to have quite the same tenacity as the sea-towers did. Any construction had to be capable of resisting waves which could hurl up to three tons of liquid pressure at any object in their way. Every one of the lighthouses built on Scottish sea rocks had stone walls at least nine feet thick; anything less and they might not have lasted the first gale of winter.

To build something under such singular pressures, at a time when the only materials available were stone, wood, glass and iron, was almost miraculous. There was no concrete or hydraulic lifting equipment; no helicopters or pneumatic drills. Dynamite, a new and fickle builder's tool, had to be treated with extreme caution. Mortar required expert mixing and split-second timing. Horses often provided the haulage, and horses would jib at precipitous cliffs. Equipment came by sailboat or (later) small steamer, which ran the risk of shipwreck on the very rock or headland to which they were ferrying men and materials. Try taking a trip round Scotland's lighthouses now. Even with the twentieth century's luxuries—cars, roads, ferries and planes—reaching the uttermost points of the northern coast is still not a simple task.

The Stevenson family built almost every one of Scotland's lighthouses. Robert Louis Stevenson is the most famous member of his family, but he was by no means the most industrious. His literary achievements have thrown a long shadow over the accomplishments of his ancestors. The 'Lighthouse Stevensons' achieved a slew of inventions in both construction and optics, and managed feats of engineering in conditions which would be forbidding even today. The driven energy that R.L.S. put into literature, his family put into lighting the dark seas.

The first beacons for mariners were either coal fires or high coastal towers in which candles burnt through the night. Only a few of these fires were ever constructed in Scotland since they consumed fuel voraciously and were usually extinguished by bad weather. Thus, by the mid-eighteenth century, the Scottish coast had become notorious for shipwrecks; in 1799, seventy vessels were lost in the Firth of Tay alone. In 1800, the writer's grandfather Robert Stevenson went into partnership with his stepfather Thomas Smith, engineer to the fledgling Board of Northern Lighthouses. The two began replacing the existing coal fires, first with oil lamps and later with a system of fixed lights using gas or oil. In 1807 Robert started work on the Bell Rock, a vicious spit of reef off Arbroath in the North Sea. Battling with the elements and an optical science still in its infancy, Robert was, if nothing else, a stubborn genius. He was also a man of a most particular time, a bootstrap businessman who combined practical skill with exceptional emotional stamina. Unusually, he had both the creative imagination to dream up new schemes and the mindset to ensure that every detail was correctly executed. He fitted in well with the temper of Enlightenment Edinburgh, and undertook all his work on the lighthouses from a resolute sense of public duty. Many of his strongest qualities were passed on—at some cost—to his sons and their successors.

Three of his five surviving children also became engineers. Alan was a classical scholar, literary, gifted, and noted for his early championing of Wordsworth. He suppressed his artistic side to go into the family firm, becoming like his father before him chief engineer to the Northern Lighthouses. His greatest professional triumph took root on a ragged clump of rocks near the Hebridean island of Tiree; Skerryvore, perhaps the most beautiful lighthouse in the world. David Stevenson, who took up Alan's position after his retirement, built the light at Muckle Flugga, the most northerly of all Scotland's lighthouses. Constructed as a temporary light to aid British naval convoys on their way to the Crimea, it was placed on the summit of a wave-washed miniature mountain. The government insisted that the light should be working within six months; David Stevenson ensured that, even with winter seas crashing 200 feet over the rock, it was finished in time.

Thomas Stevenson was responsible for the construction of twenty-seven onshore and twenty-five offshore lighthouses. He built the light at Dubh Artach, an isolated mass of rock off the island of Mull. He harnessed the new science of electricity and built a series of revolving lights, in a loop which finally enclosed the whole of Scotland. Much of the time he worked with David. The brothers complemented each other; Thomas was inventive; details suited David. Together they built reliable systems for constructing, surveying, lighting, supplying and staffing their fast-growing constellation of lights. David had two sons, David A. and Charles, both of whom refined the existing systems. Most of the remarkable feats of engineering had been completed; there seemed little for the grandchildren to do but tinker with them.

Robert despised literature, but his grandson perpetuated the family name with it. R.L.S. was trained by his father, Thomas, as an engineer and spent three summers supervising building works on various projects. Aged twenty-one, he gave it up for law and then for writing. As he later confessed, in 'The Education of an Engineer', he had not used his time as his father intended; string courses and *pierres perdues* were an interesting addition to his vocabulary, but not for him a way of life.

With age and distance, R.L.S. recovered pride and affection in the Stevenson trade. He wrote with awe of his grandfather's work on the Bell Rock lighthouse and of his father's melancholic genius for design. In essays, letters, introductions and memoirs he wrote about every aspect of his brief time as an apprentice engineer. Most of all, he transformed his experiences into his best fiction; *Treasure Island* and *Kidnapped* both salvaged traces of his early career. The further R.L.S. grew away from engineering, the more keenly he felt towards it; he was sea-marked, and he knew it. He also recognized with some discomfort that his own fame was swallowing up the recognition which his family deserved. In 1886, he wrote crossly to his American publishers:

> My father is not an "inspector" of lighthouses; he, two of my uncles, my grandfather, and my great grandfather in succession, have been engineers to the Scotch Lighthouse service; all the sea lights in Scotland are signed with our name; and my father's services to lighthouse optics have been distinguished indeed. I might write books till 1900 and not serve humanity so well; and it moves me to a certain impatience, to see the little, frothy bubble that attends the author his son, and compare it with the obscurity in which that better man finds his reward.

Robert Louis Stevenson tried hard to immortalize his family, but the Stevensons had hardly helped themselves. In four generations, not one of them took out a patent on their inventions. All of them believed that their works were for the benefit of the nation, that they were unworthy of private gain or personal celebration. They were only engineers, after all; they worked to order or conscience. What pride they had in their creations they put down to the advantages of forward planning and the benevolence of the Almighty. It was the novelist Stevenson, the builder of fantasy, who took all the fame that posterity had to give. □

THE CASE FOR BUTTERFISH
Neal Ascherson

The ship had left the port of Varna in Bulgaria, the passengers had dined and the autumn night had fallen. Suddenly word went round that the Patriarchs were about to bless the Black Sea. The crew gathered on the promenade deck. Curious passengers began to arrive from the saloons below. Somebody handed out candles, and glimmers broke out all over the expectant crowd beneath the lifeboats. Then the bearded Fathers of the Orthodox Church made their way to the rail: His All Holiness the Ecumenical Patriarch Bartholomew I of Constantinople, His Holiness Elyas of Georgia, The Most Reverend Metropolitan John of Pergamon and a train of others. They stepped up in turn to dip a spray of basil in holy water. Each chanted a prayer and then scattered the blessed droplets over the side on the sea rushing past in the darkness below.

It was near the end of the voyage. The ferry *E. Venizelos* is a huge steel box of a ship which normally runs cars and lorries between Crete and Piraeus. This time, it had been chartered to carry several hundred scientists, priests, bishops, ecological warriors, writers, philosophers and financiers on a study journey around the Black Sea. 'Symposium II' was dedicated to 'Religion, Science and the Environment: The Black Sea in Crisis'.

Nobody denies that the Black Sea *is* in crisis. Its waters have been poisoned and its fish stocks have collapsed. The big rivers— Don, Bug, Dnieper, Dniester, and above all the Danube—pour down a suffocating spew of industrial filth: excess nutrients from chemical fertilizer, spilt oil (the Danube alone discharges 110,000 tons of oil a year), toxic metal waste, pesticides, sewage. The fertilizer nutrients create 'blooms' of floating algae which kill bottom-dwelling life on the shallow coastal shelf by cutting off the light from above; they also exterminate the zooplankton on the shelf which feed young or spawning fish. Hydroelectric dams block the seasonal rise and fall of the river deltas, and prevent anadromous fish—sturgeon, shad—from swimming upstream to breed. Reckless overfishing, by the Turks above all, plunders what remains of the anchovy and bonito on their annual anticlockwise migration around the Sea. It had been the supply of fish from the Black Sea, caught and cured in the Greek colonies round its shore, which allowed the city states of the Aegean and Ionian seas to grow populous, to found maritime empires, to feed scientists and playwrights and philosophers. Now this may be the first sea in the world to become, for human purposes at least, lifeless.

Aboard the *E. Venizelos*, the cargo of wise men and women argued about how to save the Black Sea, but also about what the sea—any sea—is for. Is the sea a mandate under God, awarded to

175

the trusteeship of human beings? Is it an estate for 'sustainable exploitation' or a wilderness whose only purpose is to make us aware of our smallness and mortality? Or is it now to be regarded as a garden, and is it therefore our duty to keep its waters and creatures in some sort of order, free of weeds?

Horace said: *Exitio est avidum mare nautis*—the greedy sea is there to be a doom for sailors. That has been my view of what the sea is for, ever since a midwinter Atlantic night spent hanging over a boat's stern holding on to a broken rudder. Overhead the Northern Lights strutted their stuff across the constellations. But I did not see much of them, because a comrade was grasping me by the ankles and icy waves submerged my head every few seconds. The Greeks called the Black Sea 'Euxinos'—friendly to strangers—but only because they thought the sea was listening. The sea is nobody's friend. It wants you dead, and when its fish and crabs have done with you, spits you out contemptuously on the shore.

The savants on the *E. Venizelos* were less concerned with the greed of the sea than with the greed of men. The idea was that the religious people on board (the 'faith community' is the correct 1990s phrase) should find common ground with the scientists about man's duty to nature or place in it, and about what to do to salve the marine ecosystem. But I am not sure that they did. Plans were agreed to help the mostly bankrupt states around the Black Sea to meet the obligations to which they had signed up in the 1994 Odessa Declaration and the 1996 Strategic Action Plan. These treaties commit them to reduce pollution and 'manage' the Sea's damaged species. And yet the ethics of the business, the proper relationship of Man to Nature, could not be pinned down to our satisfaction. The scientists said: Do something, do almost anything practical before it is too late. The faith people seemed to say: If we want to do something for this sea and its creatures, we should be sure about whose name we are acting in, and by what right. And (they went on) it is the human species, rather than the fish and the dolphins and monk seals, which is the urgent case for treatment.

176

One day, the ship put in at Yalta. There was a grand welcome, with choirs hymning and patriarchs embracing, in front of the Margate Restaurant on the esplanade. (Yalta is twinned with Margate, but the restaurant, with its fading inscriptions in English—STURGEON ON SPIT. FOOD. TAKE OFF. DELICIOUS—is boarded up.) A few of us went off by taxi and then on foot to climb the Crimean coastal escarpment which towers above the port, and we rested at a waterfall halfway up the cliffs. Here the Tartars come to make wishes, bringing little rags and ribbons inscribed with prayers and tying them to the trees under the fall.

We could see our ship, a white splinter thousands of feet below. The sea was a quiet blue, fading into the misty blue of the sky at the horizon. It looked as if nothing harmful had ever happened, or could ever happen, to this immense presence. It reminded me of standing on the Lyle Hill above Gourock, where the Clyde broadens out into an estuary many miles broad. When I go there now, looking down on the empty, tranquil waters, I cannot believe that as a boy I saw it crowded with warships and liners and battered Liberty ships arrived from the Atlantic convoys, with destroyers whooping echoes off the Argyll hills, and cruisers gushing black oil-smoke, and picket launches drawing white feathers across the surface. It can seem that the sea closes over everything, erases everything and returns invulnerably to itself.

But now we know that it is not so. The last open frontier, the seas and the seabeds and the life in them, has become finite, and the death of the Black Sea ecosystem is now close enough to be imagined. Sitting on the hillside above Yalta, recollecting the intense debates on board our ship so far, I felt that we had developed two ways of imagining that end or apocalypse which did not fit together.

One was the view that Man holds the seas in trust from God. In Genesis I, it says that God created Man in his own image and gave him 'dominion over the fish of the sea, and over the fowl of the air, and over the cattle, and over all the earth, and over every creeping thing that creepeth upon the earth'. Until now, this has been held to mean that the 'natural creation' is there for Man to hunt, fish, deforest and build cities on. But in this century it has been understood as a warning. The eco-religious view is that after the Fall the sinful human race began to exploit the planet selfishly and unsustainably, contrary to the duty of care imposed on Man by his Creator.

The other approach is to get Man back into perspective. Human beings are not categorically separate from other forms of life, or even of matter. They are integral parts of the natural world, even though no other species has the power to do its own environment such short-term damage. It is no good approaching the ecological disaster of the Black Sea with an anthropocentric mindset. The Black Sea was not created to be a useful pond which could be fished recklessly for ever. But neither are its problems, in the long term, exclusively the work of guilty, greedy Homo Sapiens.

In one session, I heard a man exclaim, quite sharply: 'There is no such thing as natural pollution. Only Man can pollute!' In that remark lay all the blind conceit of our species, and the root of the problem. He implied that, for better or worse, Man is omnipotent. But of course 'Nature' does pollute. The Black Sea is almost a dead sea not because of modern toxic waste, but because ninety per cent of its water, below a depth of about 200 yards, is anoxic. It is poisoned with hydrogen sulphide, contains no dissolved oxygen and cannot support life—which swarms, or used to swarm, only in the surface layer. This condition was brought about by the big rivers which, as the last glaciation began to melt, poured silt and organic matter into the Sea until the older ecosystem was overwhelmed. About 20,000 years ago, during the latest Ice Age, the Sea's connection to the Mediterranean was blocked and it became a lake, leading to the death of all its marine species and their replacement by freshwater life forms. Then, 10,000 years later, the Ice Age ended and the Narrows leading to the Mediterranean once again broke open, producing what must have been a spectacular flood as the bigger sea rushed in and began another exchange of fauna which has been going on ever since.

These are very recent events, on the geological scale of time. Both were probably witnessed by human beings. The second event—the sea breakthrough—took place among early farmers already herding domestic animals and planting crops. But they had not the slightest share of responsibility for those cataclysms. And no ecological damage now being wreaked on the Black Sea by industrial societies can remotely compare in extent to what natural forces have done twice in the lifetime of our own species.

The point of all this is humility. 'The Black Sea is Dying' is an idiotic headline. Even the human race is not up to killing a sea. What is taking place is a rapid change in the ecological balance of life in the Black Sea, in a way which reduces quantity and diversity and seems also to threaten the future of human beings. The ecosystem will find a new balance when it is left to itself again: a marine environment is never a steady state, but always in the process of change. But it may well be a balance which humans do not like. If the rebalancing after this episode of human damage leaves only one fish species and waters clogged with inedible jelly-organisms, we will be both impoverished and distressed. It follows that it is up to us to help shape this new ecological balance. We can't ever restore the status quo, with the old numbers of anchovies and bonito and sturgeon migrating and breeding in the old way. Nature does not retrace its steps. But we can, if we want, guide the construction of a new Black Sea to our own tastes.

The key argument on that Cretan ship, for me at least, was about two Latin names. One has invaded the Black Sea; the other—so far—has not. *Mnemiopsis leidyi* is a ctenophore or comb-jelly, a small transparent creature which normally lives in eastern American estuaries. Some ten years ago, brought in as a stowaway in the water-ballast of American freighters, it 'exploded' throughout the damaged Black Sea ecosystem until it had attained a floating biomass of a billion tons. *Mnemiopsis* consumed the plankton normally eaten by other species, destroyed the shallow sea-floor environment, and helped to accelerate the collapse of one fish species after another. The other creature is *Peprilus triacanthus*, the American butterfish. This ugly, blubber-lipped little fish is the only natural predator of *Mnemiopsis* and can eat its own weight of ctenophores every hour.

So why not bring the butterfish to the Black Sea, and watch it dispel the *Mnemiopsis* nightmare? Sure, the Sea would acquire a new species, 'artificially' introduced. But at least it would be a fish, useful to somebody, and not a jelly.

Here theology jibbed, however. Not so much the clerics,

although some of them were very uneasy about the idea, but the theologians of the church of ecology. They raised two sorts of objection. The first was scientific. Who could say what introducing the butterfish might lead to, or what further, unintended damage it might do to the environment? That was a reasonable question, and the only answer is to start a test programme at once. But the other objection was dogmatic. Human intervention to modify a natural ecology is always wrong, its advocates said. Who do we think we are? Have we not done enough sinful damage to this sea, and aren't we showing unteachable contempt for the planet by proposing to interfere again?

In extreme form, this was the confrontation between 'Man-and-Nature' and 'Man-in-Nature'. It opposed the idea of stewardship, which can easily become a recipe for merely passive care, to the idea that a sea is a context to which humans and water and fish and changing currents all belong equally, in which human action to keep the sea good for ourselves is not a form of blasphemy. The Black Sea shows how empty the argument against intervention is, when the damage has already been done. As one scientist said about *Mnemiopsis*, 'Doing nothing seems to me to be the same as dumping oil into the sea and saying: Let Nature clean it up.'

There is some chutzpah about a proposal to 'garden' the ocean. But there is far worse arrogance in pretending that the future of a sea depends on how we square our consciences with God or Gaia. The rhythms of the Black Sea, like those of any sea, remain largely mysterious and unpredictable. All that we can know is that it is changing, and that it is we—not the Sea—who are dying. □

INTO THE WIND
N.A.M. Rodger

In the days of Francis Drake, the Armada and Queen Elizabeth's war with Spain, the qualities of most English warships and armed merchantmen were speed, handiness, and relatively heavy armament. The heavy armament was made possible by remarkable advances in the English iron-founding industry. Whereas Henry VIII had to import almost all his military supplies, Queen Elizabeth had a plentiful supply of iron guns at a time when few other countries had progressed beyond bronze. Bronze guns were better weapons, and easier to cast, but they were also five times more expensive. In other countries, heavy guns were princely status symbols. In England, by the 1580s, they were an everyday commodity within the pocket of any would-be pirate or explorer. This striking technical advantage, which lasted in certain respects into the nineteenth century, distinctly marked the character of overseas expansion. It made English ships, however small, unusually ready to fight other ships; and it gave the English advantages at sea which they did not have on land. It also made them more inclined to raid ships from other countries, laden with the cargo of these countries' colonies, than to develop colonies of their own.

The design of English ships, as well as their gunpower, also influenced England's behaviour at sea. Any ship represents a balance of different qualities; superiority in one has to be bought by sacrificing others. The speed and handiness of English ships came from fine underwater lines; consequently they had limited carrying capacity, particularly as much of their displacement was absorbed by their heavy armament. They were as a result ill-adapted for long ocean passages, and were often forced to spend a great deal of time searching for food and water. The Spaniards comforted themselves with the thought that the English ate so much that their ships could not carry sufficient provisions, and they were right in effect, even if they mistook the cause.

Quantity of food was not the only problem. Until the nineteenth century, the range of foodstuffs which could be preserved for use at sea remained the same: salt beef and pork, beer, pease, cheese and butter (all in cask), biscuit and salt fish. Preservation and packing was a skilled and chancy business, especially brewing beer and pickling meat, which could be done only in winter. The only English seaport with markets developed enough to victual a large expedition or a major fleet was London, and then only if money was provided early enough to pack in the right season and in good time. In terms of ship design, Elizabethan men-of-war, both royal and private, were hardly less capable of campaigning in the West Indies (or even the East Indies) than their successors in the eighteenth century. The real difference lay in two centuries of effort to improve the quality and organization of victualling. This alone explains why Queen Elizabeth's Navy could not have been an instrument of colonial conquest even if the queen had wanted it to be. It also explains many of the worst difficulties of the early English colonies. Individual ships could and did reach very far across—even around—the globe, but reliable movement on a large scale was badly hampered by the difficulty of preserving food.

Wind was another of England's disadvantages. The wind systems of the North Atlantic blow broadly clockwise from the coast of Portugal down to the Canaries, across the Atlantic to the West Indies, up the coast of North America, and back across the North Atlantic. From the Gulf of Florida to the coasts of Europe, the wind is accompanied by the powerful drift of the Gulf Stream. Within the Carribean, both wind and currents move from east to west, so that ships have to enter through the Lesser Antilles and leave through the Windward or Mona Passages (from the southern part of the basin), or through the Gulf of Florida. This pattern of winds and currents gave Spanish ships an easy passage to and from the New World. Sailing from Seville in the spring, they would run before the wind south-west and westerly across the Atlantic, enter the Caribbean through the Windward Islands, and disperse to their destinations. They could gather again in the late summer (before the hurricane season) at Havana, leave by the Florida Straits and return across the central Atlantic, breaking their voyage midway at the Azores. Unfortunately for the English, the winds of the north-eastern Atlantic are not so obliging. They are south-westerly for most of the year, forcing any ship bound to the southward or westward to beat down the English Channel and across the Bay of Biscay, losing weeks or even months before picking up the favourable trade winds.

Western ports, especially Plymouth, were popular because they were most of the way down Channel—but they were too small to supply any large force properly. Hence English ships, and especially fleets, often ran short of food and water trying to get across the Atlantic, and were forced to waste time and run the risks of landing at the Bayona Islands, the Canaries, Madeira or the Cape Verde Islands. The direct crossing to New England or Newfoundland was much shorter, but it was also directly into the prevailing winds, across the most stormy and dangerous part of the North Atlantic. This is why the Basques, with a longer but easier passage, could exploit the Grand Banks long before the English could mount an effective challenge. In practice, the most successful English crossings tended to be those which took the longer but safer southerly route; there were islands at regular intervals to supply food and water.

The wind systems also explain why, and where, the English concentrated their early colonial ventures. Because all Spanish trade ships left the Caribbean through the Florida Channel, and worked up the coast as far as the Carolinas before picking up the westerlies to blow them home, a base in or near Roanoke or Chesapeake Bay was perfectly placed for English privateers to intercept them. In the 1620s and 1630s, the English, like the French and Dutch, profited from the Spaniards' failure to settle the Lesser Antilles by acquiring footholds which eventually allowed them to control the gateway to the Caribbean basin.

The English were latecomers in overseas voyaging. Well into the 1560s, England remained an ally of Spain and the Spanish Empire, closely linked to them commercially and militarily. Even before Philip II's short reign as King of England, the English Navy was essentially an auxiliary of Spanish power, involved only to a limited extent in the Spanish and Portuguese Atlantic trades. At that time, and for long afterwards, the Spaniards and Portuguese were the acknowledged masters of oceanic voyaging, and the Scots and French were in advance of the English. English seamen were skilled pilots, familiar with the waters of northern Europe, but not deep-sea navigators. Like Chaucer's shipman, they knew every creek in Brittany and Spain—no doubt because, like the shipman (generally supposed to be based on the notorious Dartmouth pirate, the elder John Hawley), that was where they lay in wait for their victims. This sort of knowledge, derived from a lifetime of practical experience, was of little use in making ocean passages. For that the mariner needed to learn the new scientific techniques of celestial navigation. He had to be literate and numerate, familiar with the new books and instruments which were appearing with precocious speed. The Elizabethan wars at sea forced the growth of this new kind of mariner, and endowed England with a large population of highly skilled navigators, competent to carry a ship to anywhere in the world and bring her home. No commercial or colonial effort overseas would have been possible without these men and the skills they had learned.

In the early seventeenth century, with the return of peace, the English found their overseas efforts still shaped by the ships which were available to them. Heavily armed ships with limited stowage were best adapted for cargoes of small bulk and high value, carried in dangerous waters. So the English prospered in the Levant trade, where shippers were willing to pay well for insurance against the Barbary and Christian corsairs. They opened up the East India trade, where a good armament was essential to trade in the face of Dutch and Portuguese hostility. They secured a large part of the European carrying trade as neutrals in the Thirty Years War, able to defend themselves against the privateers of every nation. In all these cases, however, the English advantage lay largely in the disordered and dangerous condition of the seas; disorder which the English had done a great deal to generate. □

TRAWLING FOR FACTS
Will Hobson

Less than one-hundredth of a per cent of the deep sea has been glimpsed; astronauts have flown 384,000 kilometres to walk on the moon, but no one has actually set foot on the deepest ocean floor, eleven kilometres away.

More than a mile down, the water is perpetually dark and even artificial light is obscured by 'undersea snow'—the blizzard of falling particles from decaying animals and plants. At a depth of two miles, the temperature is only a few degrees above freezing, and the pressure on a whale's skin is one ton per square inch.

The Mediterranean was cut off from the other oceans more than six million years ago. When the sea level in the Atlantic rose, the ocean flowed over the Straits of Gibraltar in the largest waterfall ever. It took a hundred years for the Mediterranean to refill.

Ocean life began with algae over three billion years ago. There are 160,000 known species of marine animals, whereas land supports a million species (three-quarters of them insects). But the oceans contain both the smallest creatures on earth (the one-celled foraminifera and radiolarians) and the largest: the blue whale.

A blue whale's blood vessels are so broad that a full-grown trout could swim through them; its tongue is the weight of thirty-five men, its heart the size of a small car. A newborn blue whale drinks over a thousand pints of mother's milk a day.

The most abundant fish in the world is the bristlemouth, but it is small: a kitten could eat a million a week. Copepods, minuscule shrimp-like herbivores approximately the length of a hyphen (-), outnumber all the other life forms on earth put together.

Only 300 of the world's 20,000 species of fish are caught commercially. A third of the total world catch is used for fishmeal and fish oil for animal feed and fertilizer. It costs the world's fishing fleets $124 billion to earn $70 billion; the shortfall is made up by government subsidies.

Over twenty-five million tons of fish are discarded each year. Pollution and overfishing have reduced the twenty-six commercially fished species in the Black Sea to five. A nineteenth-century cod could weigh ninety kilograms; today they rarely exceed eleven.

Prawn production in Ecuador rose from 4,625 tons in 1979 to 35,000 tons in 1983; in the same period, Ecuador lost one-third of its mangrove, the natural habitat of the wild juvenile prawn.

There are 33,035 seafood-related illnesses in the US each year; in Japan, twenty people per year die after eating poorly prepared puffer fish.

Coral is used in grafts to help bones heal more quickly. The cell walls of brown algae are used in the manufacture of beer, frozen desserts, pickles, adhesives, ceramics, paper, toys and explosives. Kelp grows two feet per day, and produces a substance used in the manufacture of paint, cosmetics and toothpaste.

One-third of the world's oil and gas lies beneath the seabed. Nearly six million tons of salt are extracted from the sea every year. The sea is full of gold—sufficient to provide nine pounds for everybody on earth. The Pacific seabed is full of polymetallic nodules; it holds forty billion tons of manganese. A seabed mine costs $1.8 billion in start-up capital, and has annual operating expenses of $400 million.

The world's fleet of merchant ships has grown from 130 million gross tonnage in 1960 to 508 million gross tonnage in 1996. Japan and South Korea built sixty-eight per cent of the merchant vessels completed in 1996.

The American surf industry is valued at $1.35 billion.

There are 2,000 storms at sea in progress at any given moment.

Three hurricanes have led to insurance claims of $5 billion each.

In hotels in Manila, one can pay $350,000 to have ships stolen to order. In 1996 there were 224 recorded acts of piracy.

Half the world's people live within thirty-seven miles of the sea.

The largest man-made reef is in Truk Lagoon, off the Caroline Islands, where sixty Japanese vessels were sunk by an American air raid in 1944.

Ninety per cent of all volcanic activity occurs at sea. In 1963, a volcano erupted off Iceland and formed a new island, Surtsey. The first plant grew eighteen months later; within five years Surtsey was home to twenty-three species of birds and twenty-two species of insects.

The first known underwater concert took place in 1855, when the crew of a Russian submersible, *Le Diable-Martin*, sang along to a brass band in honour of the coronation of Tsar Alexander II.

The oil spill from the *Exxon Valdez* off the coast of Alaska in

1989 killed 36,000 seabirds, 3,000 sea otters and 150 sea eagles.

Lost or discarded nets—'ghost nets'—continue to catch fish; as many as 20,000 northern fur seals may be trapped in this way each year.

In 1987–88, half the inshore population of United States East Coast bottlenose dolphins succumbed to bacterial infections; in 1988, 18,000 harbour seals in European waters died from a distemper-like virus.

Between 1965 and 1981, eighteen nuclear reactors were scuttled by the Soviet Union.

In 1996, 179 vessels were lost at sea, killing 690 people.

Largest loss of life in peacetime: 4,386 men, women and children when the ferry *Dona Paz* collided with a coastal tanker in the Philippines, 20 December 1987.

Largest loss of life in wartime: approximately 7,700 when the liner *Wilhelm Gustloff*, carrying German troops and refugees fleeing the advancing Soviet army, was torpedoed in the Baltic by a Soviet submarine in 1945.

A one-metre rise in the sea level (predicted to occur by the year 2100) would drown eighty per cent of Majuro, capital of the Marshall Islands, and bury fourteen per cent of Bangladesh's agricultural land.

The Aswan dam on the Nile has trapped more than a million tons of nutrient-rich silt, causing a sharp decline in Mediterranean sardine and shrimp fisheries.

By the year 2000, about two-thirds of the world's total flow of water to the oceans will be controlled by dams.

Sources: UN Food and Agriculture Organization; The Smithsonian Institute; International Oceans Newsletter; US Food and Drug Administration; Lloyd's Register; International Maritime Bureau; Independent World Commission on the Oceans; National Maritime Museum; The Times Atlas and Encyclopedia of the Sea; Philips's Atlas of the Oceans; The Oceans Atlas; Encyclopaedia Britannica; The Universe Below by William J. Broad; Deep Atlantic by Richard Ellis. ☐

THE VOICE IMITATOR

104 STORIES
BY THOMAS BERNHARD

Translated by Kenneth J. Northcott

"Consisting of 104 stories, each no longer than a single page.... *The Voice Imitator* works as a mini-anthology of Bernhard's obsessions with political corruption, madness, murder, and the inability of language to capture, or relieve, the absurdity of life. Part diatribe, part black comedy and part philosophical investigation, the book strikes all the major themes in Bernhard's novels and plays....A highly artistic undertaking."—PETER FILKINS, *New York Times Book Review*

Cloth £14.20 Available at bookstores.

THE UNIVERSITY OF CHICAGO PRESS

Visit www.press.uchicago.edu to read excerpts from The Voice Imitator.

EIGHTEEN SUICIDES

SIX PAINFUL DEATHS

TWENTY-SIX MURDERS

[*one love affair*]

THIRTEEN INSTANCES OF LUNACY

TWENTY SURPRISES

FOUR DISAPPEARANCES

TWO INSTANCES OF LIBEL

THREE CHARACTER ATTACKS

FIVE EARLY DEATHS

ONE MEMORY LAPSE

FOUR COVER-UPS

TAKING THE AIR
THE NEW YORK WATERFRONT
1920 AND 1997

At the turn of the century, the city of New York met the
sea in a whirring, hooting jumble of trade. Piers jutted like
teeth into the East and Hudson rivers for most of the way
around Manhattan island: railroad and ferry piers, liner
terminals, freight wharves, stretching as far as the eye could
see and blurring with the smoke of steamers, tugs and
railroad yards. This was a great working harbour. But where
was the pleasure of the sea? Municipal philanthropists
thought that New York citizens deserved a different kind of
pier—the kind found at seaside resorts—where people might
stroll, sniff the breeze, listen to a band. At least four of these
'recreation piers' were built in Manhattan to similar design
under the supervision of New York's Department of Docks.
The pair of photographs on the following pages show the pier
at Christopher Street in 1997, and another (or possibly the
same) recreation pier in 1920, in its original form.

Unidentified recreation pier, by unknown photographer, circa 1920

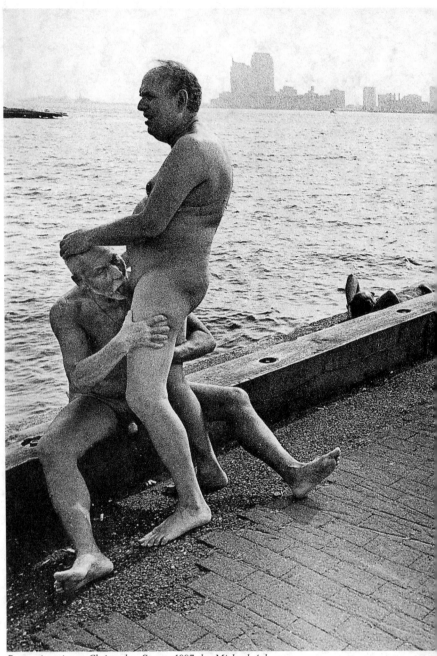

Recreation pier at Christopher Street, 1997, by Michael Ackerman

PHILIP MARSDEN
WAITING FOR
ST PETERSBURG

The Kommunar

I took the top road to Tolverne. Overhead, grey clouds chased each other across a low sky. The road pushed north, between brown autumn hedges, away from the sea. After several miles, it dropped down towards the upper reaches of the Fal river and the chain ferry that plies between its banks. It is always something of a surprise to come across the sea again, here, so far inland, to see tide-stained rocks tucked up beneath a dense mass of oak woods, to see torn-off wrack hanging from low branches. But at this point, the slaty southern coast of Cornwall has been breached. Twice a day the flood tide presses its way into a whole network of deserted creeks. The channels are narrow—no more than a couple of hundred yards wide, but they are very deep and ships of a great size are able to lie up there in complete shelter. It is the cheapest parking lot for ships in the British Isles. For many years two old carriers—the *Methane Princess* and *Methane Progress*— wintered above the ferry, kept in service solely for an annual cargo of guano from South America. In the end that contract expired too, and they were sent off for scrap.

An old concrete track led away from the ferry road and down through the woods. To the left, beyond the dark green of holly bushes and holm-oak, flashed the waters of the Fal. The Americans had built this track and ran tanks and troops down it for the Normandy landings. Grass now grew in its potholes and, dodging them, I bumped on towards the river. I stopped the car on the foreshore. The tide was out. A slope of shingle and mud led down to the waterline. A hundred yards beyond lay the Russian ship. She lay portside on, her raised bows facing downstream, the far shore so close behind that she seemed almost to be aground. KOMMUNAR was written in Latin script near the bridge and in Cyrillic on the bows. A pair of funnels, ringed with the Russian tricolour, rose from the deck. The first filaments of rust had pushed through her paintwork.

I was carrying a side of bacon and a bottle of vodka. I walked out to the end of the pontoon. I'd heard about the ship in the butcher shop. Someone was buying a side of bacon. 'For the Russians, poor bastards, stuck up the river for months on end.'

I was particularly alert to talk of things Russian, shut away as I was with the writing-up of a year in Russia, and particularly here in Cornwall, on a wind-battered November day among the chops and sausages of the village butcher. I agreed to deliver the bacon, and added some cheese and bread and vodka.

I placed the bags down on the shingle. The ship loomed large above the water. Nothing moved on board. I cupped a hand beside my mouth. 'KOMM-UNAR!' No response. I shouted again. A heron rose from the flats. High up at the ship's rail appeared a lone figure. It stood there a while, then waved and disappeared. Soon afterwards, two men came jogging down the gangway to where one of the lifeboats was tied alongside. The noise of its engine filled the creek and in this strange red craft, they ferried me aboard. I followed them up the gangway to a wooden deck and in through a series of half-lit corridors. They led me over the threshold of bulkheads, up a steep staircase and to a door saying: CAPTAIN'S CABIN. I knocked. *'Da.'*

Inside, three men sat playing cards at a table. A television was on, proffering from its high bracket the unintelligible glitz of an ITV quiz show. At a desk, hunched over a book, sat the captain. I placed the meat and drink on the desk and greeted him.

'You know Russian?'

'A little.'

'I am the captain, Shamyl. Welcome to my ship.'

For the rest of that afternoon—while outside the *Kommunar*'s salted-up windows the early winter darkness crept in with the tide—we sat around the table drinking vodka and eating *kolbasa* and cheese. We talked of the usual things—families, prices, politics; they asked me what I'd been doing in Russia and I told them about the villages of the south, the communities of religious sectarians, the Cossacks and Old Believers. 'Cossacks,' said Shamyl. 'Dangerous men.'

For their own situation these Russian seamen showed only a weary contempt. They sighed at the demise of the Communists, the bandit state their country had become. And it struck me that were they back in St Petersburg they would be doing just this— sitting in a kitchen somewhere in the high-rise hinterland of their city, television on in the background, oilclothed table scattered with plain food and drink, chattering with the ease of those who know that the levers of change are always beyond their reach.

The *Kommunar* was a fishing vessel. Six thousand six hundred tons, one hundred and twelve yards overall length, she had been built in the People's Democratic Republic of Germany in 1973, in the thick of Brezhnev's Years of Stagnation. She had put in twenty-three years' service before arriving in this Cornish backwater six months earlier. During the previous winter, she had finished her work in the fishing grounds off Shetland, then taken orders to move south. In the first days of April, she put into Falmouth for bunkers, but the launch that came alongside placed her under arrest. Two officers of the Admiralty tied a plastic-covered writ to one of the masts above the bridge. The ship's holding company in St Petersburg had, it turned out, left a long line of debts around the world. The *Kommunar* was to be held in lieu of them. Faxes began to bounce back and forth between the two ports. The weeks passed and no payment came from St Petersburg. The Falmouth harbour authorities grew tired of the *Kommunar*'s brooding presence in the bay. They took their tugs and towed her upstream. They moored her fore and aft and had both anchors dropped to secure her bows. Thirty-three men remained on board and when one night they began to riot, the police were called from Truro and a helicopter hovered above the deck. The following week, twenty-two were repatriated. The skipper, Shamyl, kept with him a skeleton shift—chief engineer, electrical engineer and eight crew members. There wasn't much for them to do. Supplies were sporadic. The shipping agents were slow to gather victuals for a penniless ship. The faxes grew rarer. A kind of stalemate was reached, which no one but the crew had much interest in resolving. Shamyl managed to raise cash by selling some of the fuel he had on board. Other than that, and the occasional charity of locals, the crew was reduced to dangling hand-lines over the stern of their fish factory to pick up whatever grey mullet or mackerel swam in on the tide.

A week or so after my first visit to the *Kommunar*, I went back. I took with me a carton of cigarettes, and beer and some Russian books I'd picked up on my travels. The afternoon was still and windless; a low sun shone on the ship's sides. Shamyl was alone in his cabin reading a Moscow mafia thriller.

'How are things, Shamyl?'

'Normal.'

He gestured to the banquette that curled around the table and I sat down. A samovar was boiling in the corner. 'Coffee, tea?'

'Tea.'

I leaned back against the blue foam seats and asked Shamyl about his life in St Petersburg and his family. He needed little prompting. I'd forgotten how quickly the old Russian stories could seep through the façade of post-Soviet life. Soon he was talking about the *Wehrmacht*'s siege of Leningrad, the starvation, and about his eldest brother, who had gone for a walk at that time, been taken from the streets, and eaten.

Shamyl's parents were Tartars. In 1911, his father had left the wide horizons of the southern steppe for the boom town of pre-war St Petersburg. A host of nameless aunts and uncles were scattered by the Revolution; two grandparents died from the diseases and famine that followed. Shamyl himself had been born in 1947, the youngest of eight. Only three of his brothers survived their childhood. He hadn't known his eldest brother but, with an exile's longing for his home town, he recounted the exact route he'd taken on that morning in 1942, on his way to see an aunt.

'She lived near the Moscow station. He crossed the Dvortsovy bridge, went down Nevsky Prospekt and turned off to the right. Somewhere behind Gostinny Dvor his footsteps disappeared. They took him and just ate him up.'

The police had found his clothes in a warehouse and arrested a group of dock workers who'd been moonlighting as human butchers. Shamyl's mother had also had a narrow escape when she'd been lured to a flat to buy shoes. When the door opened, a number of hands reached out of the darkness to drag her in. Being so thin, she managed to wriggle out of her winter coat.

'Take a man, chop him up, sell him. That's what they did in those days. Even now sometimes.'

Shamyl had been sailing for nearly thirty years. He held no romantic illusions about the sea—I could not imagine him holding romantic illusions about anything. He had one of those icily handsome Russian faces, and in it were the generations before him who'd spent their lives herding livestock on the southern steppe.

There was nowhere in the world that he had not been. He had known the pale blue waters of the Caribbean, the islands of the Pacific, the chaotic ports of Africa (which was always just 'Africa'; the continent was never distinguished by country). His favourite place was Panama, where the climate was good and the women were cheap. He had some good friends in Cape Town, and had nearly foundered off the Falklands. He did not see that among his contemporaries, who had required permission even to leave their town, this was any sort of privilege.

'It's a job. Some people are electricians, some are cooks. I am a sea captain. And now I don't get paid, just like everyone else.'

I asked him what he needed—food, drink, cigarettes. He said: 'Just talk, this is what we like. Come aboard whenever you can.'

A few days later I persuaded Shamyl to show me round the ship. He led me down a dark corridor through the bulkheads. The *Kommunar* was a monument to Soviet endeavour. Hundreds of such factory ships were built in the last, stumbling years of the planned economy. In long convoys they sailed through the Baltic and fanned out across the world's oceans, trawling in international waters or, when within exclusion limits, buying up catches from local boats. In the winters of the early Eighties they came to Falmouth Bay. I knew one or two of the fishermen who used to sell to them, tying their trawlers up alongside and striking a deal with the skipper. The Cornish remembered the Russians for their hard bargaining, the skippers' faulty English and the home-made spirits with which they closed deals.

Below *Kommunar*'s football pitch of a trawl deck lay the processing plant. A dim electric light fell on a labyrinth of conveyors and gutting trays. Everything was scrubbed clean, but patinas were forming on each of the surfaces, and nothing would ever rid this place of its dead fish smell.

The fish themselves, forty tons at a time, would come sluicing down through a hatch in the stern. A team of twelve men would then sort, top-and-tail and gut them. Cramped between the machinery they worked swiftly, airlessly, while fish blood spattered their boots and aprons and the fillets slid on a circuitous conveyor towards the freezing plant. Here they were pressed into ten-kilo bricks before being arranged in the freezers. Eleven hundred tons

Philip Marsden

of fish could be stored in this way. And every couple of months a supply ship would rendezvous with them in whatever ocean they were working, replace the crew and take away the fish.

I asked Shamyl what kind of fish they were after.

'Mackerel, cod, herring, flatfish—anything that came in with the nets. In Africa, we caught fish none of us had ever seen before. They all went into the freezers to be tinned.'

I had seen those tins, stacked in low pyramids in the state shops of Russia's landlocked interior. An anonymous fish shape decorated the label which read simply: FISH.

Shamyl took me down to the engine room where only the small auxiliary engine was still working. The laundry room, the steam baths, the redundant bridge, the radio room—he showed me all these with a muttering detachment. He shouldered open a door marked with a red cross: SURGERY. An operating table stood in the centre of the room, white coats hung on the wall. Just being in that room made me wince. It no longer smelt of antiseptic—just uncirculated air. Surgical instruments lay rusting in the sterilizer. Rows and rows of pill jars remained in one cupboard; in another was a set of gynaecological instruments. 'For women,' said Shamyl, opening a pair of forceps—though why an all-male ship should need them I wasn't sure.

He told me a story about arriving in some islands off 'the African coast'. As soon as the islands' president saw the Russian flag, he came out in his official launch. He asked to see the ship's doctor. He stood in the surgery and said he had a Russian disease. None of his own doctors had ever seen such a disease. He had caught it from a girl in Moscow and knew that only a Russian doctor could cure him. The doctor examined the president and said, yes, the disease was easy to cure: he must give the president a course of three injections, administered directly into the penis.

When the Russians left, the president ordered the ship to be supplied with as much mango and papaya and pineapple as they could take; and his brass band, playing on board the presidential launch, trailed the ship as she left the harbour.

We carried on, into the ship's cabins. Cell-like, three-berthed, they looked as if they'd been abandoned in a hurry. Blankets hung from the top berths. Tin-openers, full ashtrays, dried orange peel lay on the Formica-topped tables. Each cabin had its own icon-corner. Pinned to cupboard doors and spare stretches of wall was an array of glossy female flesh—a fairly tame selection of fashion shots and girls in swimsuits. Peering up at the underside of one of the top bunks, I expected to see something a little hotter. Instead there was a panoramic poster—an expanse of forest, swans on a river and a herd of grey horses grazing on the open steppe.

Right down in the belly of the ship, Shamyl showed me the cold store. He flicked a light switch and heaved open the door. It was practically empty—boxes in one corner, a few bits of old packaging. A freezing mist formed quickly. In the middle of the room, suspended from a meat hook, several sides of beef had begun to rot. Yellow strands of fat hung from the grey carcasses. I remember only the skeletal symmetry of the ribs before catching half a breath of that frozen air, and gagging.

Shamyl was outside. He closed the door behind me and chuckled. 'Bad smell, yes?'

Through the weeks of January and February, I paid regular visits to the *Kommunar* and her remaining crew. We played chess and watched bad Russian films and sometimes we went ashore. There was no word from St Petersburg or the Admiralty. The ship settled deeper into her torpor. The pile of rubbish in the stern grew, the rust thickened, and the Soviet smell of the corridors was overtaken by a much more powerful smell from below—the ton of fish that remained in the hold.

Late February brought the fiercest of the winter gales. Day and night the noise of the wind surrounded my cottage. Tucked away upriver in her wooded berth, the *Kommunar* had less of the weather, but Shamyl was worried about his bowlines. One afternoon he took me on to the foredeck and, above the noise of the wind, showed me the warps, which ran over the side in a shallow arc down to the water. They had been half chafed away.

'Another gale and they'll go. What can I do? I have not enough crew even to move them. Half a metre would be enough.'

There was another gale. The bowlines snapped. The ship started to swing on her anchor. Shamyl rushed ashore, telephoned Falmouth, and within an hour a crew of six arrived by launch and mended the warps. The bill for the *Kommunar* mounted. By the middle of March the strain was beginning to show. Divisions had grown up among the crew; several were not speaking to each other. Shamyl grunted orders, and was resented by everyone. On the year's first warm day, I went on board and found two of the crew sunbathing on the foredeck. Shamyl was pacing the bridge like a circus tiger. 'Shipowners, they have forgotten us. We see tribunal—we see court—we see Yeltsin. No president! No constitution! No law! No country! We do not exist.'

I had heard that there was to be a court hearing later that week. 'Perhaps there'll be some news in four days,' I said.

'Four days—four years! We'll be old men before it happens.'

But if I'd learned anything from five years' intermittent travelling in the old Soviet Union it was the pattern of progress: things happened very, very slowly, and then very, very quickly. So it was when trying to elicit information or track down a contact, so it was when turning on a tap, and so it had always been with Russian history: the botched half-measures of Tsarist reforms, the years of indolence and the days of revolt. And so it proved with the *Kommunar*. Word came through that the court hearing was suddenly a formality. The ship was to be sold, the crew repatriated. They would be back in St Petersburg within days. Shamyl did not believe it. I could hardly blame him.

A week later, I took the road to Tolverne again. Coming out on the shore I could see the *Kommunar* in exactly the same position as always. On the beach, a man was painting the seats of a pleasure steamer. The tourist season was about to start. He waved his brush at the ship. 'It's Russian, you know. Hardly surprising their country's a mess if that's how they keep their fleet.'

I walked along the shingle. The *Kommunar* still dominated the creek. Her lifeboat lay alongside. The gangway remained in place. On the funnels, amid the colours of the new Russian flag, the old insignia was beginning to show through. I could see the shape of a hammer and sickle etched out in rust.

Two weeks later the *Kommunar* was towed to Turkey, and scrapped. □

SCOTLAND'S LAST
GREAT ARTEFACT

PICTURES BY STEPHEN GILL
INTERVIEWS: IAN JOHNSTON AND
LEWIS JOHNMAN

In December 1964, the Cunard Line placed its order for the ship that turned out to be the last great transatlantic liner. It was already an anachronistic project—jet aircraft had begun to kill the seagoing passenger trade between Europe and North America in the 1950s—but the keel was laid at John Brown's shipyard at Clydebank, on the River Clyde just west of Glasgow, in July 1965. Brown's had an old connection with Cunard, which had been ordering Clyde-built steamships for the Atlantic crossing since the 1840s, and out of its yard had come some of the most celebrated and loveliest ships in maritime history. The *Lusitania*, the *Aquitania*, the *Queen Mary* and the *Queen Elizabeth* were all launched at Brown's. They were among the largest moving objects ever made, and for much of this century they reminded Scotland of its once eminent rank in the industrial world.

About 8,000 workers (almost all of them men) built the new ship, which was launched by the Queen in September 1967, and named by her the Queen Elizabeth the Second—later abbreviated, modishly, to *QE2* (Sir Basil Smallpiece, then Cunard's chairman, wrote: 'The liner is named after the monarch, but I do not feel we should use "Queen Elizabeth II", which is the official designation of the Queen as Sovereign. I thought the use of an Arabic 2, instead of a Roman II, might make a sufficient distinction . . . ').

The *QE2* sailed on her maiden voyage from Southampton to New York in May 1969, and still makes that crossing about a dozen times each way every year; the last liner in the world which has not been converted to full-time cruising. She is 960 feet long, has thirteen decks and weighs 70,000 gross tons.

The shipyards of the Clyde never made anything so grand again, nor ever will. The industry collapsed soon after. In 1908, to take one of the river's peak years, 569 ships were launched from shipyards on the Clyde; about twenty-five per cent of the world's merchant tonnage. Ninety years later, the proportion launched by all British shipyards (including the Clyde) hardly reaches one per cent. The decline was swift and steep. Even in the 1960s the upper reaches of the Clyde still looked like the 'glade of cranes' that Auden had depicted thirty years before. The photographs and interviews that follow portray some of the people who helped build the *QE2*, and whose world quite suddenly vanished.   IJ

Robert Dickie, 65, joiner

I was forty-eight years in the shipyard. I served my apprenticeship as a joiner and latterly I was a shop steward [union representative] for the joiners. At the peak of the carpentry work on the *QE2*, we had something like fifteen hundred joiners in the yard making bulkheads, ceiling panels and all the furniture for the cabins and passageways—everything except the work in the public rooms which went to outside contractors. A big problem on the *QE2* was asbestos. The bulkhead linings and ceiling panels were made of a material called Marinite, which was thirty per cent asbestos. The yard recognized there was a health problem, but Cunard insisted that the asbestos material would have to be used to meet American fire regulations. The company issued us with masks, they even built a special asbestos workshop on the ship, but when you think of the number of people working in the vicinity—not just joiners, but other trades—you can see the problem. Now we have a Clydeside Asbestosis Group in the area which helps the relatives of loved ones who have died. My brother, who was a driller in the yards, died of it. I would say that it's a real problem in Clydebank.

But they were good years. There was something about a shipyard. There was something about the characters who worked in a shipyard, something about their humour. Of course, there were lots of times when the work stopped—demarcation disputes and that sort of thing—which came from a sort of tribalism, I think, which should have been overcome. But basically I enjoyed all of those years. I never woke up in the morning thinking: 'Oh God, I've got to go and work in that place.'

You always felt a certain pride when a ship left the yard, when you completed a job and you could see it coming down the Clyde, whether it was a tanker or a liner. You know? A job well done. That was us.

Isabel Dickie, 66, data process clerk

My job was to key in men's wages and on Friday pay them out. I would personally pay out about three hundred. The timekeeper would be there and he would shout out the man's number and I would give out the pay packets. You had to be very careful in case you gave anybody the wrong one. Occasionally you would give out the wrong one. The man who had been given the small pay packet would come back, but the man with the larger would not, so you had to chase him up on Monday morning. You had six minutes to pay out three hundred men and the shop stewards used to time you. They would stand there with a stopwatch. They would come over and say: 'I am very sorry to tell you, Isabel, but I will have to tell the management that you took eight minutes today to pay out.' And I'd say: 'Well, I'm going to go to your foreman and tell him to time your job. I cannot pay out three hundred men in six minutes.'

Yes, it was a predominantly male environment. Maybe out of the eight thousand people who worked in the shipyard and the engine works, fifty or sixty would be women. But it was good fun. We had a lot of men friends. I don't mean men friends in that sense, I mean the nice, cheery men I worked beside. I met my husband [Robert Dickie] because we both worked in there. He used to wait outside the yard gate for me. [Robert Dickie interrupts: 'No, you used to wait for me.']

My first thought when the *QE2* order was announced was about Robert and his job. Years ago, every time a ship was finished, the men were off the payroll, so every time there was a new order you felt: 'Oh, that's lovely.' Many a time I used to stand at the window and watch for Robert coming up the road. If he had his toolbox, it would have meant he'd been paid off. But he never did have his toolbox.

I didn't see the Queen at the launch because I was stuck at the back of the crowd, but there was a gasp when she named the ship. Somehow we hadn't expected that it would be named after her. Later I got on board after she was finished. In the cabins I remember there was a certain lighting on the ladies' dressing tables, so it looked like daylight and you wouldn't make a mistake and put on too much make-up.

Dr John Brown, 96, managing director

I started my apprenticeship at John Brown's—the name is purely coincidental—in 1919. I remember that the battlecruiser HMS *Hood* was in the fitting-out basin nearing completion and I went on board one day and climbed to the top of the foremast, just for the fun of it.

When tenders were first opened for the ship that became the *QE2*, Cunard expressed an interest in a competitor's design which incorporated an aluminium superstructure. Our tender was for an all-steel ship—we had little experience of aluminium alloy at that time. Cunard's naval architect, Robert Wood, who was a very good friend of mine and who had been a fellow apprentice at Clydebank, worked closely with me. We needed to follow up the aluminium idea. Wood and I knew that the American liner *United States* had a lot of aluminium in her superstructure, but we needed to know how much. So we booked a passage on the *United States* from Southampton to Bremen and back. We were both equipped with a little magnet, the kind that schoolboys play with, and we went round the whole superstructure standing against bulkheads with our hands behind our backs. If the magnet stuck it was steel, if it didn't it was aluminium, and so we assessed the extent of aluminium in the *United States*.

Halfway through the design of the *QE2*, the Cunard directors thought that they would like an artist to have a hand in the appearance of the ship. Robert Wood and I were very upset that they were going to bring someone—an artist!—into what we considered to be more of a technical matter. However, the artist was appointed. At first, Wood and I didn't like his ideas but eventually I came round to them. I came to look at the ship on a calm sea as a swan in a millpond. I came to look on her as rather a lovely ship.

Joe Brown, 75, plumber and shop steward

I started my apprenticeship in 1938, then the war came and I did four years in the Royal Navy. From 1946 to 1968 I worked in John Brown's without a break.

News of the *QE2* contract got a mixed reception, because we'd had a bad experience with a liner just before—the *Kungsholm* for the Swedish-Amerika line—which turned out to be disastrous financially. The Swedes caught Brown's at a slack period in their order book and they screwed them into the ground price-wise. Then they screwed them further by taking terribly strict control of the completion of the ship.

So when the *QE2* was announced, there were some misgivings. Was another big liner going to be good news for the yard or would it be another financial disaster?

Myself and two other lads were the first workers' representatives ever to be included in an official launch party at Brown's. Until the *QE2*, no manual worker had ever been invited to attend on the platform and go to the lunch afterwards. When I first got the invitation I was a bit nonplussed because it had never happened to anybody before. I thought to myself: should we go, should we be involved in this thing, because up to that time when people came in for launches, the workers were totally disregarded. We only built the ship after all. There was no recognition that *we* were the people. We used to have shipbuilding employers at launches and they would very often take the opportunity of a public forum to attack the unions and the workers about demarcation disputes and that kind of thing. So when we got the invitation we had to discuss it. In the end it was the shop stewards' committee that decided we should go. Some of us were very hesitant, but it was decided that as this was the first time we had ever been invited we had better go. My wife would have been there as well but she was very heavily pregnant at the time. So she didn't get to the *QE2*'s launch because we were about to have our own personal launch.

214

Willie Miller, 74, timekeeper

I was a timekeeper and a piecework counter as well. I used to count for the Caulking Department. Count the work the men did each day. If they worked overtime I would check them in, check them out and keep a record of their time and pay them according to the rates.

You got to your wee office, your time box, in the morning at quarter past seven. You had about a hundred and fifty men to check in with their badge numbers. You marked them in and docked them if they were late. You did the same in the afternoon. You went back to your office and marked them two strokes for morning and afternoon. When it came to overtime they'd completed, there was a wee space on the form where you would add up their premium hours, normal hours and overtime hours. It was quite a straightforward sort of job.

When you got on the boat, you'd ask the man what he'd done and he would show you. Then you had to take a note back to the office, make a copy which the foreman signed. He would then give you a slip of paper and say: 'Give that man a penny an hour,' which was a penny extra and quite a bit back then. Then we would calculate the pay and send it to the counting house where they would take off the tax, any savings, and make up his packet.

The packet then came to the time box. The wages clerk came in with the big box. The men were outside standing in numerical order. I was there to see that the men were getting the proper packets, and you took a note of the pay packets that were left. You countersigned. Then you were away home.

Clydebank then made sewing machines and ships. The whole thing's died away now. It's all this modern stuff, small businesses. In 1968 I took over the head timekeeping job. But I had the feeling that things were sort of drifting away. Your security was getting undermined. You had a feeling that things were not well at all.

I was there for thirty-eight years. They were very pleasant years. It was a very important job in a sense—your integrity was at stake. I never had any problems with my men. They were good lads, they were rough diamonds. They would swear a lot but that was just shipyard talk.

Roddy McKenzie, 74, welder

I started in Brown's after the war. When things got quiet, I was paid off and just drifted—Grangemouth, the Isle of Grain, Birkenhead, then away to Kuwait, Iran and Iraq. Then I came home and started back in Brown's because I liked the atmosphere there. When I was paid off again, I went to Perth in Western Australia to work on a refinery. When I came back from that, I went to Brown's and never moved until I retired. So I was in there for fifteen years of constant work without being paid off.

When I worked on the *QE2*, I was getting about thirteen to fifteen pounds a week which was good money compared to other trades. There was always a bit of jealousy between the finishing trades, the platers and caulkers. The welders always seemed to be that little bit ahead by a few pounds. But that was piecework, you were in there to graft and to earn.

Mostly we worked on the keel and the shell of the *QE2,* both inside and out. You knew it was something special. You could see what the drawings were like and what height the ship was going to go up to. You felt it would never end. We had a feeling that Brown's was the best yard in Great Britain and that we were a lucky yard. There always seemed to be work to do.

The majesty of the launch, and seeing the ship pulled into the dock, was terrific. You were pleased that everything had gone right but sorry because your job on the ship was over. You might have had the odd wee bit still to do on board, but once the ship was in the hands of the finishing trades, you were bundled off it right away.

I worked on quite a lot of boats, the royal yacht *Britannia*, *Arcadia* for the P & O. The workmanship on the *Britannia* was fantastic, the ship's shell buffed to a polish, and the finish on the *QE2* was equally good. I don't think they could get that workmanship now. Not tradesmen of that calibre. I think that's why these boats have lasted so long.

Lord Aberconway, 86, company chairman

I succeeded my father as Chairman of John Brown's when my father died in 1953. I retired in 1986 by which time John Brown's had been acquired by Trafalgar House.

I remember signing the contract for the *QE2* with Cunard in the John Brown boardroom. In the course of the signing ceremony in front of the press, there were photographers lying on the floor or standing on the mantelpiece to photograph us. I said to one very pleasant but persistent photographer who was standing on the mantelpiece: 'Are you never going to run out of film?' He drew himself up to his full height and said: 'Sir, the *Daily Express* never runs out of film.' Rather charming. The contract was signed.

The launch of the *QE2* itself was a great occasion; the Queen and the Duke of Edinburgh were there. It was the Queen's sixth launch at Clydebank. The Queen Mother had already launched six ships there, so that day it became level pegging. The Royal Family seldom go to the same affair together, but the week before Princess Margaret sent me a telegram asking if it would be all right if she came along too. Certainly, I replied. I then wrote to the Queen Mother and asked her too. She graciously replied that she couldn't. I know her, of course, from the Chelsea Flower Show.

Most of us felt that shipbuilding was becoming thoroughly uncompetitive in this country. Restrictive practices really killed British shipbuilding. Let me give an example. A lot of pipework for the water supplied to the cabins and so on used to be done in ordinary zinc pipes—a plumber's job. But then it became more efficient to do them in copper pipes, which was the work of coppersmiths. The unions quarrelled over whose job it should be and the eventual compromise was that it had to be done by a coppersmith with a plumber standing by doing nothing. Thoroughly uneconomic, but the unions were very intransigent and short-sighted and that was that. There was little regret within the John Brown Group when we stopped building ships because the other parts of the group did not like their profits being whittled away to subsidize the losses of Clydebank. So the group as a whole was quite happy to get rid of that drag on our fortunes, even if many of us were devastated to lose our link with the romance of shipbuilding.

Willie Clydesdale, 72, welder

I started my time in the shipyards in Stephens of Linthouse as an electric welder and then moved to Fairfields of Govan. I ended up in John Brown's in 1950. To be quite honest, I wasn't really interested in working in a shipyard again. It was just a case of passing the time until I got a better job. But Brown's wasn't like the other yards I'd worked in, there was more of a family feeling to it, so I got married and stayed. Eventually we got a John Brown's house in Clydebank and we've lived here ever since.

In the late Sixties, around the time of the *QE2*, I became a shop steward. You could see how things were changing abroad. You'd listen to your union's national full-time officials, who were going to places like Japan and Holland, coming back with stories about flexible working in the shipyards, but we wouldn't change, we still held the reins. I blame myself as much as anyone else. Instead of looking forward, trying to get the best arrangement so that you could retain jobs rather than let them go to Japan or Germany, we held on right to the end. No flexibility. We allowed very little. We held up progress. We were the same as the Luddites.

I always believed that management gave in too easily. They must have seen what was going to happen but were too frightened to face up to it. That's my opinion. They were frightened to have a face-to-face confrontation. That was what was required for the whole industry. Someone had to say: 'Look, this is the way it's going to be and if you don't like it then your jobs are going to disappear.'

I became a full-time union official in 1978 and Mrs Thatcher became prime minister in 1979. At the start of my time, I had a list of firms to look after the length of both my arms. By the time I retired, it was down to a handful.

Tom McKendrick, 49, loftsman

I teach art now and I paint, but in Brown's when the *QE2* was being built I was an apprentice loftsman, which was like being a full-scale draughtsman. In the loft, you worked from a full-size plan of the ship, making up all the individual shapes and frames, enormous things which would be perfectly worked out to within a ninth of an inch. It was just like making the whole ship in wood beforehand. There was no more accurate way of building a boat. It was a good job, but when the work took you outside it could be dangerous.

During one summer, myself and a guy called Big Allan Lang—a tremendous guy, ex-Merchant Navy—were hanging off the side of the bow of the *QE2*, which has this tremendous rake [curve] as it slopes in under you. We were up on a six-inch plank with the absolute minimum of safety measures by way of barriers when all of a sudden, about twenty feet above us, welders started to burn out the holes for the bollards. I'm standing there with my shirt off because it's a boiling hot day when I hear this noise, psssh, phsssh, which turns out to be coming from my hair and the skin on my back because I'm being sprayed with red-hot slag. Then Big Allan said: 'Look at the state of you.' I was seventeen then and what really worried me was my hair—my scalp had been turned into patchwork. I eventually got carried across to the ambulance room, which was so primitive it wasn't true. The guy there said: 'Right, get yourself down on that chair,' and I sat astride it, the old cowboy bit, biting the bullet, while the same guy took a pair of tweezers and picked the slag fragments out of my back and put on a bit of plaster and gauze. And that was you, you went back to your work! The lesson was: never ever take your shirt off in a shipyard, you stupid bastard.

Two other guys who worked there were utterly unbelievable. One was a plater and the other his helper, and they were called the Two Rabs—fat Rab and skinny Rab. Their big thing was fighting. In the pub on a Friday night, during the day, they would fight over the sandwiches and at their tea break. They were inseparable. It was: 'Ya bastard, fuck you.' Raindrops, boats, folk, fitba', politics, religion—they fought over anything and fell out—always an inch from blows. There would be total silence, then this incredible outburst of battle. It would start out with a minor disagreement, for example: 'Have you got the French chalk?'

HARUKI MURAKAMI
THE SEVENTH MAN

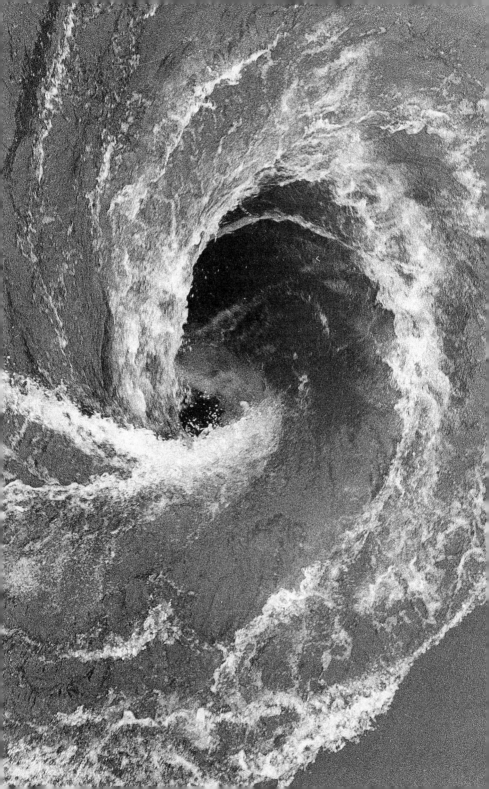

'A huge wave nearly swept me away,' said the seventh man, almost whispering. 'It happened one September afternoon when I was ten years old.'

The man was the last one to tell his story that night. The hands of the clock had moved past ten. The small group that huddled in a circle could hear the wind tearing through the darkness outside, heading west. It shook the trees, set the windows to rattling, and moved past the house with one final whistle.

'It was the biggest wave I had ever seen in my life,' he said. 'A strange wave. An absolute giant.'

He paused.

'It just barely missed me, but in my place it swallowed everything that mattered most to me and swept it off to another world. I took years to find it again and to recover from the experience—precious years that can never be replaced.'

The seventh man appeared to be in his mid-fifties. He was a thin man, tall, with a moustache, and next to his right eye he had a short but deep-looking scar that could have been made by the stab of a small blade. Stiff, bristly patches of white marked his short hair. His face had the look you see on people when they can't quite find the words they need. In his case, though, the expression seemed to have been there from long before, as though it were part of him. The man wore a simple blue shirt under a grey tweed coat, and every now and then he would bring his hand to his collar. None of those assembled there knew his name or what he did for a living.

He cleared his throat, and for a moment or two his words were lost in silence. The others waited for him to go on.

'In my case, it was a wave,' he said. 'There's no way for me to tell, of course, what it will be for each of you. But in my case it just happened to take the form of a gigantic wave. It presented itself to me all of a sudden one day, without warning. And it was devastating.'

I grew up in a seaside town in the Province of S. It was such a small town, I doubt that any of you would recognize the name if I were to mention it. My father was the local doctor, and so I led a rather comfortable childhood. Ever since I could remember, my best friend was a boy I'll call K. His house was close to ours, and he was a grade behind me in school. We were like brothers, walking to and from school together, and always playing together when we got home. We never once fought during our long friendship. I did have a brother, six years older, but what with the age difference and differences in our personalities, we were never very close. My real brotherly affection went to my friend K.

K. was a frail, skinny little thing, with a pale complexion and a face almost pretty enough to be a girl's. He had some kind of speech impediment, though, which might have made him seem retarded to anyone who didn't know him. And because he was so frail, I always played his protector, whether at school or at home. I was kind of big and athletic, and the other kids all looked up to me. But the main reason I enjoyed spending time with K. was that he was such a sweet, pure-hearted boy. He was not the least bit retarded, but because of his impediment, he didn't do too well at school. In most subjects, he could barely keep up. In art class, though, he was great. Just give him a pencil or paints and he would make pictures that were so full of life that even the teacher was amazed. He won prizes in one contest after another, and I'm sure he would have become a famous painter if he had continued with his art into adulthood. He liked to do seascapes. He'd go out to the shore for hours, painting. I would often sit beside him, watching the swift, precise movements of his brush, wondering how, in a few seconds, he could possibly create such lively shapes and colours where, until then, there had been only blank white paper. I realize now that it was a matter of pure talent.

One year, in September, a huge typhoon hit our area. The radio said it was going to be the worst in ten years. The schools were closed, and all the shops in town lowered their shutters in preparation for the storm. Starting early in the morning, my father and brother went around the house nailing shut all the storm-doors, while my mother spent the day in the kitchen cooking emergency provisions. We filled bottles and canteens with water, and packed our most important possessions in rucksacks for possible evacuation. To the adults, typhoons were an annoyance and a threat they had to face almost annually, but to the kids, removed as we were from such practical concerns, it was just a great big circus, a wonderful source of excitement.

Just after noon the colour of the sky began to change all of a sudden. There was something strange and unreal about it. I stayed outside on the porch, watching the sky, until the wind began to howl and the rain began to beat against the house with a weird dry sound, like handfuls of sand. Then we closed the last storm-door and gathered together in one room of the darkened house, listening to the radio. This particular storm did not have a great deal of rain, it said, but the winds were doing a lot of damage, blowing roofs off houses and capsizing ships. Many people had been killed or injured by flying debris. Over and over again, they warned people against leaving their homes. Every once in a while, the house would creak and shudder as if a huge hand were shaking it, and sometimes there would be a great crash of some heavy-sounding object against a storm-door. My father guessed that these were tiles blowing off the neighbours' houses. For lunch we ate the rice and omelettes my mother had cooked, waiting for the typhoon to blow past.

But the typhoon gave no sign of blowing past. The radio said it had lost momentum almost as soon as it came ashore at S. Province, and now it was moving north-east at the pace of a slow runner. The wind kept up its savage howling as it tried to uproot everything that stood on land.

Perhaps an hour had gone by with the wind at its worst like this when a hush fell over everything. All of a sudden it was so quiet, we could hear a bird crying in the distance. My father opened the storm-door a crack and looked outside. The wind had stopped, and the rain had ceased to fall. Thick, grey clouds edged across the sky, and patches of blue showed here and there. The trees in the yard were still dripping their heavy burden of rainwater.

'We're in the eye of the storm,' my father told me. 'It'll stay quiet like this for a while, maybe fifteen, twenty minutes, kind of like an intermission. Then the wind'll come back the way it was before.'

I asked him if I could go outside. He said I could walk around a little if I didn't go far. 'But I want you to come right back here at the first sign of wind.'

I went out and started to explore. It was hard to believe that a wild storm had been blowing there until a few minutes before. I looked up at the sky. The storm's great 'eye' seemed to be up there, fixing its cold stare on all of us below. No such 'eye' existed, of course: we were just in that momentary quiet spot at the centre of the pool of whirling air.

While the grown-ups checked for damage to the house, I went down to the beach. The road was littered with broken tree branches, some of them thick pine boughs that would have been too heavy for an adult to lift alone. There were shattered roof tiles everywhere, cars with cracked windshields, and even a dog-house that had tumbled into the middle of the street. A big hand might have swung down from the sky and flattened everything in its path.

K. saw me walking down the road and came outside.

'Where are you going?' he asked.

'Just down to look at the beach,' I said.

Without a word, he came along with me. He had a little white dog that followed after us.

'The minute we get any wind, though, we're going straight back home,' I said, and K. gave me a silent nod.

The shore was a 200-yard walk from my house. It was lined with a concrete breakwater—a big dyke that stood as high as I was tall in those days. We had to climb a short flight of steps to reach the water's edge. This was where we came to play almost every day, so there was no part of it we didn't know well. In the eye of the typhoon, though, it all looked different: the colour of the sky and of the sea, the sound of the waves, the smell of the tide, the whole expanse of the shore. We sat atop the breakwater for a time, taking in the view without a word to each other. We were supposedly in the middle of a great typhoon, and yet the waves were strangely hushed. And the point where they washed against the beach was much farther away than usual, even at low tide. The white sand stretched out before us as far as we could see. The whole, huge space felt like a room without furniture, except for the band of flotsam that lined the beach.

We stepped down to the other side of the breakwater and walked along the broad beach, examining the things that had come to rest there. Plastic toys, sandals, chunks of wood that had probably once been parts of furniture, pieces of clothing, unusual bottles, broken crates with foreign writing on them, and other, less recognizable items: it was like a big candy store. The storm must have carried these things from very far away. Whenever something unusual caught our attention, we would pick it up and look at it every which way, and when we were done, K.'s dog would come over and give it a good sniff.

We couldn't have been doing this more than five minutes when I realized that the waves had come up right next to me. Without any sound or other warning, the sea had suddenly stretched its long, smooth tongue out to where I stood on the beach. I had never seen anything like it before. Child though I was, I had grown up on the shore and knew how frightening the ocean could be—the savagery with which it could strike unannounced.

And so I had taken care to keep well back from the waterline. In spite of that, the waves had slid up to within inches of where I stood. And then, just as soundlessly, the water drew back—and stayed back. The waves that had approached me were as unthreatening as waves can be—a gentle washing of the sandy beach. But something ominous about them—something like the touch of a reptile's skin—had sent a chill down my spine. My fear was totally groundless—and totally real. I knew instinctively that they were alive. The waves were alive. They knew I was here and they were planning to grab me. I felt as if some huge, man-eating beast were lying somewhere on a grassy plain, dreaming of the moment it would pounce and tear me to pieces with its sharp teeth. I had to run away.

'I'm getting out of here!' I yelled to K. He was maybe ten yards down the beach, squatting with his back to me, and looking at something. I was sure I had yelled loud enough, but my voice did not seem to have reached him. He might have been so absorbed in whatever it was he had found that my call made no impression on him. K. was like that. He would get involved with things to the point of forgetting everything else. Or possibly I had not yelled as loudly as I had thought. I do recall that my voice sounded strange to me, as though it belonged to someone else.

Then I heard a deep rumbling sound. It seemed to shake the earth. Actually, before I heard the rumble I heard another sound, a weird gurgling as though a lot of water was surging up through a hole in the ground. It continued for a while, then stopped, after which I heard the strange rumbling. Even that was not enough to make K. look up. He was still squatting, looking down at something at his feet, in deep concentration. He probably did not hear the rumbling. How he could have missed such an earth-shaking sound, I don't know. This may seem odd, but it might have been a sound that only I could hear—some special kind of sound. Not even K.'s dog seemed to notice it, and you know how sensitive dogs are to sound.

I told myself to run over to K., grab hold of him, and get out of there. It was the only thing to do. I *knew* that the wave was coming, and K. didn't know. As clearly as I knew what I ought to be doing, I found myself running the other way—running full speed towards the dyke, alone. What made me do this, I'm sure, was fear, a fear so overpowering it took my voice away and set my legs to running on their own. I ran stumbling along the soft sand beach to the breakwater, where I turned and shouted to K.

'Hurry, K.! Get out of there! The wave is coming!' This time my voice worked fine. The rumbling had stopped, I realized, and now, finally, K. heard my shouting and looked up. But it was too late. A wave like a huge snake with its head held high, poised to strike, was racing towards the shore. I had never seen anything like it in my life. It had to be as tall as a three-storey building. Soundlessly (in my memory, at least, the image is soundless), it rose up behind K. to block out the sky. K. looked at me for a few seconds, uncomprehending. Then, as if sensing something, he turned towards the wave. He tried to run, but now there was no time to run. In the next instant, the wave had swallowed him.

The wave crashed on to the beach, shattering into a million leaping waves that flew through the air and plunged over the dyke where I stood. I was able to dodge its impact by ducking behind the breakwater. The spray wet my clothes, nothing more. I scrambled back up on to the wall and scanned the shore. By then the wave had turned and, with a wild cry, it was rushing back out to sea. It looked like part of a gigantic rug that had been yanked by someone at the other end of the earth. Nowhere on the shore could I find any trace of K., or of his dog. There was only the empty beach. The receding wave had now pulled so much water out from the shore that it seemed to expose the entire ocean bottom. I stood alone on the breakwater, frozen in place.

The silence came over everything again—a desperate silence, as though sound itself had been ripped from the earth. The wave had swallowed K. and disappeared into the far distance. I stood there, wondering what to do. Should I go down to the beach? K. might be down there somewhere, buried in the sand . . . But I decided not to leave the dyke. I knew from experience that big waves often came in twos and threes.

I'm not sure how much time went by—maybe ten or twenty seconds of eerie emptiness—when, just as I had guessed, the next wave came. Another gigantic roar shook the beach, and again, after the sound had faded, another huge wave raised its head to strike. It towered before me, blocking out the sky, like a deadly cliff. This time, though, I didn't run. I stood rooted to the sea wall, entranced, waiting for it to attack. What good would it do to run, I thought, now that K. had been taken? Or perhaps I simply froze, overcome with fear. I can't be sure what it was that kept me standing there.

The second wave was just as big as the first—maybe even bigger. From far above my head it began to fall, losing its shape, like a brick wall slowly crumbling. It was so huge that it no longer looked like a real wave. It was like something from another, far-off world, that just happened to assume the shape of a wave. I readied myself for the moment the darkness would take me. I didn't even close my eyes. I remember hearing my heart pound with incredible clarity.

The moment the wave came before me, however, it stopped. All at once it seemed to run out of energy, to lose its forward motion and simply hover there, in space, crumbling in stillness. And in its crest, inside its cruel, transparent tongue, what I saw was K.

Some of you may find this impossible to believe, and if so, I don't blame you. I myself have trouble accepting it even now. I can't explain what I saw any better than you can, but I know it was no illusion, no hallucination. I am telling you as honestly as I can what happened at that moment—what really happened. In the tip of the wave, as if enclosed in some kind of transparent capsule, floated K.'s body, reclining on its side. But that is not all. K. was looking straight at me, smiling. There, right in front of me, so close that I could have reached out and touched him, was my friend, my friend K. who, only moments before, had been swallowed by the wave. And he was smiling at me. Not with an ordinary smile—it was a big, wide-open grin that literally stretched from ear to ear. His cold, frozen eyes were locked on mine. He was no longer the K. I knew. And his right arm was stretched out in my direction, as if he were trying to grab my hand and pull me into that other world where he was now. A little closer, and his hand would have caught mine. But, having missed, K. then smiled at me one more time, his grin wider than ever.

I seem to have lost consciousness at that point. The next thing I knew, I was in bed in my father's clinic. As soon as I awoke the nurse went to call my father, who came running. He took my pulse, studied my pupils, and put his hand on my forehead. I tried to move my arm, but I couldn't lift it. I was burning with fever, and my mind was clouded. I had been wrestling with a high fever for some time, apparently. 'You've been asleep for three days,' my father said to me. A neighbour who had seen the whole thing had picked me up and carried me home. They had not been able to find K. I wanted to say something to my father. I *had* to say something to him. But my numb and swollen tongue could not form words. I felt as if some kind of creature had taken up residence in my mouth. My father asked me to tell him my name, but before I could remember what it was, I lost consciousness again, sinking into darkness.

Altogether, I stayed in bed for a week on a liquid diet. I vomited several times, and had bouts of delirium. My father told me afterwards that I was so bad that he had been afraid I might suffer permanent neurological damage from the shock and high fever. One way or another, though, I managed to recover—physically, at least. But my life would never be the same again.

They never found K.'s body. They never found his dog, either. Usually when someone drowned in that area, the body would wash up a few days later on the shore of a small inlet to the east. K.'s body never did. The big waves probably carried it far out to sea—too far for it to reach the shore. It must have sunk to the ocean bottom to be eaten by the fish. The search went on for a very long time, thanks to the cooperation of the local fishermen, but eventually it petered out. Without a body, there was never any funeral. Half crazed, K.'s parents would wander up and down the beach every day, or they would shut themselves up at home, chanting sutras.

As great a blow as this had been for them, though, K.'s parents never chided me for having taken their son down to the shore in the midst of a typhoon. They knew how I had always loved and protected K. as if he had been my own little brother. My parents, too, made a point of never mentioning the incident in my presence. But I knew the truth. I knew that I could have saved K. if I had tried. I probably could have run over and dragged him out of the reach of the wave. It would have been close, but as I went over the timing of the events in memory, it always seemed to me that I could have made it. As I said before, though, overcome with fear, I abandoned him there and saved only myself. It pained me all the more that K.'s parents failed to blame me and that everyone else was so careful never to say anything to me about what had happened. It took me a long time to recover from the emotional shock. I stayed away from school for weeks. I hardly ate a thing, and spent each day in bed, staring at the ceiling.

K. was always there, lying in the wave tip, grinning at me, his hand outstretched, beckoning. I couldn't get that picture out of my mind. And when I managed to sleep, it was there in my dreams—except that, in my dreams, K. would hop out of his capsule in the wave and grab my wrist to drag me back inside with him.

And then there was another dream I had. I'm swimming in the ocean. It's a beautiful summer afternoon, and I'm doing an easy breaststroke far from shore. The sun is beating down on my back, and the water feels good. Then, all of a sudden, someone grabs my right leg. I feel an ice-cold grip on my ankle. It's strong, too strong to shake off. I'm being dragged down under the surface. I see K.'s face there. He has the same huge grin, split from ear to ear, his eyes locked on mine. I try to scream, but my voice will not come. I swallow water, and my lungs start to fill.

I wake up in the darkness, screaming, breathless, drenched in sweat.

At the end of the year I pleaded with my parents to let me move to another town. I couldn't go on living in sight of the beach where K. had been swept away, and my nightmares wouldn't stop. If I didn't get out of there, I'd go crazy. My parents understood and made arrangements for me to live elsewhere. I moved to Nagano Province in January to live with my father's family in a mountain village near Komoro. I finished elementary school in Nagano and stayed on through junior and senior high school there. I never went home, even for holidays. My parents came to visit me now and then.

I live in Nagano to this day. I graduated from a college of engineering in the City of Nagano and went to work for a precision toolmaker in the area. I still work for them. I live like anybody else. As you can see, there's nothing unusual about me. I'm not very sociable, but I have a few friends I go mountain climbing with. Once I got away from my home town, I stopped having nightmares all the time. They remained a part of my life, though. They would come to me now and then, like debt collectors at the door. It happened whenever I was on the verge of forgetting. And it was always the same dream, down to the smallest detail. I would wake up screaming, my sheets soaked with sweat.

This is probably why I never married. I didn't want to wake someone sleeping next to me with my screams in the middle of the night. I've been in love with several women over the years, but I never spent a night with any of them. The terror was in my bones. It was something I could never share with another person.

I stayed away from my home town for over forty years. I never went near that seashore—or any other. I was afraid that if I did, my dream might happen in reality. I had always enjoyed swimming, but after that day I never even went to swim in a pool. I wouldn't go near deep rivers or lakes. I avoided boats and wouldn't take a plane to go abroad. Despite all these precautions, I couldn't get rid of the image of myself drowning. Like K.'s cold hand, this dark premonition caught hold of my mind and refused to let go.

Then, last spring, I finally revisited the beach where K. had been taken by the wave.

My father had died of cancer the year before, and my brother had sold the old house. In going through the storage shed, he had found a cardboard carton crammed with childhood things of mine, which he sent to me in Nagano. Most of it was useless junk, but there was one bundle of pictures that K. had painted and given to me. My parents had probably put them away for me as a keepsake of K., but the pictures did nothing but reawaken the old terror. They made me feel as if K.'s spirit would spring back to life from them, and so I quickly returned them to their paper wrapping, intending to throw them away. I couldn't make myself do it, though. After several days of indecision, I opened the bundle again and forced myself to take a long, hard look at K.'s watercolours.

Most of them were landscapes, pictures of the familiar stretch of ocean and sand beach and pine woods and the town, and all done with that special clarity and coloration I knew so well from K.'s hand. They were still amazingly vivid despite the years, and had been executed with even greater skill than I recalled. As I leafed through the bundle, I found myself steeped in warm memories. The deep feelings of the boy K. were there in his pictures—the way his eyes were opened on the world. The things we did together, the places we went together began to come back to me with great intensity. And I realized that his eyes were my eyes, that I myself had looked upon the world back then with the same lively, unclouded vision as the boy who had walked by my side.

I made a habit after that of studying one of K.'s pictures at my desk each day when I got home from work. I could sit there for hours with one painting. In each I found another of those soft landscapes of childhood that I had shut out of my memory for so long. I had a sense, whenever I looked at one of K.'s works, that something was permeating my very flesh.

Perhaps a week had gone by like this when the thought suddenly struck me one evening: I might have been making a terrible mistake all those years. As he lay there in the tip of the wave, surely K. had not been looking at me with hatred or resentment; he had not been trying to take me away with him.

And that terrible grin he had fixed me with: that, too, could have been an accident of angle or light and shadow, not a conscious act on K.'s part. He had probably already lost consciousness, or perhaps he had been giving me a gentle smile of eternal parting. The intense look of hatred I thought I saw on his face had been nothing but a reflection of the profound terror that had taken control of me for the moment.

The more I studied K.'s watercolour that evening, the greater the conviction with which I began to believe these new thoughts of mine. For no matter how long I continued to look at the picture, I could find nothing in it but a boy's gentle, innocent spirit.

I went on sitting at my desk for a very long time. There was nothing else I could do. The sun went down, and the pale darkness of evening began to envelop the room. Then came the deep silence of night, which seemed to go on for ever. At last, the scales tipped, and dark gave way to dawn. The new day's sun tinged the sky with pink.

It was then I knew I must go back.

I threw a few things in a bag, called the company to say I would not be in, and boarded a train for my old home town.

I did not find the same quiet, little seaside town that I remembered. An industrial city had sprung up nearby during the rapid development of the Sixties, bringing great changes to the landscape. The one little gift shop by the station had grown into a mall, and the town's only movie theatre had been turned into a supermarket. My house was no longer there. It had been demolished some months before, leaving only a scrape on the earth. The trees in the yard had all been cut down, and patches of weeds dotted the black stretch of ground. K.'s old house had disappeared as well, having been replaced by a concrete parking lot full of commuters' cars and vans. Not that I was overcome by sentiment. The town had ceased to be mine long before.

I walked down to the shore and climbed the steps of the breakwater. On the other side, as always, the ocean stretched off into the distance, unobstructed, huge, the horizon a single straight line. The shoreline, too, looked the same as it had before: the long beach, the lapping waves, people strolling at the water's edge. The time was after four o'clock, and the soft sun of late afternoon embraced everything below as it began its long, almost meditative, descent to the west. I lowered my bag to the sand and sat down next to it in silent appreciation of the gentle seascape. Looking at this scene, it was impossible to imagine that a great typhoon had once raged here, that a massive wave had swallowed my best friend in all the world. There was almost no one left now, surely, who remembered those terrible events. It began to seem as if the whole thing were an illusion that I had dreamed up in vivid detail.

And then I realized that the deep darkness inside me had vanished. Suddenly. As suddenly as it had come. I raised myself from the sand and, without bothering to take off my shoes or roll up my cuffs, walked into the surf to let the waves lap at my ankles.

Almost in reconciliation, it seemed, the same waves that had washed up on the beach when I was a boy were now fondly washing my feet, soaking black my shoes and pant cuffs. There would be one slow-moving wave, then a long pause, and then another wave would come and go. The people passing by gave me odd looks, but I didn't care.

I looked up at the sky. A few grey cotton chunks of cloud hung there, motionless. They seemed to be there for me, though I'm not sure why I felt that way. I remembered having looked up at the sky like this in search of the 'eye' of the typhoon. And then, inside me, the axis of time gave one great heave. Forty long years collapsed like a dilapidated house, mixing old time and new time together in a single swirling mass. All sounds faded, and the light around me shuddered. I lost my balance and fell into the waves. My heart throbbed at the back of my throat, and my arms and legs lost all sensation. I lay that way for a long time, face in the water, unable to stand. But I was not afraid. No, not at all. There was no longer anything for me to fear. Those days were gone.

I stopped having my terrible nightmares. I no longer wake up screaming in the middle of the night. And I am trying now to start life over again. No, I know it's probably too late to start again. I may not have much time left to live. But even if it comes too late, I am grateful that, in the end, I was able to attain a kind of salvation, to effect some sort of recovery. Yes, grateful: I could have come to the end of my life unsaved, still screaming in the dark, afraid.

The seventh man fell silent and turned his gaze upon each of the others. No one spoke or moved or even seemed to breathe. All were waiting for the rest of his story. Outside, the wind had fallen, and nothing stirred. The seventh man brought his hand to his collar once again, as if in search of words.

'They tell us that the only thing we have to fear is fear itself; but I don't believe that,' he said. Then, a moment later, he added: 'Oh, the fear is there, all right. It comes to us in many different forms, at different times, and overwhelms us. But the most frightening thing we can do at such times is to turn our backs on it, to close our eyes. For then we take the most precious thing inside us and surrender it to something else. In my case, that something was the wave.' □

Translation by JAY RUBIN

ROBERT DREWE
NEWS SHARK

By the time I was nineteen I was in a spin: hyperactive with self-consciousness, excitement, sadness and suddenly assumed—and ill-fitting—maturity. Within the passage of twelve months I'd left school, won a much-desired newspaper job, got my Catholic girlfriend pregnant, faced fierce parental opposition to our marriage (and small-town gossip) but nevertheless acquired both a new wife and baby. And then I'd seen my mother die.

Cerebral haemorrhage, the doctor said. 'We can't do anything.' Aneurysm. The brain was swimming in blood. My mother's headache began at eight o'clock on the first morning that Mary and our baby were home from hospital. She quickly became unconscious and was dead, aged forty-seven, by four p.m.

She'd predicted as much. 'This is too much for me,' she said when we announced the pregnancy in front of the evening stove. Mary's face was as pale and smooth as marble. She'd used a lot of powder but she still looked like a nun. My mother kept crying and shouting, 'This is more than I can handle.' Lamb cutlets were burning. She stirred the peas so vigorously they flew out of the saucepan on to the stove top. 'This is more than the body can bear.' A few days later she moaned, 'This is worse than adultery.' It was too much. I snapped back, 'Actually, we're single.'

Perhaps I misunderstood her, misinterpreted her remark. Perhaps she was comparing the way she felt now to her emotional and physical reactions on another occasion. Because the look she gave me at that moment was deeper than scorn, more complex than anger. 'Furious grief' could only begin to describe it.

She saw the baby when he came home from hospital. One glimpse of the little sleeping red boy. 'Looks like his dad,' she remarked. Next day she was dead in her own hospital bed even before she was dead. There was no resilience in her flesh. Her shoulder muscle didn't give when I hugged it. Her cheek was cool. Her eyes weren't quite shut; the open bits didn't look like normal eye tissue. She was lying on her side, her knees jackknifed under her, and her hip beneath the hospital blanket felt like wood.

After the funeral the doctor asked to see me in his surgery. He was the family GP and a family friend, Dr Guy Hancock. He'd been treating her insomnia and depression (caused by me) with phenobarbitone. 'Sit down,' he said grimly, more like a doctor in a movie—Gregory Peck in stern mode—than one abutting a newsagent's and fruit shop. 'I won't keep you long.'

I waited, much more a child than a father: dizzy, embarrassed and sad all at once. My head swam. 'I want you to know,' Dr Hancock announced, 'that you didn't necessarily kill your mother.' He fingered some silver instrument or other. 'We have no way of knowing, of course.'

My face must have surprised him—here was I thinking he'd just stood by ineffectually while she died!—because he prescribed some phenobarbitone for me as well.

Despite the phenobarbitone I couldn't sit still. I had to keep busy. When Mary and I weren't marvelling at the baby or making love, I was submerged in work or in the ocean. We were living near Swanbourne beach in the one-bedroom, lamb-smelling 'residence' attached to the butcher's shop in North Street (the butcher having wisely moved elsewhere). I swam each summer's day before going to work in the Fremantle branch office of the *West Australian*, only six stops or fifteen minutes down the train line.

In the previous century, Fremantle harbour had been blasted out of the coastal limestone where the wide Swan river estuary narrowed and twisted and flowed into the Indian Ocean, thirteen miles downriver from the State capital, Perth. As Australia's first and last port of call for shipping from and to Asia, Africa and Europe, as well as the home of the State's fishing fleet, it had always been a rough-house town. Fremantle was rarely short of the more raffish type of news.

A young chaser of ambulances and fire engines (and police-court reporter and shipping-list compiler) walked the night-time wharves and streets with caution. The waterfront pubs were bloodhouses. Most mornings, Polish and German seamen appeared before the court after assaulting each other—and their Aboriginal pick-ups in the Cleopatra Hotel—with marlinspikes and vodka bottles. At night, and all weekend, the sons of Italian and Greek fishermen and Croatian vegetable growers prowled the port in their hotted-up cars looking for girls and fights with the sons of Irish wharf labourers.

Fremantle was nonetheless a cohesive place, oddly independent for a town situated so close to the capital that it was really a suburb. Power was more or less evenly divided between the Waterside Workers' Federation and the city councillors (second- and third-generation shipping and general merchants), between communists and conservatives, between Catholics and Masons, between the South Fremantle and East Fremantle football clubs. It was a town whose population, maritime aspect and leached stone buildings gave it a distinctive Mediterranean flavour. Its most imposing building, once an asylum for insane women, had housed US navy officers during the war, and become a notorious sexual rendezvous. A high, stark limestone wall dominated and hemmed in the town. This was the boundary wall, warders' quarters and gatehouse of Fremantle Gaol, the State's largest and oldest prison. Murderers were sometimes executed there, for some reason always on a Monday morning at eight o'clock.

It was somehow appropriate that this sombre wall seemed as frightening and ageless as murder and retribution, that over the years the fierce sea winds had given it a patina of dusty, salty misery and that it looped around the neck of the port like a noose.

My mother was a swimmer. She'd also been a life-saver as a teenager, at a time when female surf-club members were a rarity. She still knew her resuscitation methods and rescue drills. When I was small I'd pretend to be drowning and yell out, 'Help!' She'd throw her left arm diagonally over my chest and under my armpit or cup my chin in her hand and, breathing steadily, sidestroke me into the safety of the shallows.

Some grown men and women remember their mothers as the scent of face powder and the inside of handbags, or perhaps as a particular rustle of fabric after the goodnight kiss. My mother was the smell of salt water, tanned flesh and the satiny femaleness of her swimming costume. She was the faint, sweet, perished-rubber odour of her bathing cap.

The family albums showed her happy, vigorous adolescence. She'd represented the State in tennis, recovered from a broken pelvis as a showjumper and enjoyed highboard diving. This last had come as a surprise to me when I was twelve or thirteen—old enough to have few illusions about parental heroism. She'd never mentioned it.

We were picnicking one Sunday at Yanchep and went swimming in the pool of the Yanchep Inn to cool off after lunch. Suddenly my mother left the water without saying a word, climbed the thirty-foot diving tower, stood poised high above us, and jackknifed perfectly into the pool. We were in the shallow end— my pale outclassed father, my brother and sister and I. No one spoke. After that, whenever I saw the Jantzen swimwear trademark of the diving woman in the bathing cap I thought of her.

In the *West Australian* office, on the corner of Adelaide and Queen streets, a reporting staff of two senior and two junior reporters worked out of a small room on the west of the building between the classified advertisements counter and the salesmen's tearoom.

The other junior's name was Russell Hazard, in my mind the perfect byline for an intrepid journalist. Each afternoon one of us would prise the daily shipping list from the reluctant sausage fingers of the harbour master, Captain Urquhart, whose phobia— the waterfront equivalent of worrying whether he'd left the gas on—led him to check and recheck the sailing times in case 400 passengers missed the *Fairstar* to England. Then, in the two hours where our shifts crossed and the late afternoon sun made our desks uninhabitable, Hazard and I would play game after game of office cricket in the shady corridor, with a ruler for a bat and balls made out of copy paper and Scotch tape, and cheerfully ponder ways to out-scoop each other.

A Fremantle boy born and schooled, Hazard had the advantage of local knowledge and an easier way with cops. (My relations with the local police never recovered from my enquiries into the aftermath of the retiring inspector's farewell party: the inspector's car mounted the pavement, struck an Italian family of three and accelerated away.) But Hazard's casual street-wisdom and detective-room banter was matched by my hunger for the big coastal story. I thought about the story all the time, even off-duty, jogging the beach each morning from Swanbourne to Cottesloe and willing a passing crayfish boat or container ship on to the rocks. I wanted the story so much that I studied for it.

In the *West Australian*'s library in Perth I read all the clippings and microfiche files on shark attacks, shipwrecks and disasters on the coast since the colony's first European settlement. And in the Fremantle city library, a hundred yards across King's Square from the office, I read all the books, too, going back to the early Dutch mariners.

I'd no idea, back then, what had set me off on this course. All I knew was that some cogs seemed to be sliding into place. For the past year life had left me dazed and uncomprehending, but now I was fascinated and excited by its potential. Hazard might have understood the port itself better than I did, but I knew I had the drop on him when it came to the sea. Hadn't I spent my whole childhood and adolescence at the beach, surfed all the waves between North Beach and Fremantle, trained as a life-saver? Hadn't I even killed a shark myself with a hand-spear when I was just fourteen? It was only a four-foot wobbegong, and it was dozing on the sea floor at the time, but it was indeed a shark, as I'd congratulated myself at the instant of impalement, all my new teenage strength forcing the spear through the flesh of its motionless, carpet-patterned head. Yes, certainly a shark, I continued to tell myself as I trudged and panted the three miles back along the scorching limedust road to our Rottnest holiday cottage. Those teeth were strong enough to crush a crayfish or crab. They could give you a nasty bite. You could lose a finger.

I made it back to the cottage, the leathery, boneless weight drooping and thudding around my neck, the fishy blood seeping down my chest and thighs attracting clouds of flies but, sadly, not the admiring female glances I'd anticipated. All the shark's weight had fallen into its head. I threw the stinking body into the bushes.

Whenever I dived into the sea I thought of sharks. Not that their existence made any difference to whether I went swimming or not. I thought about them, then put them out of my mind. More or less. Coming over the Eric Street hill at North Cottesloe any hot, still midday and seeing that human bodyslick floating three or four hundred yards out to sea (all that sweat and coconut oil), I couldn't help thinking of berley, the greasy groundbait fishermen tossed in the water to attract fish. Same principle. And weren't sharks supposed to have a miraculous sense of smell?

The shark isn't buried deep in our collective unconscious for nothing. It's amazing what any swimmer can see in the back-froth of a snapping wave or in the darker patchwork surges of weed and reef. Is that really just the wake of a swiftly diving shag, the sudden shadow of a passing cloud? Or the first, last, hint of the white pointer's charge?

My friends and I had grown up on the ocean and river shores. Everyone was a capable swimmer and surfer, pretty good with boats and boards, with crab and prawning nets—even, in less-cool younger days, with the *gidgee* and *kylie*: the fish-spear and fish-boomerang modelled on the old Aboriginal ones and favoured by gawky twelve-year-olds. We knew the tides and reefs, the hot easterlies and blustery south-westerlies of our patch of coastline. We swam in school and club teams. We crewed on small, brisk, plywood yachts: ancient varnished Gwen-12s and VJs and creaking fourteen-foot dinghies. Some of my friends, like Nelson Mews, lived on the riverbank and came from families who'd been boatbuilders for four generations. A couple of brothers, Peter and Max McWilliam, came from an old pearling family who operated a fleet of luggers out of Broome in the far north-west and had sent their sons south for their education.

One Saturday late that summer, Max and I and three or four other beach cronies went body-surfing. Max was two years younger than me but, in the way of teenage friendships, overcame this handicap by being confident and amiable. He was a joker, a good sport, a natural swimmer. Because of the poor surf elsewhere we were trying to catch waves, this particular afternoon, on a smooth reef between Cottesloe and North Cottesloe known locally, because of its carpet of mossy weed, as the Slimy.

Even at low tide, when only a few inches of water covered the reef's spongy surface, body-surfers could skim over the Slimy with no worse injury than an occasional grazed knee or toe. I'd only an hour's surfing time to spare. I had to get home to my marriage, to my new family. I didn't say this to Max, of course. I was hypersensitive about my new condition. It wasn't the teasing so much, but the total incomprehension. No one, certainly not a kid like Max, could understand why I'd insisted on marriage, why I hadn't tried to get out of it.

The Slimy was nothing to write home about but at least its waves were usually dependable. By four-thirty, however, the tide was rising and the sea rolling over the reef was rough and cloudy and swirling with kelp and sand. The Slimy was no longer slimy. The surf began dumping dangerously on the rocks. We started using the back of the reef as a foothold to launch ourselves obliquely into those waves breaking on its outer edge. The idea was that they'd carry us off the rocks and into the deeper and safer sandy-bottomed basin beyond.

This plan wasn't a success. The waves, as the local saying went, had too much water in them. The tide was too high. On the reef the water was shoulder-deep and murky. We had to feel for the reef with our feet, thrust them down into the weedy depths and search for a crevice with our toes and heels. Who knew what was down there? In the currents the kelp seemed alive, one moment silkily caressing our thighs and stomachs and pressing insistently against us, the next scratching and lashing out.

Buffeted by the surf and undertow and the rolling kelp, swearing and dancing and stumbling over the slippery weed and rocks, it was hard to get any purchase, even harder to position yourself on a wave. Impossible to concentrate on anything other than the next breaker and your own sudden intentions.

As if conditions weren't difficult enough, three surfboard riders on big, plywood boards, fifteen-footers, had the same idea and began cutting in on us. These heavy, knife-nosed monsters were the last straw. With every wave-surge one or other of us gave up and half swam, half rolled, through the froth to the beach. I was the last of us to reach the shore, or so it seemed. By the time I got there everyone else had gone.

Night changes the sea. The following morning, it was calm and slick as I cruised the coast road in the office Ford Anglia, desperate for a story to make this humdrum Sunday day-shift worthwhile. And, from a rise where suburbanites were beginning to build new brick houses in the sandhills, I looked out into the low swell of the ocean and saw dark shapes gliding there.

At last I had my story. I followed it north up the West Coast Highway, with the two-way radio crackling and the sun glinting off the white dunes and sandy verges, off the roadside bottles, off every approaching windscreen and the glassy sea itself.

Along the way I kept the chief-of-staff primed with the progress of events. I called him from City Beach and Scarborough and a couple of stops in between. He didn't remind me that my territory stopped at Cottesloe. He was impressed by people sticking to a story. 'Tigers,' I informed him knowledgeably, trying to keep the self-consciousness out of my voice when I said 'Come In!' and 'Over and Out!' Then I stomped through the sandhills in my work shoes once more, training the office binoculars on the unbroken sea just beyond the surfline.

On the western horizon Rottnest Island was, as usual, mysteriously transformed by summer's atmospheric conditions into a misty string of mirage-islands which hovered like spacecraft above the Indian Ocean, six or eight miles south of Rottnest's real whereabouts. As I searched for fins in the smooth rise of each breaking wave, for those sinister, thrilling shadows in the swells, glistening women smelling of coconut oil glanced drowsily up at me from their towels. Children squinted into the glare to see what this fully clothed boy was peering at. Languid adults' faces said: what do you think you're doing?

Willing you to be eaten, I could have said, and the sooner the better. Well, not a kid, maybe, but at least a well-known businessman or sun-dried old socialite. If possible, I wanted even more than a shark attack on a noted victim. I knew my news values. I wanted the shark in question to be of great size and uncommon species, and I needed the reaction of a garrulous old-timer witness like Ted 'Sharky' Nelson, every reporter's favourite 'contact' for shark stories. ('It rushed at him like a Metro bus, bit him in half and swallowed him in two bites. Never seen one that big this far north. The poor bastard never had a chance. I'll never forget the look on his face.')

Frankly, I hoped for still more. Not just that this bloody

Sunday would turn out to be the victim's birthday or golden wedding anniversary, or that he'd just won the lottery (news editors adored poignant coincidences). As a second-year reporter I wanted more than to break news: I wanted to be in the news.

My fantasy front-page lead—shark attack or boating disaster or freak rip tide—was an adventure story in which I would be the hero. Of course it would take unforeseen dramatic circumstances for me to step outside the neutral-observer's role, a role stressed by my paper, and quietly but heroically intrude. (Frantic captain of surf life-saving club, through loud hailer: 'There's still a little girl on a floatie out there! All my guys have major arterial bleeding. Does anyone on the beach have their bronze medallion for life-saving?' Me: 'Well, if there's a kid's life at stake . . .')

Just as my dream exclusive required the loss of a life, it required me to save one, too. And, importantly, to risk my own. Then, dripping water, and possibly blood, over the Anglia's dashboard (and modestly postponing news of my feat until the third or fourth paragraph), I'd dictate the story over the two-way for the first edition.

A spluttery motor sounded above the shallows. The shark-spotter plane, a barnstorming little show-off Moth, was after them, too. There went my scoop. I could've cried. Even if the plane didn't chase them out to sea, the local surfboats would. Already the shark alarm was sounding on Scarborough beach.

I lost them then anyway, in the dunes between Scarborough and Trigg. The afternoon sea-breeze, the Fremantle Doctor, was shirring the ocean surface. I could see the pattern and colour of the sea changing through the binoculars, small choppy waves darkening from turquoise to blue. On the two-way, the chief-of-staff was philosophical. 'You've still got a story. Shark Pack Threatens Beaches. Get some quotes. Over and out.'

I drove back south to Fremantle on the coast road, writing the story in my head. Passing Cottesloe on the way, I noticed four surfboats strung out in a line on the reef, riding the light chop, the oarsmen keeping them more or less motionless and parallel to the beach. There was no sign of either physical effort or excitement on the boats. Maybe the crews were trying some new training manoeuvre. Anyway they were so still they certainly weren't chasing any sharks out to sea. Their movements were so calm and measured they could have been fishing.

The sun was between me and the horizon, which made it about three o'clock. Over and beyond the stationary surfboats I saw that Rottnest Island had shed its mirages and returned to its proper anchorage. The south-westerly had lifted the heat haze and brought reality back.

I got quotes all right. I went overboard. I was both poetic and pragmatic. I quoted everyone from William Blake ('Tyger Tyger, burning bright,') to Ted 'Sharky' Nelson. And I'd gathered most of my background material already. The shark story I filed was less a snappy news item than a very long, information-soaked feature article. For 'colour' I dropped in the comments from the ubiquitous Mr Nelson. But my coup was to bring in science.

I got the State's 'leading ichthyologist', Dr Byron McEntee, to leave his Sunday barbecue to declare that my sharks were from the family *Carcharhinidae*, otherwise known as requiem sharks. Requiems included some of the biggest and most voracious sharks: the tiger, whaler, bull shark, blue shark and grey reef shark, and were characterized—Dr McEntee pointed out—by 'a nictitating membrane and a heterocercal tail'.

This requiem business was intriguing. As he nonchalantly remarked: 'Requiem sharks are everywhere.' Active swimmers, they travelled long distances each day and migrated according to seasonal changes. They had the widest possible range of habitats, from river estuaries and intertidal pools to the open ocean; from muddy bays and hypersaline estuaries to coral and rocky reefs. These fellows weren't put off by freshwater rivers or lakes, and were found throughout all tropical and temperate seas.

In my ichthyologist's words, 'The requiem group dominates the world's shark fauna in diversity of species and numbers of individuals.' He said, and I wrote, that the biggest requiem sharks (tigers) could reach a length of twenty-four feet and were among the most important marine predators, eating a 'broad spectrum of prey': bony fishes, other sharks and rays, crustaceans, carrion, sea turtles, sea snakes, seabirds and large marine mammals.

'And humans,' I said.

'Let's not sensationalize that aspect.'

I asked him about their name and on this he was pleased to oblige. 'Obviously, with its funereal associations "requiem" is much more stirring than "tiger" or "whaler".'

'Can you elaborate?'

'It's from the obsolete French *requiem,* a variant of *requin* "shark", and is influenced by the gloomier associations of the word "requiem" as we understand it.'

'Gloomy?' This was more like it.

'A requiem is music for dead people.'

'So their name comes from their habit of killing people?' I said eagerly, adding: 'What are the chances of a West Australian beach-lover being eaten by a shark?'

His sigh was loud. 'You've got more chance of dying from a bee sting or a lightning strike. A hundred thousand times more chance of dying in a car crash on the way to the beach.' He paused. 'I do hope you people aren't going to beat this thing up.'

When I arrived back at Fremantle, Russell Hazard grunted, 'There you are. I need the Anglia,' and sped off down Queen Street. I wrote my article, knocked off work at seven and went home to sit by the phone in case the sub-editors needed to check something. I imagined that there might be one or two queries.

Next morning I was at the newsagent's at dawn to get the paper. The suspense, the anxiety, the excited anticipation: it's hard to think and walk straight while simultaneously flicking ever more urgently through a newspaper on whose crisp judgement at that moment your life depends. Well, the sub-editors had cut my shark story—it was more than filleted, more than slashed, it was flensed—to ten paragraphs. It ran on page seven, with a single-column stock picture of Ted 'Sharky' Nelson, not a word from my ichthyologist or William Blake, and the heading SHARK HUNTER WARNS OF SUMMER THREAT.

Hazard, however, had got himself a story on page three: STUDENT DROWNED AT COTTESLOE. And suddenly I knew—don't ask me how—that it was going to be about Max. I felt peculiarly calm. I wasn't numbed by the story; I had to struggle to keep my attention on it. My mind kept veering off in other directions. It was more than an absence of surprise; I had this strange feeling of retrospective premonition. Once again I'd had a hand in someone else's disaster while being unable to do anything at all about it.

Hazard's piece was only five or six paragraphs. It was not particularly well written. His only source seemed to be the standard police report. He had no knowledge of Max's family background in the pearl industry, no inkling that his whole life had been determined by the moods of the sea. He clearly had no idea who his companions had been when he drowned. All he said was that Max's body, shrouded in kelp, was found the day after he disappeared, half a mile north of where he'd been swimming. (Actually, Hazard didn't say 'shrouded'; he said 'covered'.)

The body had a bump on its head, and other abrasions that may have been caused by rocks. No fish had touched it. I was rather surprised. I'd always believed that there were these tiny sea lice that could reduce a body to bones in twenty-four hours. □

GRANTA

JOHN BIGUENET
AND NEVER COME UP

W*as there a story?*
Yes, there was always a story.
Did you write this one down?
I've written them all down.
Will you read it to me?
It wasn't really his story. I thought it was. I thought it had something to do with him—or one of his shipmates, at least. That it had happened on a boat he knew. But then I was reading to my son one night, and there it was in this book of sea stories.
Exactly the same?
No, just the idea. All the details were different.
Stories get passed on. Maybe your father heard it somewhere.
Maybe. But he made me believe it was no story. I thought it was true.
Why?
Because of what he said after he told it to me.
Read it to me. Please.
If you like.

The freighter was three days out of New Orleans on its run to Panama when the wife and the daughter of the ship's captain both succumbed, in the space of a few hours, to a fever from which they had suffered since their first day at sea.

As the bodies of the handsome woman and the little girl were wound in canvas for burial, old salts, shaking their heads, repeated to the younger hands the ancient injunction against sailing with women. 'It's a terrible shame, but we're lucky it weren't worse,' the bosun confided to the third mate, who had brought the sorrowful news to the bridge.

The captain, with twenty years' experience of the vagaries of the sea, was not so bold a man as to have been indifferent to the superstition. In fact, he had for a year denied the repeated entreaties of his daughter to take her with him on a voyage. Only as a special birthday present to this child whom he adored without measure had he relented. His wife, delighted that at least once in her life she would not have to bid farewell to her beloved husband from the edge of a dock, spurred him to live up to his promise.

And so, on 2 September, with the assurance of the harbour

master that the Gulf threatened no hurricane at the moment, the captain ushered aboard his ship the child and her mother. Having slipped its moorings, the freighter nosed down the Mississippi under the command of a river pilot. At the mouth of the river, the pilot disembarked, remarking to his fellows when he had returned to Pilottown on the captain who had taken the whole family to sea. 'He some crazy, huh?' the pilot's father observed.

Already the woman and her child were faint with their illness. 'It's to be expected,' the captain told them, and he tried to comfort them with tales of his own seasickness on his first trip out. But the onset of fever late that afternoon alarmed him; they were not seasick.

The ship, of course, had no doctor, but the second mate did what he could to ease their discomfort. When they grew too weak to swallow the aspirins he had taken from the medicine locker, he crushed the pills beneath his thumb in the bowl of a spoon and added a few drops of water so they might drink the medicine. But their decline was so steady and seemed to him so certain that he had shaken his head over them a good day before they finally died.

The captain, having seen his share of death in the war, trembled but held his composure as his first officer read from his Kingspoint manual the liturgy for burial at sea. The crew, unpractised in this drill, stumbled in sliding the bodies over the side. The ship's navigator, as required by maritime custom, shot the sun and fixed the location of the burial, noting it on the ship's chart and conveying it to the captain for entry in the log.

The remainder of the voyage was uneventful. One of the sailors got into a bit of trouble on shore leave, but the local authorities were glad to release him to the custody of an officer of the ship.

The freighter, now laden with coffee, retraced its route back to New Orleans. Two days out of Panama, in the middle of the third watch, an officer called the captain to the bridge.

Fifty yards off the starboard bow, the water rose up in the shape, vaguely, of two figures—one somewhat taller than the other. The captain dropped his binoculars. 'Sir,' the navigator nearly whispered, 'we're very close to the spot, very close.'

As the ship slid past, the watery figures trembled in the bright sunlight. Finally, the watch saw the two columns of water collapse after the stern had passed them.

By the time the ship docked in New Orleans, the captain had been locked in his cabin. Orderlies from St Simon's Asylum led the man down the gangplank in restraints.

New Orleans is one of the great ports of the world. The story easily found its way to the pages of the local papers. Intrigued by the tale, the *Item* sent a photographer on the Panama run when the ship embarked a week later.

Again two watery figures rose up.

In a quiet dinner at Antoine's a few days after the photo's publication, in the face of a threatened strike by the seafarers' union, the owners of the four lines that traded with Panama agreed to re-route their ships to a more easterly course. The new route they plotted that night has been followed for the last half-century.

In all that time, no ship has passed within ten miles of the location fixed by the navigator that melancholy afternoon. Whether the sea remains calm there or whether a mother and her daughter have risen up like pillars of water each day for the last fifty years no man can say.

That's your version?

That's how I wrote it down.

But that's not how he told it.

No, it's not the way he told it. To be the same, it would be whispered so close to your face you could smell the breath that carried it, but in darkness so black you couldn't even see the lips that were telling it.

You're resorting to poetry again.

No, no, I'm not. That's exactly how it was, the night I heard the story. That's the absolute truth.

How is that possible? Where were you?

We were deep in the marsh, back down one of those winding canals off the ship channel. We'd been hauling in speckled trout hand over foot for better than an hour when they stopped biting. It was already nearly three, so my father tried to start the engine. He pulled on the cord till I thought he would rip the top off the motor, but it didn't even cough.

You'd been fishing?

Yeah, we had a little fourteen-foot plywood runabout my father and grandfather had built, the kind with fibreglass tape at the seams. Everybody made their own in those days. My grandfather wasn't with us, though, out in the marsh. I think maybe he was already in the hospital by then.

How old were you?

I don't know. Nine. Maybe ten.

You were just a baby.

No, I wasn't a baby. I was ten years old.

Oh, you were a baby. Ten years old.

OK, I was a baby. We had this huge outboard on the back—my father won it somehow playing pinochle—and when you leaned on the throttle, the boat just about jumped out of the water. So we called it the *Mullet*.

Mullet?

It's this little fish that jumps out of the water when something big is chasing it. You can't catch them with a hook. Their mouths are too small.

So what did your father do?

Bobbing there in our little boat, Daddy changed the spark plugs, cleaned the lines, checked the pumps, went through the whole drill. But when he popped the cover back on and tugged the cord again—nothing. We were stuck. And hunkered back in the marsh the way we were, we hadn't seen another boat in a couple of hours. It was so hot by then if your hand brushed a cleat you got burned. So there weren't many damn fools still out.

Then what did your father do?

What he always did. He pulled a bottle out of the ice chest.

But what about you? You must have been frightened, a little child like you.

There used to be a saying around here when I was a boy: 'Nobody but God can whup my daddy, and God better watch his step.' As long as Daddy was leaning back against the bow drinking Dixies, it was just another fishing trip as far as I was concerned. I knew Mama would be upset, our being late and all—and I was worried about that because I knew what would happen if she made too much of a fuss when we got home. But afraid of being stranded out in the marsh? I didn't have the slightest idea how much trouble we were in.

Your father knew what he was doing, didn't he?

Sure. In all the times we went out there, I never once saw him check a chart, and anybody'll tell you what a labyrinth those canals are. Nothing but sawgrass and water as far as you can see.

And your father had been a sailor, hadn't he?

Yeah, that's right. He was in the Merchant Marine until I was born and my mother made him come home. He sailed damn near everywhere. I don't know how many winter runs he made in the North Atlantic. The water's so cold that time of year, if you fall overboard you're dead in twenty seconds. At least, that's what he used to tell me. He dodged submarines in the Pacific during the war, took a ship through the Suez, rode out a typhoon in the South China Sea.

He must have seen some things.

He said you could walk to shore on the backs of the sharks they were so thick in Manila Bay. In fact, he lost one of his shipmates when they were unloading in the Philippines near the end of the war. The idiot got drunk and decided to go for a swim, right there where they were anchored.

Didn't anybody try to stop him?

I asked my father about that once, when I was still small. That's the thing about sailors, he explained. They'll warn you off of trouble, but not a one of them will ever stop you. You want to take your boat out in weather like this? One of them will tell you, 'Might get a little wet today.' By which he means, 'If you're damn fool enough to go out on a day like this, the crabs'll be scraping the flesh from your bones at the bottom of the sea before you're done.' But nobody's going to stop you. It's your boat.

You don't have to be so grisly.

That's the way Daddy put it. He said deep down they all expected to drown sooner or later themselves, so they didn't see any point in going to a lot of trouble to keep someone from drowning sooner.

This is the kind of story your father told a ten-year-old?

Ten? He was telling me his stories before I went to school. They weren't any worse than fairy tales.

Crabs eating the flesh from your bones?
Wolves eating up grandmothers and inviting children into
their beds?
So what about the man who went swimming?
My father said his buddy hadn't been in the water half a
minute before a shark took his legs. But it was quiet, he said; they
never even saw the shark. The man rolled like a ship broaching—
that's the way he always put it, and running in those Pacific
convoys for two years, he saw plenty of ships broach—and the
guy just bobbed there upside down for a moment or two, bloody
stumps in the air, then slid under, gone.
There's really no need to—
He hated the Indian Ocean—the storms lasted so long down
there they'd eat cold mess three days running because it was too
rough for the cooks to make hot food. But you know what was
the most dangerous thing he ever did at sea? Haul molasses from
the Caribbean to the East Coast.
Molasses? What's so dangerous about that?
I'll tell you how dangerous it is. Molasses carried the highest
premium for hazardous cargo. That's why he did it, for the money,
the bonus. And we needed the molasses for explosives, so there
was a lot of demand during the war.
But what's so dangerous about it?
It's heavier than water. If a ship was hit and went down, the
molasses took everything with it to the bottom of the sea. Down
where the crabs were waiting.
No survivors.
None. My father was a real sailor, all right. So he knew what
he was doing on the water. Of course, he told me one night when
he was good and drunk that the best advice he'd gotten in a dozen
years at sea was from an old sailor on the first ship he sailed, the
Howard Handstrom I think it was. You've probably heard this
saying before. 'Never learn to swim—it only prolongs the
drowning.' I remember when he told me he took another swig of
bourbon and then, with one eye open, swore, 'But, goddamn it, I
already knew how to swim.'
So what happened to you out in the marsh?
My father and I sat there till dusk. I tried fishing some, but

the water was too hot and the tide was out. Daddy kept drinking. We had some kind of cheese spread my mother had made and soda crackers, so that was our dinner. Every once in a while, Daddy would stand up on the bench and look for another boat, but nobody else was still out, and we were too far off the channel to catch a tow with the shrimp boats coming in from the Gulf. He was still in a pretty good mood, though. After he'd taken a look, he would say, 'I'd better send up a flare.' And he'd unzip his pants and take a piss, standing up on the seat. I guess it was all the beer he'd been drinking.

And what about you?

I'd kept my Dodgers baseball cap on the whole day, and, of course, we both were wearing long-sleeved shirts. But by the time the sky in the east began to turn purple, I'd had too much sun. Hot as it was and even though I was still wearing one of those big, old-fashioned life jackets, I started getting chills. Fever, I guess.

Keep a child out there all day on the water till he gets sick?

I was sick all right, but we had a bigger problem to deal with. I could already hear them lifting out of the grass before I could see them. At first I thought it was an engine. Dizzy as I was, I stood up on the bench. I was sure we were saved. I was really proud, too. Daddy had fallen asleep in the bow. I was going to be the lookout that spied a boat and saved the crew. But there weren't any boats when I looked, just small dark clouds hovering, twitching over the mudflats. I didn't know what they were— smoke, fog? But as the roaring got louder, I looked down at my hands. They were seething with mosquitoes. It was weird, I hadn't felt a thing. Maybe it was the fever, I don't know, but I watched these bugs crawling all over themselves like it was somebody else's hands they were biting. And then, very calmly, I plunged both arms into the water. With my face close to the canal, the racket from all those little wings overhead was unbelievable. I reached behind me to shake my father awake by the leg. He didn't stir. That was when I began to be afraid. So I crawled beside him, and when I got close enough to see him in the dark, his face and neck were so thick with mosquitoes he looked like he had a black beard. I tried to call out to wake him, but my mouth was full of them before I could even say his name. I choked on mosquitoes, spitting them out into the water. My coughing woke him up. By then, they were in our eyes. I think my eyelids were starting to swell shut from all the bites. The next thing I knew, Daddy had thrown me overboard and jumped in beside me.

My God.

He was spitting out the bugs even as he shouted at me. He got his shirt off and threw it over my head like a little tent. Then I felt him underwater, loosening my life jacket and working my own shirt off. I couldn't see him till he came right up in front of my face under the tent of his shirt. 'Vicious little bastards, aren't they?' he shouted at me even though he was just inches away. And then he said, 'Here, you put your own shirt over your head when I tell you to.' His hand brought up the sopping shirt my mother had buttoned on me that morning when it was still dark outside. I remember it had cowboys with lariats all over it. I think they were on horseback. Daddy said the first thing we had to do was tie the sleeves in knots so the mosquitoes couldn't get in. And we had to make sure that the edges of our shirts stayed in the water.

You had your life vest on?

Yeah, of course. I wasn't allowed in the boat without a life jacket. Anyway, Daddy was working in the dark on all this. It had gotten pitch black under the shirt. The brim of my baseball cap kept the fabric off my face when Daddy submerged. He had helped me slip my shirt under his own. It was a much smaller little tent. I hadn't realized how big my father was. His shirt had been huge, but I could barely keep the edges of mine in the water. In fact, it was so dark it was hard to tell where the water began. My father said to keep dipping my head under so the shirt would stay wet. 'They find you by your heat,' he whispered, as if they might hear. 'Stay wet and they won't know where you are.' That worried me. I was afraid my fever would give us away. But the water was making me feel better.

That's horrifying.

It gets worse.

Worse?

Little by little, Daddy had felt his way along the edge of the boat until he found some footing on the bottom. He could stand with his head out of the water. He had tightened the straps on my life jacket and drawn his shirt over himself and me, so I was under two shirts. It was the strangest feeling, floating there in the darkness. I'd get panicked every now and then, when I couldn't hear him breathing—we were only a few inches apart. Then he'd talk to me, calm me down. I got used to it after a while, I guess, because I was slipping in and out of sleep, a few hours later, when something brushed my leg and made me jump. Like I said, Daddy was standing up, probably sunk to his ankles in the muck. That still left a good five feet of water. I asked him if he had felt anything. He hadn't. But just as he said no, something hit us both at the same time, coming between us, I think. Daddy staggered back a step or two, slipping on the bottom.

A shark?

Probably. You always saw them there, a fin slicing through the water out in the channel. You looked for a second fin following the first, that's how you could tell it was shark. Otherwise, it was just a dolphin with that horizontal fluke of a tail they've got. But that afternoon I'd seen the double fin easing through the water, maybe fifty feet out, sliding back and forth as easy as you please. It wasn't all that big a shark, maybe four foot or five, but big enough, I knew. So there I was, floating in the dark, remembering what I'd seen that afternoon and thinking about all the shark stories he'd ever told me. Not to mention that we weren't under the same shirt any more. I called out for him; I didn't know what had happened. I wanted him to hold me, so I started paddling forward, trying to find him. But then I heard his voice shouting to stay still. That's when I felt it again, its side scraping my khaki pants like sandpaper. I was crying, I remember, with Daddy half-whispering, hush, hush, they'll hear you. That really scared me. It hadn't occurred to me there might be more than one shark. 'And don't take a crap,' he warned, 'they love the smell of shit.'

So what happened?

Nothing. We didn't move for a minute or two—in the dark inside that shirt, all by myself, it felt like hours—and that was it. Gone. Daddy grabbed me and got us organized again. Only this time I stayed under his shirt, hanging on his neck till he said I was going to choke him. That's when he told me the story.

You were just ten years old?
Worse things happen to kids. It did make me sad, though, the story. I didn't know who I felt worse for, the captain or his little girl. But that's how we got through the night. That and the singing.
Singing?
After all those hours in the water, the life jacket wasn't working so well. Like everything else in the boat, the vests were army surplus, so God knows how much they'd been used already when we got them. I was floating lower and lower in the water; I had to tilt my head back after a while to keep it out of my mouth, the water. The cork had absorbed too much, I guess. I put my hands on my father's shoulders to keep from slipping deeper. Pretty soon, the life jacket was useless, but I kept it on for the sharks. At least, that was what I was thinking as I hung on to my father. He was having a hard time staying awake, so he started singing. It was the only song I ever heard him sing.
What was that?
I don't know its name, but it goes like this:

> If the ocean were whiskey,
> and I were a duck,
> I'd swim to the bottom
> and never come up.

> But the ocean's not whiskey,
> and I'm not a duck,
> so I'll play the jack of diamonds
> and trust to my luck.

He just kept singing those same verses over and over again, like a chant more than a song. Then I started singing. It must have sounded strange out there in that dark marsh, those two voices carrying across the water. We kept at it a long time, waiting for the light.
The whole night in the water?
The whole night. Then, when the sun rose, we hauled ourselves up into the boat. There were a few, straggling mosquitoes buzzing around us. I made a point of killing every one of them while Daddy tried the motor again. There was nothing

doing, though, so Daddy tied a line to a bow cleat and, with water up to his chest, dragged the boat along the shelf of the mudflats for hours, it seemed, until he had hauled us to the mouth of the canal, where it joined the ship channel. He was so exhausted by the time we reached the edge of the flats he couldn't lift himself into the boat right away. He hung on by the gunnel, half-floating for a few minutes until he had the strength to swing his leg over the side. I pulled him into the boat, and he lay on the deck like a fish. Lying there, he heard the trill of a motor off in the distance. Then, out in the channel, we saw a shrimper, its butterfly nets up and drying in the sun after a night of trawling. We got up on the benches and swung the life vests over our heads, shouting in the still air. I've never known another feeling like the one when the shrimp boat, still a hundred, two hundred yards out, swung its bow towards us.

And they towed you in?

Yeah. Daddy offered the skipper twenty dollars for his trouble and fuel. '*Oui, mon ami,*' he said—it was all still half-French and half-English back then—'but not for money.' So he towed us in to Pointe à la Hache. We tied the boat up, walked down a shell road, and found a little diner that was just opening. Daddy called home, told Mama to come get us. Then we started eating, and when she got there an hour and a half later, we were still eating.

My God, what a night.

Well, it wasn't over yet. We still had to drive back to Delacroix, where we'd launched, to get our other car and the trailer. Then, Mama and I drove home to New Orleans together while Daddy went back to Pointe à la Hache to get the boat. Every now and then she'd look at me and start crying. But it was funny. I wasn't hers any more.

So that's how it happens? That's how they turn sweet little boys into big, mean men?

Something like that.

What was it he said? About the story, the story about the captain and his wife and daughter? You said that's what made you believe it.

When he got to the end of it, he said they had the photograph from the *Item*—the picture of those two columns of water, the one that ran in the paper—in some kind of archive on the third floor of the main library, down on Tulane Avenue.

Maybe that was part of the story he had heard?

No. What he said was all his own. He told me he had seen it once, the photograph, he and his father both. That's why I believed the story.

And that was all he said about it?

No, he said one other thing. Years later.

What was that?

He said they all end the same way, those sea stories. In madness or in death.

And what about this story?

It's not a story. It's true.

But how will it end?

End? With him singing, I guess, with the two of us singing—a man's deep, weary voice and a boy's thin little soprano, the voice of a drowned child, singing about whiskey and cards and a drunken duck—adrift in that black water, in that dark marsh, the mosquitoes hovering over our heads like death, and the two of us singing, singing until the sun comes up. □

NOTES ON CONTRIBUTORS

NEAL ASCHERSON's books include *The Polish August* and *Black Sea*. He is writing a book about Scotland for Granta Books.

BELLA BATHURST is writing the story of the 'Lighthouse Stevensons', to be published next year by HarperCollins.

JOHN BIGUENET lives in New Orleans and teaches at Loyola University.

JULIA BLACKBURN'S latest book, *The Leper's Companions*, will be published by Cape in the autumn. She lives in Suffolk.

ROBERT DREWE's most recent novel, *The Drowner*, was published by Granta in 1997. He is writing a memoir set on the west coast of Australia.

STEPHEN GILL was born in Bristol in 1971. He is a member of the Independent Photographers Group and lives in London.

JAMES HAMILTON-PATERSON lives in Italy. His books include *Seven-Tenths*, *Gerontius* and *Playing with Water* (re-issued by Granta).

LEWIS JOHNMAN is an economic historian at the University of Westminster. IAN JOHNSTON teaches at the Glasgow School of Art. Both are writing histories of British shipbuilding.

PHILIP MARSDEN's most recent book is *The Spirit-Wrestlers: A Russian Journey*, published by HarperCollins. He lives in Cornwall.

HARUKI MURAKAMI lives near Tokyo. He was recently awarded the Yomiuri Literary Prize. His latest novel, *The Wind-Up Bird Chronicle*, is published by Harvill in the UK and Knopf in the US.

CHARLES NICHOLL's account of a cockfight in Martinique appeared in *Granta* 23. His latest book is *Somebody Else*, a study of the poet Arthur Rimbaud's life in Africa.

ORHAN PAMUK's novels include *The White Castle*, *The Black Book* and *The New Life*, all published by Faber. He lives in Istanbul.

N.A.M. RODGER is Anderson Fellow of the National Maritime Museum in London. 'Into the Wind' is drawn from his chapter in the first volume of the *Oxford History of the British Empire*, to be published by Oxford University Press this year.

GEORGE ROSIE is a writer and television journalist. His play *Carlucco and the Queen of Hearts* won several awards at the 1991 Edinburgh Festival. He lives in Edinburgh and is writing a novel.

WILLIAM SCAMMELL left school at fifteen and worked as a photographer on Cunard liners. He has published eight books of poetry.

PAUL THEROUX's most recent novel is *Kowloon Tong*, published by Hamish Hamilton in the UK and Houghton Mifflin in the US. He lives in Hawaii.

JUSTIN WEBSTER is a freelance writer. He lives in Barcelona.